Franziska Quabeck

The Lawyer in Dickens

Law & Literature

Edited by
Daniela Carpi and Klaus Stierstorfer

Volume 18

Franziska Quabeck

The Lawyer in Dickens

DE GRUYTER

Funded by the German Research Foundation
SFB 1385 "Law and Literature"

ISBN 978-3-11-075270-0
e-ISBN (PDF) 978-3-11-075450-6
e-ISBN (EPUB) 978-3-11-075459-9
ISSN 2191-8457

Library of Congress Control Number: 2021939062

Bibliographic information published by the Deutsche Nationalbibliothek
The Deutsche Nationalbibliothek lists this publication in the Deutsche Nationalbibliografie; detailed bibliographic data are available on the Internet at http://dnb.dnb.de.

Typesetting: Integra Software Services Pvt. Ltd.
Printing and binding: CPI books GmbH, Leck

www.degruyter.com

Contents

1 The Law: An Introduction

It has often been said that *David Copperfield*, written from 1849 to 1850, constitutes a turning-point in Dickens's works. The farcical nature of the earlier works has gradually disappeared and this, his most personal novel, constitutes a trajectory towards the 'dark' Dickens, who has been the focus of scholarly interest in recent years. From the perspective of law and literature, this turning-point does not seem quite so obvious as *David Copperfield* has also often been described as one of Dickens's least political or most domestic novels.[1] Dickens's critique of the law, so harsh in texts like *Bleak House* or *Great Expectations*, seems virtually absent from the novel and many critics have attested Dickens's expression of his particular dislike for the legal system and its representatives as explicit only in the novels following *David Copperfield*. Within existing law and literature scholarship, Dickens plays a major role, yet *David Copperfield* is rarely the subject in such discussions. There are simply many major works that make their critique of the law an overt topic; to the extent that Dickens's alleged 'disgust' for the law has become almost proverbial and a critical investigation into the matter rarely dispenses with quoting the most famous epithet about the Court of Chancery that introduces the main theme of *Bleak House*: "Suffer any wrong that can be done you, rather than come here!" (*BH*, ch. 1, p. 4)[2] Critics are mostly unanimous in their diagnosis of Dickens's antipathy towards the law. J. Hillis Miller was most explicit in defining what he regarded as Dickens's unequivocal condemnation of the subject:

> Dickens detests lawyers, the legal system, and most legally operative speech acts. He has no confidence in the benign power of the written word in its official, public, legalized form. Lawyers' performatives are, for him, the most infelicitous felicities that could be imagined. They are a pollution of the body politic . . .[3]

From *Pickwick v. Bardell* in the *Pickwick Papers* to the Artful Dodger's 'shop for justice' in *Oliver Twist*; from Sampson Brass in *The Old Curiosity Shop* to Mr Vholes in *Bleak House*; from the Circumlocution Office in *Little Dorrit* to the Old Bailey in *Great Expectations*; Dickens seems to have nothing uplifting to say

---

1 See John O. Jordan, "The Social Sub-text of *David Copperfield*," *Dickens Studies Annual* 14 (1985): 61–92, 61.

2 Charles Dickens, *Bleak House*. Wordsworth Classics. Ware: Wordsworth Editions Limited, 1993. All further quotations will be taken from this edition, abbreviated as *BH*, and given parenthetically by reference to chapter and page number.

3 J. Hillis Miller, "Moments of Decision in *Bleak House*" in *The Cambridge Companion to Charles Dickens*, ed. John O. Jordan. Cambridge: CUP, 2001: 49–63, 56.

https://doi.org/10.1515/9783110754506-001

about lawsuits, lawyers, institutions or the law in and of itself. The epitome of all these horrific aspects of 'the law' in its most general terms is of course *Bleak House*. The novel's main theme is the destructive, even lethal, force of the law, its system and its representatives. Characters involved in the lawsuit at the novel's centre die in abundance – either at their own hand, driven to despair by the futility of it all or slowly wasting away, eaten up by the powers that be. In this famous novel, Dickens accuses the system of institutional failures, but extends his criticism towards those individuals who use the system to absolve themselves from the responsibility for their own actions:

> Its criticisms centre on three main areas: the failure of the courts, enmeshed in procedural rules which fail to provide an even playing field and threaten to obscure judicial decision-making; the failure of the legal profession, whose representatives are at best ineffectual windbags and at worst parlous villains; and a broader social failing, which is responsible for pervasive poverty and widespread misery.[4]

'The law' or, to be more specific, Chancery, creates a narrative arc for the novel that twists and turns not only each single plotline, but also almost each single character's fate. Legal enforcement by institutions as well as people is given a power in the novel, which seems dangerously omnipotent and most critics have noted this consuming power of the law in many of Dickens's representations.

Usually, one cannot help but note at this point that Dickens himself experienced the legal system as such a negatively connoted power, so much so that "Chancery was for Dickens a symptom of ubiquitous corruption in the legal profession."[5] As has often been mentioned, he made the experience of a suit in Chancery in person in the attempt to secure his copyright for *A Christmas Carol* and most scholars presume that it was this personal experience that ruined his belief in the system and generated the famous epithet quoted above.[6] Historically speaking, he certainly had a point: by the early nineteenth century, the English legal system that had once prided itself on the division of courts for different forms of justice could no longer proclaim any efficiency in its equity court. Due to lengthy proceedings and the need to document all movements in even the most banal Chancery suit, the Court had long become famous for its bureaucratic horror:

---

4 James E. Boasberg, "Chancery as Megalosaurus: Lawyers, Courts, and Society in *Bleak House*," *University of Hartford Studies in Literature* 21 (1989): 38–60, 38/39.

5 Dieter Paul Polloczek, *Literature and Legal Discourse. Equity and Ethics from Sterne to Conrad*. Cambridge: CUP, 1999.

6 See Paul Schlicke (ed.), *The Oxford Reader's Companion to Dickens*. Oxford: OUP, 1999: 71.

> By the eighteenth century [. . .] most of the advantages had been lost by abuse. Chancery pleadings had become verbose and complex, and the use of minutely drafted interrogatories served only to hinder proceedings. The documentation produced by most Chancery suits was elephantine.[7]

Thus, even the domineering Jarndyce and Jarndyce consumes itself in worthless documentation: ". . . great bundles of paper began to be carried out – bundles in bags, bundles too large to be got into any bags, immense masses of papers of all shapes and no shapes, which the bearers staggered under, and threw down for the time being, anyhow, on the Hall pavement, while they went back to bring out more." (*BH*, ch. 65, p. 730) J. Hillis Miller has contributed one of the most important readings of *Bleak House* by arguing that the crucial question of the novel is that of interpretation itself and thus this excessive documentation is in the end not funny, but another social threat: "The villain is the act of interpretation itself . . ."[8] At the same time, Dickens certainly aspires to being historically accurate in describing the hells of Chancery bureaucracy, but whether or not he is, has often been a point of discussion. After all, the very many years of common complaints against the Court of Chancery had led to the Chancery Amendment Act, passed in 1852, so in the end quite punctual for Dickens's *Bleak House*. It therefore cannot be argued that the novel contributed in any way to the long-awaited reform, even if Dickens himself might have wanted to think so. In fact, early reviews already indicate that the public was somewhat bored with the ins and outs of the Court and the legal arc Dickens created for the novel was no longer considered timely, as George Brimley wrote in *The Spectator*:

> This great suit is lugged in by the head and shoulders and kept prominently before the reader, solely to give Mr Dickens the opportunity of indulging in stale and commonplace satire upon the length and expense of Chancery proceedings, and exercises absolutely no influence on the characters and destinies of any one person concerned in it. The centre of the arch has nothing to do in keeping the arch together.[9]

Brimley anticipates a common twentieth-century criticism of the novel as lacking in a coherent narrative structure – a criticism that has been countered too well to deserve much commentary here.[10] More to the point is the fact that Dickens's

---

7 J. H. Baker, *An Introduction to English Legal History*. Second Edition. London: Butterworths, 1979: 97.

8 J. Hillis Miller, "Interpretation in *Bleak House*" in *Bleak House. Contemporary Critical Essays*, ed. Jeremy Tambling. New Casebooks. Basingstoke: Macmillan, 1998: 29–53, 39.

9 Philip Collins (ed.), *Dickens: The Critical Heritage*. London: Routledge and Kegan Paul, 1971: 283.

10 See above all Robert A. Donovan, "Structure and Idea in *Bleak House*," *ELH* 29.2 (1962): 175–201.

critique of the legal system seemed already stale even to his contemporaries. Reforms were desired by all and well under way by the time he began the instalments of *Bleak House* in 1852.

It seems too easy, therefore, to attribute Dickens's long-standing interest in the law and its resulting portrayal in so many of the novels to his general reputation as a reformer. One need not dispute that Dickens was extraordinarily committed to improving the conditions of his society, but whether or not the law and its reforms take the same place among his other interests may be a legitimate question. Certainly, the lack of romance in the law and the modern systematic oppression of certain groups it represents make for a fruitful fictional background, as Jan-Melissa Schramm has argued: "It suits Dickens's agenda for the moral aggrandizement of fiction to argue that the law is inattentive to the 'romance of life,' and this is a critique that he sustains throughout his fiction . . ."[11] The legal system, the Court of Chancery and all their representatives can easily be employed as personified villains and an overpowering evil on account of which one can create heroes and heroines: "Because Chancery fails to serve its presumed purpose, that of deciding lawsuits, it appears to have a will of its own, like the cruel, creeping, anthropomorphized fog to which it is initially compared."[12] Victorious are only those, who have shied decidedly away from getting involved in this corruption and shine as moral superiors to others, such as Esther Summerson, who has been seen by many critics as the embodiment of equity itself. In his seminal work, Kieran Dolin astutely identifies a crucial distinction: Dickens looks not only to the system, but to the individual.[13] While systematic justice may be a contemporary impossibility, individual responsibility can be and should be taken. In many of his novels, the heroes and heroines are those, who deliberately undermine a system that seems to relieve them from their own social responsibility for others and so their personal actions defeat a systemic apathy.

Taking this particular angle into consideration, it seems fairly reasonable to assume, as many critics have done, that Dickens takes no favourable view of the representatives of systems in *Bleak House* and beyond. One such kind of representative is of course the lawyer and characterisations of this type are indeed no insubstantial part of Dickens's 'stage society.' The lawyer seems personified

---

11 Jan-Melissa Schramm, "Dickens and the Law" in *A Companion to Charles Dickens*, ed. David Paroissien. Oxford: Wiley-Blackwell, 2011: 277–293, 281.

12 Suzanne Daly, "Belligerent Instruments: The Documentary Violence of *Bleak House*," *Studies in the Novel* 47.1 (2015): 20–42, 28.

13 See Kieran Dolin, *Fiction and the Law. Legal Discourse in Victorian and Modernist Literature*. Cambridge: CUP, 1999: 87.

systematic failure, for his belief in the law necessarily conditions a disinterest towards the human in Dickens's world:

> To the lawyer the law is intellectual, abstract, and beautiful, like a game of chess, and it is just here that the fundamental ground of Dickens' quarrel with him lies. Justice for Dickens was generally open and palpable. He couldn't understand why man's natural emotional response to injustice wasn't sufficient impetus to lead him to correct it if he could.[14]

Given Dickens's affinity for stock characters and caricatures, it is fairly easy to see in representatives such as Vholes or Jaggers mere variants of the despicable lawyer as type – a type and an image of a cultural figure that Dickens did not invent, but nevertheless certainly used and perpetuated. Long before the nineteenth century, lawyers already suffered from a questionable reputation and they do so to this day as the butt of innumerable lawyer jokes. In order to see clearly what Dickens does with the type, however, it is necessary to distinguish more specifically between certain branches of the profession, for Dickens shows a possibly idiosyncratic preference for the solicitor over the barrister.

The barrister was a type of lawyer who was allowed to argue in court and whose role drastically increased with the Prisoner's Counsel Act of 1836. Until the act, defendants were allowed to speak for themselves, but were not given the right to have a professional argue their case. The solicitor, on the other hand, was not called to the Bar and hence did not argue in the criminal court, but worked both to prepare documents for legal trials and functioned in the equity trials in the Court of Chancery. The separation between the two branches of the profession of 'lawyer' already carried an inherent segregation, for barristers were considered of a higher social order than solicitors: "The Bar had cut itself off from those members of the legal profession whom it stigmatised as ministerial persons of an inferior nature and had committed itself to the courts as the main sphere of its activity."[15] Historians have emphasised that the profession of the solicitor was considered questionable and inferior from the start, although as is so often the case, the barrister's hauteur towards the solicitor was equally arbitrary, for neither had legal training, let alone a university degree:

> It is a sad reflection on law faculties that most of the distinguished lawyers between about 1850 and 1950 were not university graduates at all or had read subjects other than law. The state of legal education was constantly debated. In 1846 [. . .] it was recommended that universities should teach the elements of legal science and that professional law schools should teach the practice. The profession responded first, by establishing the

14 Donovan, "Structure and Idea," 179.

15 Harry Kirk, *Portrait of a Profession. A History of the Solicitor's Profession, 1100 to the Present Day*. London: Oyez Publishing, 1976: 19.

> Council of Legal Education in 1852 to serve the inns of court; [. . .] but lectures were voluntary and were soon virtually superseded by crammers, and examinations for the bar were not compulsory until 1872.[16]

Thus, barristers had no more legal training than solicitors and their higher professional status was merely conventional. This perceived superiority becomes even more equivocal, when one considers what it took in truth to become a barrister in the nineteenth century. If they wanted to be called to the Bar eventually, aspiring lawyers merely had to join one of the Inns of Court, which required a certain capital:

> If he had enough money to pay the appropriate fees it was fairly easy to join one of them for usually, during the nineteenth century, there was no very meticulous investigation into the character of applicants. Anyone who wished to go beyond this stage and actually be 'called' to the Bar had to consume a number of more or less edible dinners at the Inn and (after 1852) attend a few lectures . . .[17]

The professional 'distinction' of having been called to the Bar, therefore, in truth offered no qualification and the binary system of barristers and solicitors (or attorneys)[18] was merely founded on a formality, yet had severe social implications. As much as lawyers generally suffered from a questionable reputation, solicitors were even worse off: "The attorneys and solicitors in the nineteenth century were acutely sensitive about their social status and their reputation. [. . .] They found the contrast in their situation in this respect and that of the Bar particularly irksome . . ."[19]

Whether or not barristers looked down on solicitors with any professional justification, as lawyers they all shared an existence as frequent butts of jokes even long before the nineteenth century: "From ancient Greece and the New Testament to our own day, lawyers have long been objects of derision. [. . .] In early modern England, lawyers were condemned for avarice and greed, for stimulating unneeded litigation and then prolonging it."[20] Such prejudice lies at the heart of both Shakespeare's line "The first thing we do, let's kill all the lawyers" in *2Henry VI* and Dickens's own "The one great principle of the English law is, to

16 Baker, *English Legal History*, 149.

17 Raymond Cocks, *Foundations of the Modern Bar*. London: Sweet & Maxwell, 1983: 1/2.

18 See Cocks, *Modern Bar*, 3: "Attornies had similar achievements to their credit – indeed until the 1870s, when Parliament decided that they should in future be regarded as solicitors, the terms 'solicitor' and 'attorney' could be used very loosely and might even refer to the same man."

19 Kirk, *Portrait of a Profession*, 169.

20 Marc Galanter, *Lowering the Bar. Lawyer Jokes & Legal Culture*. Madison: The University of Wisconsin Press, 2005: 3.

make business for itself" (*BH*, ch. 39, p. 466). The disdain towards lawyers is so common and long-standing that this might be one of the reasons why Dickens's despicable lawyers have received relatively little attention. Lawyers had long suffered from their uncertain standing in society and as the nineteenth century made absolutely no exception, Dickens might have simply employed the prejudice. As this is not a history of the legal profession, but rather an investigation into how Dickens uses the type for the construction of his characters, I will not delve too deeply into asking for reasons for the almost unanimous rejection of lawyers, but there are two aspects that must be mentioned here, for they seem to play a crucial role in Dickens's position towards the profession – money and education:

> Money is a constant theme running through the history of the profession. Hardly had attorneys started being paid for their services than there were complaints about their avarice [. . .]. Money has always been one of the most important criteria of a solicitor's success and was for long the means by which he escaped from the toils of the profession and climbed the social ladder; money has in any event always been the subject-matter of most of the profession's business.[21]

Given their dubious status both within and outside their profession, solicitors only had an opportunity to advance their station in society through the accumulation of money – at the same time, pecuniary means in and of themselves were obviously morally dubious in Victorian society. While social advancement through worldly gains was no longer frowned upon, the sheer intention to better oneself on financial grounds was nevertheless regarded as highly arbitrary. There is no need to reiterate here the hundreds of examples in Dickens's novels of the corruptive power of money and the moral ambiguity of wealthy characters. One need only think of the memorable exchange between Dombey and Son or the theme of greed in *Our Mutual Friend*: "From the first [. . .] the story is explicitly about money, which Dickens represents as something which fastens on living life and corrupts and kills; he figures money as fatal to the quality of life and even to life itself."[22] In Dickens's novels, "obsession with money and position has a malevolent effect . . ."[23] It is hardly surprising therefore that Dickensian lawyers such as Vholes and Jaggers are unsympathetic characters per se, considering that their primary intention is to accumulate money. Dickens seems to reflect the historical discourse of the lawyer's greed rather uncritically in his adherence to Victorian ethics.

21 Kirk, *Portrait of a Profession*, 83.

22 Christina Crosby, "Financial" in *A Companion to Victorian Literature and Culture*, ed. Herbert F. Tucker. Oxford: Wiley-Blackwell, 1999: 225–243, 237.

23 Leon Litvack, "*Our Mutual Friend*" in *A Companion to Charles Dickens*, ed. David Paroissien. Oxford: Wiley-Blackwell, 2011: 422–432, 434.

The other prejudice that worked very much to the legal profession's disadvantage was the factual lack of education. As already indicated, being called to the Bar preconditioned no legal training before 1870 and professional lawyers could easily be men without any notable education whatsoever: "The standard general education in the profession was abysmally low, and even among the better sort there were hardly any with a university education."[24] While this lack of formal education certainly did not speak for the qualification of the profession, from a hierarchical point-of-view it offered another problem as to where to place the lawyer in the social order. After all, without a respectable family tree, only a proper education could enable one to achieve the status of gentleman. Whether or not solicitors, no matter how wealthy, could therefore properly be regarded as gentlemen, was a reasonable point of discussion. Formally, they had to be considered gentlemen because of the Act 'for the better Regulation of Attorneys and Solicitors' from 1730:

> Those whose names were admitted to the role of solicitors became officers of the Court of Chancery and enjoyed the same privileges as the attorney who from time immemorial had been regarded as officers of their respective courts. Accordingly they became entitled to call themselves 'gentlemen.' This is the origin of the jibe that solicitors are gentlemen by Act of Parliament.[25]

The discrepancy between the *formal* status of gentleman and the *ethical* status of gentleman as a man of good breeding and education seems to lie at the heart of the solicitor's questionable position in society – along with the general prejudice that money was their only objective. This is certainly not an offer of an exclusive or exhaustive explanation for why the lawyer has suffered from an unflattering image in so many cultures, but it shall nevertheless provide more insight into the more or less conscious elements that feed into Dickens's creation of his various lawyer figures.

Given Dickens's profound interest in and critique of the law in so many of his novels, it is surprising that we have not paid more attention to those characters he created that represent that law or deal in it. In what must probably count as the first investigation into Dickens and the law, Williams Holdsworth's seminal *Charles Dickens as a Legal Historian* from 1929, the author provides us with an overview of Dickens's legal practitioners in respect to their proper place in the professional system. As Holdsworth argues, Dickens once again seems to focus on what he knows:

---

24 Kirk, *Portrait of a Profession*, 204.
25 Michael Birks, *Gentlemen of the Law*. Stevens & Sons Limited, 1960: 136.

> Dickens's practical acquaintance with the law in the offices of Charles Molloy, and Ellis and Blackmore, had given him an extensive knowledge of the lower ranks of the legal profession. He knew well the sheriff's officers, the law stationers, and the hack copyists whom the law stationers employed. He had an equally wide acquaintance with many different types of attorneys and solicitors. But his knowledge of the higher ranks of the legal profession is less extensive. Neither barristers nor king's counsel play any great part.[26]

The lawyer characters who figure most prominently are solicitors, rather than barristers, such as Tulkinghorn and Vholes. Jaggers belongs to the same branch of the profession, although he might be mistaken for a barrister since he is referred to as acting in court too. These figures, which belong more strictly to the lawyer profession than stationers such as Snagsby or clerks such as Micawber, play an ambiguous role in Dickens's novels. On the one hand, it seems safe to argue that they are certainly minor characters, or, to put this even more mildly, there is no lawyer protagonist in Dickens, with the exceptions of Sydney Carton and Eugene Wrayburn, whose positions in *A Tale of Two Cities* and *Our Mutual Friend* will require close attention in chapter 5. As strongly as Victorian legal institutions and their elements are represented in the works of Dickens, they are negatively marginalised in unwholesome narrative arcs or unlikeable minor characters. This negative stance towards the law and lawyers is often critically construed as historical accuracy. This is certainly what Holdsworth tried to show when he used the novels as examples of legal historiography as so many legal historians have done since. In this sense, Dickens's generally critical stance taken towards this particular profession and its representatives is hardly surprising as the systematic shortcomings of the Victorian era discussed above gave him ample opportunity.

However, while I have already indicated that Dickens's proverbial disgust of the law might be a simplification, his portrayal of the representative figures is even more ambiguous as is his position towards the legal profession in general. In the 1830s he was, after all, still determined to enter the Bar himself.[27] It is not unreasonable to assume, therefore, that Dickens's relationship with the law was more complicated than the critique immanent in the novels would suggest: "[T]here is also another Dickens, the one who contemplated practising at the Bar, who wanted to become a stipendiary magistrate, who was a friend of judges, lawyers, stipendiary magistrates, detectives and prison governors . . ."[28] And there is also the Dickens, who was concerned with his own social status and

---

26 William S. Holdsworth, *Charles Dickens as a Legal Historian*. New Haven: Yale University Press, 1929: 43.

27 See Michael Slater, *Charles Dickens*. New Haven and London: Yale University Press, 2009: 46.

28 Schlicke (ed.), *Oxford Dickens*, 323.

the question of what exactly made a gentleman. It is highly significant, therefore, that he was not seldom derided in contemporary reviews of his novels for his alleged *lack* of legal knowledge:

> The literary barrister, and later judge, James Fitzjames Stephen, who delighted to lambaste Dickens in *The Saturday Review* from the mid 1850s on, crushingly (and snobbishly) observed in 1857 that Dickens's 'notions of law, which occupy so large a space in his books, are precisely those of an attorney's clerk'.[29]

This might have been a heavier blow to Dickens's self-esteem than one might think, considering the 'place' Stephen puts Dickens in. After all, it is very well known that Dickens struggled with his own insufficient education and the resulting uncertainty of his social status. Given that his financial wealth could not make him an unquestionable gentleman in his own eyes, the placement far below gentleman's status in the legal system might have been a very grave injury indeed. When Fitzjames Stephen proclaims heartily in a review of *Bleak House* that Dickens "knows absolutely nothing of law or politics,"[30] one can sense that he not only finds Dickens's legal expertise wanting, but also means to put him in his place beneath the educated elite of Victorian London. It should be imperative, therefore, to discuss Dickens's treatment of the law and its representatives with a view towards what this meant both for him and his characters in terms of class. Struggling with his own uncertain social station and constantly caught up in the attempt to better himself, it is not unreasonable to presume that Dickens treats the uncertain social status of lawyer figures in his fiction ambiguously. It is also possible to look closely at these representatives of the law as not simply standing for the system itself, but as more rounded, even more powerful characters, who have a more independent presence in their novels.

It seems that Dickens frowned upon the law and its representatives enough not to make them heroes of his fiction, but the 'minor' characters he inserts so often are in all likelihood more than just stereotypes or even only types, although this is certainly a difficult statement to make when it comes to Dickens. There is a long tradition of Dickens scholarship that has laboured under the (mis-)apprehension that Dickens's forte is certainly not the construction of character. Ever since George Eliot complained of a lack of psychological depth, many critics have assumed that one will not find a good deal of substance under the ostentatious surface of many characters in the novels.[31] There is a reason why Forster would make Dickens his prime example for the distinction between flat

29 Slater, *Dickens*, 29.
30 Collins, *Critical Heritage*, 349.
31 See Collins, *Critical Heritage*, 343.

and round characters and many have accepted the fact that Dickens works substantially with ultimately flat characters. However, these days, scarcely fewer scholars would argue that to rely on the commonplace of one-dimensional Dickensian characters is just as simplistic. Natalie McKnight makes an excellent case when it comes to Dickens's portrayal of men, women and gender stereotypes:

> It is easy to overemphasize Dickens's reliance on Victorian gender stereotypes, but to do so is to miss the richness of his fictional characterizations. Does Dickens rely on gender stereotypes? Certainly. Does he reveal the contradictions and dangerous tensions in these stereotypes? Absolutely. Does he transcend the gender stereotypes? Almost always.[32]

I would like to propose that we pay the same attention with the same caveats Dickens's minor characters and in this particular case, his lawyers. Considering that so many of these lawyer figures seem to be flat characters at first sight, one might assume that they are nothing more than representatives of the system, but such a reading hardly overcomes the historical prejudice.

When Dickens writes in *Bleak House* that "[t]he one great principle of the English law is, to make business for itself" (*BH*, ch. 39, p. 466) he does so, of course, in reference to Vholes, who squeezes Richard Carstone dry in a hopeless case merely for his own gain. In this sense, Vholes is a representative of the oppressive power of Chancery and many critics have argued exactly that. The same is true for Tulkinghorn and Jaggers, Dodson and Fogg. In the early works, lawyers seem to be caricatures of systemic representatives, in later works they seem simply villains, who are embodiments of the evil the English law is capable of inflicting on its subjects. However, I argue that Dickens's conception of the lawyer character changes substantially throughout his career. His earliest lawyers, for instance, can hardly be considered characters in their own right. Both Dodson and Fogg in *The Pickwick Papers* and Sampson Brass in *The Old Curiosity Shop* are evil qua profession and there is nothing to their natures that is not 'lawyer.' They are exclusively types built on prejudice. In fact, many critics have struggled with the fact that it is difficult to conceive of *The Pickwick Papers* as a novel to begin with, for after all, it is more of a mystery than a novel.[33] As John Bowen has claimed, strictly speaking, it is not a novel.[34] The only aspect of the text that lends it structure is the lawsuit *Bardell v. Pickwick* itself, as Jonathan Grossman has argued in his wonderful analysis of *The Pickwick*

32 Natalie McKnight, "Dickens and Gender" in *A Companion to Charles Dickens*, ed. David Paroissien. Oxford: Wiley-Blackwell, 2011: 186–198, 197.
33 For an analysis of its 'lack' of structure see Steven Marcus, "Language into Structure: Pickwick Revisited," *Daedalus* 101.1 (1972): 183–202.
34 John Bowen, *Other Dickens. Pickwick to Chuzzlewit*. Oxford: OUP, 2000: 47.

Papers and the law court: "Pickwick's visits to the law offices and the law courts are less about legal reform than about the novel's form and the establishment of the middle-class, professional author at the outset of the Victorian period."[35] Consequently, the 'novel's lawyer characters are no more than types, born from extreme prejudice and the wish for satire. The novel is "notorious for its disparagement of lawyers,"[36] but their profession matters less than their proverbial predisposition for interpretation and bending the truth: "With the introduction of the lawyers, what was merely a dilemma of conflicting interpretations becomes a study in the manipulation of interpretation."[37] Technically, the lawsuit in *The Pickwick Papers* functions only on a 'simple' satire of the breach-of-promise trial.[38] Moreover, as Alexander Welsh pointed out long ago, the trial also serves as a source of humour for the novel's contemporary audience through its "topical satire of the Norton-Melbourne case,"[39] which seems to have been the inspiration for Dickens's imagining Serjeant Buzfuz and his extraordinary argument in court. Thus, the lawyers involved are stereotypes that confirm Dickens's society's worst prejudices against their profession: "The trial scene repeats in broad burlesque terms the same pattern of action: innocent reality in the hands of Dodson, Fogg, and Justice Stareleigh takes on an erroneous aspect of villainy . . ."[40]

I do not mean to disparage the early Dickens, but it is hardly disputable that these early lawyer characters do not serve an in-depth analysis. They are fully marginalised in the text as representatives of an evil system that does not distribute justice, but obstructs justice. In this sense, it is perfectly possible to see in *The Pickwick Papers* a source for *Bleak House*, as Sean Grass has done, especially when it comes to the constructedness of the prison.[41] Themes that would prove highly influential for many of Dickens's later novels are obviously already anticipated in the *Pickwick Papers* and the law is no exception. In this

35 Jonathan Grossman, *The Art of Alibi. English Law Courts and the Novel*. Baltimore and London: The Johns Hopkins University Press, 2002: 84.

36 Grossman, *Art of Alibi*, 100.

37 Grossman, *Art of Alibi*, 177.

38 See Mara H. Fein, "The Politics of Family in *The Pickwick Papers*," *ELH* 61.2 (1994) 363–379: 371.

39 Alexander Welsh, "Waverley, Pickwick, and Don Quixote," *Nineteenth-Century Fiction* 22.1 (1967): 19–30, 26.

40 William Axton, "Unity and Coherence in *The Pickwick Papers*," *Studies in English Literature* 5.4 (1965): 663–676, 673.

41 See Sean Grass, "Pickwick, the Past, and the Prison," *Dickens Studies Annual* 29 (2000): 17–39.

early novel, as in many of the later ones, the law serves as "an instrument of the brutality of society," a society which tends to force people "into artificial meaningless roles that deny their identity."[42] The solicitors in the novel are thus representatives of this oppressive force and according to their historical reputation, which Dickens implements in the novel, they are highly self-aware and unashamed of their dealings. Consequently, an inquiry into a psychologically more complex conception of these characters warrants little merit. While the text's important themes may recur in novels as intricate as *Bleak House*, the difference between the construction of characters such as Dodson and Fogg and Mr Tulkinghorn seems too vast to even speak of them in the same vein.

The same is true for Sampson Brass, an early lawyer in Dickens, who is little more than a foil for every conceivable prejudice against lawyers, including his highly 'unnatural' sister. As Saber Hamdi has it, "in a purely Dickensian spirit of poetic justice, the Brasses are reduced to pure allegories of the legal monster they serve."[43] As is so typical of the early Dickens, the representatives of the law in *The Old Curiosity Shop* are no characters in their own right, but only sources of evil – in Rosemary Coleman's words, they are "the embodied spirits of Disease and Vice."[44] In their carceral office, Dick Swiveller's suppressed aggression against Sally Brass serves as comic relief and his character shines by comparison – despite the fact that he is an early version of the ne'er-do-well that Dickens can make quite depressing and sinister as he does in Harold Skimpole or Tip Dorrit. It has often been observed that Dick's character might have been very close to Dickens's heart as a possible alter ego,[45] so it comes as no surprise that Swiveller finds himself disgusted with the law and its representatives – a disgust that oozes from the novel onto all of Dickens's later works, it seems. Dick serves as the most important counterpart to the evil embodied by Brass and Quilp,

42 James R. Kincaid, "The Education of Mr. Pickwick," *Nineteenth-Century Fiction* 24.2 (1969): 127–141, 136/137.

43 Saber Hamdi, "Of 'Household Gods' and Devils: Fetishism in *The Old Curiosity Shop*," *Anglia* 137.3 (2019): 411–433, 420.

44 Rosemary Coleman, "Nell and Sophronia – Catherine, Mary, and Georgina: Solving the Female Puzzle and the Gender Conundrum in *The Old Curiosity Shop*," *Dickens Studies Annual* 36 (2005): 33–55, 49.

45 See, for example, Paul Schlicke, "Embracing the New Spirit of the Age: Dickens and the Evolution of *The Old Curiosity Shop*," *Dickens Studies Annual* 32 (2002): 1–35, 26; James Buzard, "Enumeration and Exhaustion: Taking Inventory in *The Old Curiosity Shop*," *Dickens Studies Annual* 39 (2008): 17–41, 33; Carra Glatt, "Genre and the Counterfactual in *The Old Curiosity Shop*," *Dickens Quarterly* 31.2 (2014): 113–126, 122; and Hamdi, "Fetishism in *The Old Curiosity Shop*," 429.

who function not only as melodramatic villains, but also as early precursors of Dickens's recurring critique of "the everyday practice and underlying philosophy of coercive, mercenary, and ultimately unimaginative social relations . . ."[46]

While neither group of lawyers in these two early novels can serve as sources for an understanding of the complexity Dickens will employ in his creation of the character type, they can certainly be regarded as blueprints that bear a variety of aspects that hardly any of Dickens's later lawyers will escape. Their tendentiously evil, greedy, mercenary and merciless nature recurs in prominent figures such as Tulkinghorn and Jaggers, who are equally representative of a system that seems to be an almost natural breeding ground for corruption in Dickens. As Robert Garis wrote in 1965, "[i]n Mr. Tulkinghorn's business-like tone, 'like a machine', we hear the accents of System itself."[47] Or as Brenda Welch writes much more recently, "Tulkinghorn is the embodiment of English law making business for itself; he is the embodiment of those in the legal profession who are the cause of the unrest – the overreaching, self-indulgent, self-serving and abusive lawyers . . ."[48] Given that all lawyers are minor characters, it is not unreasonable to presume that they simply stand for something else, that they are pawns in an overarching political message in which Dickens generalises all those who have dealings in or with the law. In his particular focus on *Bleak House*, Gary Watt has therefore argued that in his plea for equity, Dickens makes all characters symbols of the legal conflict: "Dickens' [. . .] technique of personification is to embody abstract vices and virtues in human form. Tulkinghorn is an embodiment of the vice of all-consuming legalism and formality. Esther Summerson is equity personified . . ."[49] Yet, we also know that Dickens is a writer of contradictions as Kate Flint has shown at length.[50] The idea that all lawyers are only symptomatic of a terrible system seems a little too coherent – especially when one considers that the representation of the system itself is far from coherent. This at least is the result of D. A. Miller's famous analysis of *Bleak House*: "[T]he text at once claims that this system is and isn't efficient, is and isn't everywhere, can and can't be reformed."[51] Furthermore, it is impossible not

---

46 Sarah Winter, "Curiosity as Didacticism in *The Old Curiosity Shop*," *Novel* 34.1 (2000): 28–55, 47.

47 Robert Garis, *The Dickens Theatre. A Reassessment of the Novels*. Oxford: Clarendon Press, 1965: 137.

48 Brenda Welch, "Tulkinghorn and Professional Responsibility in *Bleak House*," *Dickens Quarterly* 35.1 (2018): 47–62, 59.

49 Gary Watt, *Equity Stirring. The Story of Justice Beyond Law*. Oxford and Portland: Hart, 2009: 167.

50 Kate Flint, *Dickens*. Brighton: The Harvester Press, 1986.

51 D. A. Miller, *The Novel and the Police*. Berkeley: University of California Press, 1988: 65.

to see that Dickens's critique in the novel is not only of the system and possibly its representatives, but also of the denial of human responsibility. He draws attention to those individuals, such as Skimpole, for instance, who rely on the system to relieve them of their personal obligation to behave ethically towards others. In other words, Dickensian 'villains' in a legal context are villains when they shy away from personal responsibility and this is blatantly reproached in the narrative of *Bleak House*, as Joseph Fradin has noted: "Chancery practice presents us with a paradigm of the ways in which civilized men are responsible for one another, and fail in that responsibility."[52] The great evil of the system therefore lies in the fact that it enables what Bruce Robbins has called "organised, legitimated irresponsibility": "It is by means of their profession that the Chancery lawyers evade the responsibility for their actions, that they shoot their daily arrows in the air without being obliged to consider on whom the arrows are falling."[53] In that sense, these lawyers in and beyond *Bleak House* are villains, but it is not possible to view them as one homogenous sub-group of Dickens's evil minor characters. For one, even within this single novel, they are not the same, as J. Hillis Miller already remarked in his famous first reading of the novel: "In this system of reference and counter-reference the differences are, it is important to see, as essential as the similarities. Each lawyer in the novel is different from all the others."[54]

This book is supposed to unravel not just the similarities between the lawyers in Dickens, but also their differences. They may be minor characters, but they do not represent a single coherent image. Most lawyers in Dickens seem to be incarnations of evil. They obstruct the happiness of others, they are mostly completely unlikeable and they serve as objects whose defeat contributes to the happy ending. They are often associated with the devil, darkness and despair; they are ugly to look at, which reflects their ugly insides, and the text somehow or other 'kills' them for the greater good.[55] This is all true, but there are two things to consider. First, types in Dickens are rarely consistent. Two, characters have a means of getting away from their fictional destiny. As to the first, the number of critics, who have remarked on Dickens's subversions of melodramatic types are

52 Joseph I. Fradin, "Will and Society in *Bleak House*," *PMLA* 81.1 (1966): 95–109, 98.

53 Bruce Robbins, "Telescopic Philanthropy: Professionalism and Responsibility in *Bleak House*" in *Bleak House. Contemporary Critical Essays*, ed. Jeremy Tambling. Basingstoke: Macmillan, 1998: 139–162, 143/144.

54 Miller, "Interpretation," 33.

55 For the significance of the physical appearance of Dodson and Fogg, for instance, see Juliet McMaster, "Visual Design in *Pickwick Papers*," *Studies in English Literature* 23.4 (1983): 595–614.

too numerous to validate another elongated effusion on the subject.[56] For the purposes of this book it is worthwhile remembering John Kucich's "second class of villains" in Dickens, for his distinction is astute:

> Despite the familiar assumption to the contrary, villainy does not make up a single category in Dickens. [. . .] But there is a second class of villains who are less tied to Dickens' economic and political satire, and who are the real melodramatic antagonists. These villains threaten irrational, violent danger that does not have a narrowly economic motive [. . .] – these are irredeemable, confirmed villains.[57]

As much as Dickens lets his lawyer figures reflect the contemporary prejudice concerning the greedy solicitor, who actively pursues hopeless cases for his own gain, I will argue that the evil within the lawyers is not simply the desire for economic profit. In fact, their desires are much more human. In order to be able to show this, however, one has to attribute more literary significance to the so-called 'minor' character than is often customary.

Character studies are outdated, to say the least. Ever since structuralists drew attention to the fact that a character first and foremost cannot 'be' a person, cannot act or think like a human being, but can only fulfil their function within the genre they have been placed in, the *raison d'être* of character studies has suffered a severe blow. Classic character studies, as summarised by Hélène Cixous, simply does not work from a structuralist perspective:

> By definition, a 'character,' preconceived or created by an author, is to be figured out, understood, read: he is presented, offered up to interpretation, with the prospect of a traditional reading that seeks its satisfaction at the level of a potential identification with such and such a 'personage' . . .[58]

In this sense, we only have a choice between a 'psychological' and a systematic reading of a character and in the aftermath of structuralism, most 'psychological' readings come across as hopelessly naïve. However, there is a certain revival of character studies to be observed in the twenty-first century that finds the appropriate angle in dispensing with the idea that the author is in control of their characters. After all, we have every right with Roland Barthes to question whether a character is "preconceived or created by an author" as Cixous has it, into a predetermined existence that leaves only a predetermined generic fate. If we assume as poststucturalists that the author is not in control of their text, character studies

56 See above all else Natalie McKnight, *Idiots, Madmen and Other Prisoners in Dickens*. New York: St. Martin's Press, 1993.
57 John Kucich, *Excess and Restraint in the Novels of Charles Dickens*. Athens, Georgia: University of Georgia Press, 1981: 61.
58 Hélène Cixous, "The Character of 'Character'," *New Literary History* 5.2 (1974): 383–402, 385.

assumes a new significance. From this perspective, characters are simply always both: both referents in a structured universe and creatures of the text's subconscious. As Alex Woloch has argued in his seminal work on the significance of minor characters, "the literary character itself is divided, always emerging at the juncture between structure and reference."[59] The inherent ambiguity in the being that is customarily referred to as 'literary character' possibly becomes most clear when one returns to one of the very first theorists on the subject, E. M. Forster himself. In *Aspects of the Novel* he lays the groundwork for structural analyses that foreground the construction into flat or round, protagonist or antagonist, and yet, Forster the writer, rather than the theorist, already anticipates that a literary character is never fully in the hands of their creator:

> The characters arrive when evoked, but full of the spirit of mutiny. For they have these numerous parallels with people like ourselves, they try to live their own lives and are consequently often engaged in treason against the main scheme of the book. They 'run away', they 'get out of hand'; they are creations inside a creation, and often inharmonious towards it; if they are given complete freedom they kick the book to pieces, and if they are kept too sternly in check they revenge themselves by dying, and destroy it by intestinal decay.[60]

It may be the case that Forster the theorist thus makes the distinction between flat and round to help Forster the writer to keep those characters in check who will otherwise get away from him – this is conjecture, but Forster clearly perceives that his characters have a life of their own and as a writer, he somehow needs to find ways and means to control them. Thus, again, characters are always both: pillars in a preconceived structure and creatures that tend to break away from it, subverting the author's power over their own work.

The literary character's ambiguous existence creates an interesting condition for minor characters, which is Woloch's premise. Whether or not a character is, in fact, minor, can be determined only by the text itself:

> The minor character rests in the shadow-space between narrative position and human personality: an implied human being who gets constricted into a limited role, but who has enough resonance with a human being to make us aware of this constricted position as limited.[61]

So whether a minor character is in fact also *flat* the text equally determines. One can easily make the mistake of equating flatness with minorness, but this

59 Alex Woloch, *The One vs. the Many. Minor Characters and the Space of the Protagonist in the Novel*. Princeton and Oxford: Princeton University Press, 2003: 17.
60 E. M. Forster, *Aspects of the Novel*, ed. Oliver Stallybrass. London: Penguin Books, 2005: 72.
61 Woloch, *The One vs. The Many*, 40.

could only be true if characters were indeed controlled by their creators. A flat character, as Forster imagines it, would then necessarily be one-dimensional and easily recognisable, as Maria DiBattista writes: "We can easily spot those characters destined to remain flat, never to curve into the round characters who, because they have no appreciable contour to them, do not arouse our anxiety or curiosity."[62] This is only true, however, if these flat characters also comply with their position on the margin, which is not necessarily the case. The minor character, on the other hand, may evolve beyond their predestined role: "The strange resonance of minor characters [. . .] stems from the intricacy of this narrative process; from the character who is *not* directly or fully represented in the narrative, and who comes to command a peculiar kind of attention in the partial occlusion of his fullness."[63] Dickens's lawyers are then only flat *and* minor, if they are truly nothing but symbolic representations of the legal system. In fact, many of them are minor characters, who will not adhere to their position and who rebel against their structural flatness – instead, they unfold "the untold tale into the telling."[64]

It is of course very easy to regard Dicken's minor characters as flat; this has to do with his particular mode of characterisation. Audrey Jaffe has pointed out that Dickens's characters first and foremost seem to be 'material' characters: "Dickens's characters are famously marked: eccentric in appearance and character, doomed in general to repeat the same phrases, whistle the same tunes, twitch the same twitches throughout their lives as characters, even if and when they exhibit a capacity for change."[65] This is perhaps even more obvious when his characters so clearly represent a socio-cultural type such as the lawyer: many aspects of his outward appearance and formal or social misdemeanour seem predetermined by the intention to make him recognisable as a Victorian lawyer. However, it makes sense to look through these external markings and consider what these minor characters truly do to the text. There is too much development and too much ambiguity in Dickens's works to let the lawyers rest as a particularly unlikeable category of minor character. Thus, the lawyer deserves the same caveat that critics often place ahead of their analysis of Dickens's types:

62 Maria DiBattista, *Novel Characters. A Genealogy*. Oxford: Wiley-Blackwell, 2010: 12.

63 Woloch, *The One vs. The Many*, 40.

64 Woloch, *The One vs. The Many*, 41.

65 Audrey Jaffe, *Vanishing Points, Dickens, Narrative, and the Subject of Omniscience*. Berkeley: University of California Press, 14.

> Naturally some of Dickens's characters are as simple and straightforward as they appear to be. Often, however, especially in his mature novels, polysemous descriptive prose, divided personalities, images of doubling and inversion, and problematic relations between character and structure create elusive fictional beings.[66]

Mr Micawber is a case in point. Micawber is a material character, who is clearly visually marked by Dickens and reiterates easily recognisable discursive patterns, thereby pushing himself through repetition towards a memorable figure in *David Copperfield*. However, his progress in the novel and the role he plays in the eventual resolution of the major conflict and the defeat of the villain, elevate him far above the status of a flat or minor character. In fact, Micawber's role as a law clerk greatly enhances his role in the novel's overall system, as I shall try to show in chapter 2.

This brings me back to the alleged turning-point in Dickens's career and the novel's seeming insignificance for a discussion in law and literature. It is true that *David Copperfield* seems to be a mostly domestic novel, but it bears much greater significance for Dickens's development of the lawyer figure than has hitherto been thought. After all, it carries the archetype of this particular type of villain: Uriah Heep. I will argue in the following that Uriah Heep is the origin of Dickens's conception of the evil lawyer figure and that his role as a Double for David tells us a lot about Dickens's conflicted position towards the law and its representatives. While early figures such as Serjeant Buzfuz or Sampson Brass are little more than caricatures, Dickens goes to the full length of developing a round character in Uriah Heep, who is synonymous with the law and serves as an archetype for the creation of all subsequent lawyer figures. The fact that Heep is the first villain of the law becomes even clearer when we contrast him with Mr Micawber, who acts according to the principles of equity. The often-observed conflict between the law and equity in Dickens, which seems to be introduced as an elaborate theme in *Bleak House*, in fact takes its beginnings in *David Copperfield*, so that it is possible to consider this novel a turning-point even through the particular lens of law and literature.

---

66 Brian Rosenberg, *Little Dorrit's Shadows. Character and Contradiction in Dickens*. Columbia, Mo. and London: University of Missouri Press, 1996: 24.

2 The Nemesis

Dickens's complex discussion of the law and its representatives does not begin with *Bleak House*, it begins with *David Copperfield*. Uriah is the archetype of the evil lawyer; Micawber is equity personified. The juxtaposition of the two exemplifies Dickens's deeply ambiguous feelings towards the law, his identification with its representatives and the principal difference between the law and equity that is crucial for many of his subsequent novels. For most of the narrative, Uriah is of course only a lawyer's clerk and the fact that his employer, Mr Wickfield, is essentially a good man, shows how Dickens approaches the lawyer as a subject from conflicting viewpoints. The most complicated perspective the text offers us towards Uriah is that of David's nemesis, a figure he proclaims to hate and yet cannot help identify with for reasons that are not always self-evident. Therefore, Uriah Heep has long been recognised as David Copperfield's Double, to whom he is 'attracted in repulsion,' because the protagonist recognises his own abject desires in the villain and antagonist. Uriah represents for David both his repressed wishes and his repressed fears and his first-person narrative is crucially influenced by the need to control Uriah as an opposed power within it. Uriah is therefore a paradigmatic character who gets away from the author, developing a life of his own due to his strong repercussions with both David's and Dickens's subconscious. Uriah is also a necessary plot element, a trigger for David's fall of fortune, and his unconscious motive to prove himself in times of crisis; the villain he can triumph over in the end; and the needed rival that brings about his sexual desire for Agnes, which turns her from sister to wife and thereby allows the hero's heterosexual happy ending: "Uriah Heep is a Doppelgänger [. . .] in whom the aggressive and sexual demands of the hero are strangely absorbed and whose criminal doings, as eventually exposed, clear the hero of blame."[67] David needs Uriah's desire for Agnes in order to allow his own feelings for her to become sexual, which triggers the crucial turning-point in the love plot of the novel.

Uriah has desires and motives that the narrator shares, but that the latter does not want to reveal to the reader, because they do not comply with his ethics. David presents Uriah as a despicable creature, because he represents a lower class background that David feels self-conscious about. In his definitive reading of the novel, John O. Jordan has shown that Uriah Heep represents for

67 Alexander Welsh, *From Copyright to Copperfield. The Identity of Dickens*. Cambridge, Mass.: Harvard University Press, 1987: 143.

https://doi.org/10.1515/9783110754506-002

David "the class entanglement he most strongly seeks to avoid."[68] Due to his class complex, having barely avoided dropping from a respectable middle-class upbringing to an existence as a street-child, David needs Uriah to divert the reader from his own designs on upward mobility. Uriah's scheme to replace Wickfield in the business through embezzlement and the 'acquisition' of the lawyer's daughter is constructed as clearly unethical to delude from the fact that David's intentions towards Dora Spenlow are almost exactly the same. The narrator thus needs his doppelganger to direct the reader's attention away from his own questionable motives: "the whole conception of Uriah Heep as the 'umble' hypocrite shadows darkly Copperfield's rise in the world through earnestness and hard work."[69]

The parallel Dickens has created between his narrator and the antagonistic villain is too obvious to be overlooked, yet this stance towards the novel also belittles Uriah as a flat character, who merely serves a function. In fact, a closer look at Uriah Heep reveals that he is the precursor of Dickens's later lawyer figures. From the first, the 'material' conception of the character employs motifs that will recur in creatures such as Tulkinghorn, Vholes, or Jaggers. Uriah is of course uncommonly ugly, "high-shouldered and bony" and dressed "in decent black, with a white wisp of a neckcloth," as becomes a future lawyer (*DC*, ch. 15, p. 246).[70] More importantly, Uriah is the first character in Dickens remotely associated with the law, who makes those in relation to him extraordinarily uncomfortable through the fact that it seems impossible to hide from his eyes:

> Though his face was towards me, I thought, for some time, the writing being between us, that he could not see me; but looking that way more attentively, it made me uncomfortable to observe that, every now and then, his sleepless eyes would come below the writing, like two red suns, and stealthily stare at me for I dare say a whole minute at a time, during which his pen went, or pretended to go, as cleverly as ever. I made several attempts to get out of their way [. . .] but they always attracted me back again; and whenever I looked towards those two red suns, I was sure to find them, either just rising or just setting. (*DC*, ch. 15, pp. 248/249)

Uriah's eyes penetrate David's conscience, for he has a secret to hide after all. It is vital for him that Uriah do not find out that the social distance between them is much vaguer than the lawyer's clerk presumes. Consequently, David

---

68 John O. Jordan, "The Social Sub-Text of *David Copperfield*," *Dickens Studies Annual* 14 (1985): 61–92, 63.

69 Welsh, *Copyright to Copperfield*, 144.

70 All references to *David Copperfield* are to the following edition and will be given parenthetically: Charles Dickens, *David Copperfield*. Penguin English Library. London: Penguin Books Ltd., 2012.

feels observed by Uriah at all times, dreams of his threatening eyes and wishes to destroy him.

In this sense, Uriah the villain is in fact a representative of the law's surveillance and his panoptical observation confronts the narrator with the uncomfortable truths he has to hide. Uriah simply comes to embody everything that David fears, hides and desires, a powerful Id in constant negotiation with his super-ego. Hence, Uriah lives in a close, almost symbiotic relationship with his mother, a union David both desires and despises, which becomes clear when he chooses as first wife a woman who is exactly like his mother. In their union, Uriah and his mother become particularly dangerous for David, for he feels most vulnerable when confronted with the love between mother and son that he has lost. One should not overlook, however, that what he describes in his first encounter with them is that he does not feel caught out as a loving and rivalrous son, but that his description of their cross-examination of him over dinner resembles a trial in court: "They did just what they liked with me; and wormed things out of me that I had no desire to tell, with a certainty I blush to think of; [. . .] I found myself perpetually letting out something or other that I had no business to let out . . ." (*DC*, ch. 17, pp. 287/288) David's 'recollection' of his inferiority and bewildering helplessness in the face of Uriah's interrogation very clearly repeats itself when Pip describes his evenings with Jaggers. Uriah's powerful eyes recur in Mr Tulkinghorn's, which are pinned uncomfortably on Lady Dedlock; and Uriah's 'cadaverous' appearance will be re-enacted by Vholes.

David never forgets to mention that Uriah is not only symbiotically intertwined with his mother, but also with the law. Upon first being made acquainted with the fact that Uriah is "going through Tidd's Practice," David asks three questions like the three prophecies for Macbeth: "I suppose you are quite a great lawyer?"; ". . . you'll be a regular lawyer, I suppose?" and "[p]erhaps you'll be a partner in Mr Wickfield's business." (*DC*, ch. 16, pp. 262/263) In other words, David clearly foresees what he will come most to fear: that Uriah will succeed to an even social footing and in that triumph of evil, becoming a lawyer is synonymous with claiming Agnes as his rightful property. Uriah's potential progress is therefore inextricably linked to his career as a lawyer and his triumph over David that the latter almost masochistically anticipates in this moment can only ever be achieved on the ladder the law provides. The clerk can only seize the business when he has become a 'regular' lawyer and as a partner in the business, he can then 'seize' just as easily the business partner's daughter. So, while Uriah is David's nemesis, it is the law David has most reason to fear, since it is the prerequisite for all of Uriah's criminal achievements. Uriah is a source of evil and the law is his accessory – when David pretends to ask innocently, 'I suppose you are quite a great lawyer?' he therefore anticipates the climax of the central struggle in the novel, for although Uriah seems to be both a flat and a minor character, the central plot concerning David's personal achievements and misfortunes twists and turns with Uriah's duplicitous accomplishments. If Uriah is not only David's nemesis, but also a representative of the law, then it is not unreasonable to argue that David's main antagonist in the novel is the law, although he does not see it.

David witnesses that the law enables Uriah to attempt everything David wishes for himself, yet he comes to equate such legal means with immoral behaviour. It comes as no surprise, therefore, that he severs his own remote ties with the legal profession by leaving Doctors' Commons. His professional position as an aspiring proctor is too closely associated with the class he desires to distance himself from, which he realises when he listens to Steerforth's condescending explanation of what a proctor is:

> 'Why, he is a sort of monkish attorney,' replied Steerforth. 'He is, to some faded courts held in Doctors' Commons – a lazy old nook near St Paul's Churchyard – what solicitors are to the courts of law and equity. He is a functionary whose existence, in the natural course of things, would have terminated about two hundred years ago. (*DC*, ch. 23, p. 384)

While Uriah is the negative foil of everything David wishes to avoid in terms of social station, Steerforth is of course the positive image he aspires to: "What David seeks in this friendship is the protection and sponsorship of a gentleman and hence, ultimately, confirmation that he too is acceptable in Steerforth's social class."[71] If the profession is too far beneath Steerforth's position, it is much too close to Uriah's, David gives us implicitly to understand. While the exchange about this menial profession takes place even before David has been articled, it is a well-timed warning that this will not be David's chosen path in life, for it is not steep enough in its social ascension. The only perceptible use of his position as an articled proctor would be to marry his superior's daughter – a scheme which is prevented through David's loss of fortune and Spenlow's death, so that the parallel between David's and Uriah's designs remains opaque. David the narrator can thus pretend to be unaware of what they have in common: "Both as a character and as a narrator, David tends to disavow his social ambition and aggression. Instead, he projects them onto Uriah and condemns them, meanwhile pursuing his own parallel course under the cover of moral superiority."[72]

---

71 Jordan, "Social Sub-text," 68.

72 Jordan, "Social Sub-text," 78. See also Jordan, "Social Sub-text," 77: "From his later position as the practical, self-disciplined husband of Agnes, David can expose the foolishness of his youthful infatuation, while at the same time relishing its narrative re-creation. From neither perspective, however, does he recognize that his falling in love with Dora is motivated, initially at least, by a desire to improve his social station."

The need to present himself as Uriah's opposite in both social station and moral behaviour naturally lets David create a reduced picture of the villain and his strategies. The narrator simultaneously denies and acknowledges the power Uriah Heep holds in the life of David Copperfield and this power is rooted to a considerable extent in Uriah's legal career. It is all the more important for David, therefore, not to become a proctor, which endangers an association with Uriah's profession. Moreover, it is David's professed wish to become a 'gentleman.' While he is not as explicit about the wish as Pip, this motive still drives his narrative, for it is the only solution to his repressed social anxiety. Thus, he needs not only to accumulate money, but he also needs to define himself through a profession and the law, in its widest sense, is too ambiguous about the question whether this makes a man a gentleman. As already mentioned in chapter 1, solicitors in Chancery were regarded gentlemen by Act of Parliament,[73] which is a label that is too arbitrary for David. After all, his whole narrative proves that Uriah can be a lawyer and *not* a gentleman – a moral evaluation David desperately seeks to avoid, which lets him abuse Uriah almost obsessively as his social inferior. As John O. Jordan has shown, "David's abuse is a form of class oppression":

> Every dropped H in the narrative is the mark of a significant social distinction made by the middle-class narrator for his presumably middle-class audience. Verisimilitude in representing Heep's accent thus supports David's program of legitimizing middle-class superiority.[74]

It seems that as long as Uriah can be visibly and discursively described as lower class, David can secure his status as gentleman. Thus, Uriah's impending and seemingly unstoppable career in the law, ironically prophesied by David himself, poses a considerable threat to David's own social station and prevents him from choosing the profession for his own progress.

Uriah Heep's villainy is considerably increased by the fact that he is a lawyer, for the legal knowledge conditions his professional position and this position allows him to exercise the power over others that haunts the novel. He infiltrates and transgresses into houses, professions, trusts and minds. He violates every sphere of living, but his most important power is that over the minds of other characters, most importantly Mr Wickfield and David himself. He is an "appropriator of persons," gradually coming to own his employer and seeking to own the latter's daughter.[75] Uriah's increasing competence in the law allows him to press Mr Wickfield into the shape of a ventriloquist's puppet and

---

73 See Birks, *Gentlemen of the Law*, 136.

74 Jordan, "Social Sub-text," 79.

75 Terence Wright, "Caresses that Comfort, Blows that Bind – Sex, Sentiment and the Sense of Touch in *David Copperfield*," *English* 48.190 (1999): 1–16, 5.

appropriate the business as well as advance in social station. In a sense, he is a classic villain, as David Thiele has argued, especially in reference to the threat he poses for Agnes, who is entrapped by him both literally and metaphorically: "In order to claim his female prize and crush the spirit of his favored rival, he must employ the kinds of methods (short of rape and murder) which Gothic villains always employ – subterfuge, captivity, torture, and invasion."[76] In Uriah's case, these methods derive from his legal qualification: his competence allows him to ensnare Mr Wickfield and coerce him into thinking that he has lost control over the business. The promotion to partner then allows him to invade not only the professional, but also the domestic sphere, which in turn enables him to unfold a veil of possession over Agnes. The narrator rarely attributes the danger Uriah poses for Agnes to his significant progress in the law. Rather, Uriah's designs on Agnes are described as perverted and animalistic. David casts the two in the roles of the virgin to be seized and violated by the beast. He can never abstain from likening Uriah to an animal, be this a fox, vulture, or eel, and thus foregrounds his presumed bestiality resulting from his 'unnatural' desire for Agnes.[77] In many ways, the horror the narrator feels at the thought of a union between Agnes and Uriah Heep echoes the first act of Shakespeare's *Othello*, but the most important attribute Uriah receives is that of the vulture: the creature who feasts on others' carcasses as Vholes will be accused of doing in *Bleak House*.

The sexual rivalry between David and Uriah is more than a plot element that ought to clarify for David who the real object of his affection is. In terms of narrative strategy, Uriah's competition turns Agnes from an angel into a desirable woman for David, but it is important to note that even for the heroic narrator, she is little more than a prized possession, acquired to fulfil his ideal fantasy of becoming a gentleman. She is the last piece of the puzzle in his construction of his identity and serves as the answer to whether he will be the hero of his own narrative. In this sense, David's objectification of her is almost obvious and only concealed by his outrage at Uriah's leering towards her. In fact, both characters want the same thing: appropriate the woman as the jewel missing in their professional and social career and complete the domestic heterosexual fantasy that cannot be missing from the construction of the perfect gentleman. In the process, Agnes is nothing more than a ball in the game over who will win the social competition.

---

76 David Thiele, "The 'transcendent and immortal . . . HEEP!': Class Consciousness, Narrative Authority, and the Gothic in *David Copperfield*," *Texas Studies in Literature and Language* 42.3 (2000): 201–222, 211.

77 For the analogies to racist stereotyping see Tara Macdonald, "'red-headed animal': Race, Sexuality and Dickens's Uriah Heep," *Critical Survey* 17.2 (2005): 48–62.

In order to divert the reader from the fact that his 'love' for Agnes is this materialistic, David places all the emphasis on Uriah's transgressive presence in her life, creating the image of her as a victim of torture at the hands of Uriah, which he presents as torturing *him*: "Whenever I fell into a thoughtful state, this subject was sure to present itself, and all my uneasiness was sure to be redoubled. Hardly a night passed without my dreaming of it. It became a part of my life, and as inseparable from my life as my own head" (*DC*, ch. 26, p. 430/431).

While Agnes suffers in silence from the actual oppression and sexual transgression made towards her in her own home, David's suffering takes precedence in his story. The irony is increased even, when one remembers that the reader knows after all that Agnes suffers doubly: not only Uriah Heep causes her pain in her daily life, but David Copperfield does too. After all, the reader knows what David proclaims to be unaware of. Agnes's unrequited love for David already causes her unnecessary pain and her compliance with the role of 'sister,' a role he repeatedly and cruelly reminds her of, greatly increases her domestic nightmare. David knows this – as he admits only before he claims her as his rightful possession. At this point, the narrative is replete with references to the fact that he does not only know it now, but that he has always known it:

> I could not forget that the feeling with which she now regarded me had grown up in my own free choice and course. That if she had ever loved me with another love – and I sometimes thought the time was when she might have done so – I had cast it away. [. . .] If she had ever loved me, then, I should hold her the more sacred; remembering the confidences I had reposed in her, her knowledge of my errant heart, the sacrifice she must have made to be my friend and sister, and the victory she had won. (*DC*, ch. 58, pp. 916/917)

The 'confidences' he refers to are the many moments in the narrative when he has shared with her a love for other girls. He clearly emphasises that it has been a 'sacrifice' for her to be cast in the role of sister, while desiring him as a future husband. Now that he believes he has lost her, he could not more openly admit that he knows that he has contributed considerably to her suffering. Hilary M. Schor has pointed out that when Agnes admits that she has always *loved* him, she simultaneously and finally admits to her lifelong pain – a pain that she shares with other women in the novel: "Agnes's gentle admission of her own pain, of the story she has lived while David was off leading his own life, of her labor and dispossession, is one with a series of female narratives throughout the novel."[78] As in all other instances of his own questionable behaviour, David thus needs Uriah to hover predatorily over Agnes in order to cover up the fact that he lets her dangle for as long as is convenient

78 Hilary M. Schor, *Dickens and the Daughter of the House*. Cambridge: CUP, 1999: 12.

for him. Agnes is simply tortured by both men in her life, whether or not one is presented to the reader as an infinitely more attractive mate.

It is important to note that David shares Uriah's propensity to regard the woman as an object that can be acquired for personal gain and they also seem to share a certain pleasure in their sadistic torture of her. After all, they both acquire the help of other women to increase the pain for Agnes: Uriah moves his mother into Agnes's house, David moves his wife into her heart. Agnes has often been regarded as the most unlikely of all of Dickens's angelic women: the devotion she shows others and the self-control she exhibits despite her many sufferings simply seem too overwhelming to be borne by anyone this quietly. Thus, most critics have concluded that she can only be understood as a character if seen as the epitome of Dickens's ideal of femininity – such is Iain Crawford's solution, for instance:

> She can perhaps best be understood if she is seen as a variation upon a type of femininity that Dickens idealizes throughout his fiction, that of the earnest heroine [. . .]. Agnes is clearly the example par excellence of this type, and she finds it quite impossible to be anything other than earnest in all she does.[79]

However, this assumption often seems to express the reader's or critic's wish that they need not pity this character for her actual pain. Her endurance seems to make her an unlikely human being, but to reduce her to a type also provides the comfort of ignoring David's cruelty towards her. It is simply the case that the suffering both Uriah and David inflict on her is quite inconsistent with the narrator's claim to be both narrator and gentleman. His behaviour towards her, which includes the expectation that she not only endures his marrying another woman but becoming a sister even to *her*, is no less cruel than Uriah's sexual harassment – the only difference is that David is in control of how visible his own torture of the woman is and since he has Uriah, he can almost fully hide behind him.

Significantly, both Uriah and David are also perversely intrigued by what they believe to be Annie Strong's sexual depravity or infidelity: "David's own suspicions are projected onto Heep, as the unwitting observer tries to distance himself from the eagerly grasping spy, a character in whom both suspicion and sexuality can be disowned as perversion . . ."[80] When Uriah approaches the subject and tries to defame the woman, David acts shocked at such ungentlemanly

79 Iain Crawford, "Sex and Seriousness in *David Copperfield*," *The Journal of Narrative Technique* 16.1 (1986): 41–57, 47.
80 James Eli Adams, "Reading with Buzfuz" in *Contemporary Dickens*, eds. Eileen Gillooly and Deirdre David. Columbus: The Ohio State University Press, 2009: 231–244, 242.

behaviour, yet cannot escape being implicated when Uriah openly calls him on his own lewd (and unfounded) suspicions:

> I turned upon him, and asked him how he dared refer to me!
>
> 'Oh! it's very kind of you, Copperfield,' returned Uriah, undulating all over, 'and we all know what an amiable character yours is; but you know that the moment I spoke to you the other night, you knew what I meant. You know you knew what I meant, Copperfield. Don't deny it! You deny it with the best intentions; but don't do it, Copperfield!'
>
> I saw the mild eye of the good old Doctor turned upon me for a moment, and I felt that the confession of my old misgivings and remembrances was too plainly written in my face to be overlooked. It was of no use raging. I could not undo that. Say what I would, I could not unsay it. (*DC*, ch. 42, pp. 689/690)

David cannot help the unwanted alliance with Uriah at this moment, for their interest in Annie Strong's potential sexual misconduct is equally strong, which he is forced to admit here. Entwined in their battle for Agnes, Uriah and David also share their desire to punish female sexual transgression elsewhere, both exhibiting a sadistic attitude towards the women in their circle that displays an equal propensity towards cruelty. Moreover, the emphasis on Annie Strong as a fallen woman is increased through Uriah's openly proclaimed wish to purge her from the society of Agnes's purity to preserve the latter's desirability as his future wife – a wish David is complicit with, although he cannot admit it.

The plot that centres on Annie Strong's alleged sexual deviance brings back the discomfort to both narrator and reader that Uriah's constant surveillance of others causes. He involves David in the scheme to catch out the deviant female by announcing what he believes to have seen: "Now, I ain't one of your lady's men, Master Copperfield; but I've had eyes in my ed, a pretty long time back. We umble ones have got eyes, mostly speaking – and we look out of 'em" (*DC*, ch. 42, p. 680). David feels observed by those "sleepless eyes" (ch. 15, p. 249) again, just like he did upon first meeting Uriah, only now he feels confirmed in his discomfort, for Uriah proves that these eyes see everything. It is not only a perceived threat, but an actual threat to be in the focus of the lawyer, as Lady Dedlock has to discover in *Bleak House*. Ironically, when it comes to the negative connotation of observation, David cannot pretend to be innocent – after all, in Annie Strong's behaviour he has seen what Uriah sees and he has prepared the reader for his suspicions from the start. When he relates her ribbon missing after Jack Maldon's departure, he lays the groundwork to return to this narrative thread as someone in the know. In his suspicions, he is therefore to no extent morally superior to Uriah. In fact, the two men act together in their attempt to bring the woman down; a woman, who serves as a placeholder for the as yet unattainable Agnes. Naturally, it is at this moment of alliance and identification that David gives in to his desire for physical assault and strikes Uriah to force a discrimination from him that is in all other respects impossible – they are much too alike. In doing so, David once again puts his own happiness before Agnes's; hitherto he has claimed to show restraint towards Uriah's villainy in order to spare Agnes from his increased wrath, but now the desire to save the image of himself by assaulting Uriah is stronger. Agnes is therefore not only a victim of Uriah's schemes, but suffers just as much from David's egotism to prove himself the hero of his own story. David Copperfield is united in his secret dislike of women with his own worst enemy. Uriah's and David's open aggression towards Annie Strong reveals a hidden misogyny in both men that they also exhibit covertly against the women they have instrumentalised. They both turn against them once they are no longer of use. Uriah disowns his mother as a fellow schemer as soon as he realises that he has been brought down by Micawber – David criticises Dora once he sees that she cannot perfect his domestic happiness. He becomes openly regretful about his undisciplined heart in an act that can only be described as disloyal towards his betrothed. Both Uriah and David discard the women they have used to torture Agnes with unsentimentally and in socially acceptable manner direct their urges for physical violation only against each other.

While David's competition with Uriah constitutes an overt element of the novel's plot, it is easy to overlook David's covert alliance with his nemesis, because the narrator commonly casts himself in the role of victim, especially in view of Uriah's inquisitiveness. The need to know everything and the skill to worm it out of everybody is Uriah's most dangerous asset, but unlike later works by Dickens, this text does not openly ascribe these dangerous strategies to Uriah's profession as a lawyer yet. The jibes against lawyers so typical of later novels only rarely appear at the surface of the text in *David Copperfield* and when they do, they are most often formulated by the lawyer figure himself: "'Why, though I am a lawyer, Master Copperfield,' he replied, with a dry grin, 'I mean, just at present, what I say.'" (*DC*, ch. 42, p. 679) David considers himself a victim of Uriah's without yet harping on the fact that Uriah's despicable nature is inextricably linked to his profession. There is only one other instance in which Uriah refers to himself as a lawyer, which comes significantly very shortly before he drops his mask. Asked about the amount of business he has managed to make for himself, he answers "[n]ot so much so, as I could wish. But lawyers, sharks, and leeches, are not easily satisfied, you know!" (*DC*, ch. 52, p. 834) It is difficult to determine whether this is spoken fully in character – on the one hand, it foreshadows Uriah's brutal honesty beyond his humble role that will determine the rest of the chapter and the novel's climax. On the other hand, it is an epithet unusual for a text that otherwise stays so completely away from the typical satire of the lawyer's profession that is common in Dickens's later works. It is as if shortly before the cruel extent of Uriah's villainy is revealed, the reader ought to be reminded that David's nemesis has been enabled by the law itself.

Overtly, David's dislike of Uriah is maybe not exactly idiosyncratic, but through the narrative perspective certainly very subjective and it has been noted that the extent to which Uriah is an object of hatred might seem remarkable on the surface: "[T]here is something excessive in the abuse that he receives from David and the others."[81] The chapter in which Uriah openly and sarcastically refers to himself as a lawyer of the worst kind, however, provides the reader with the whole truth about his embezzlement and truly criminal behaviour. Thus, shortly before David is proved right in his excessive hatred of his antagonist, we find an emphasis on the law as a breeding ground for such depraved human beings. Uriah is the worst kind of lawyer, he proves all prejudices against the profession and he is one of the most famous villains in all of Dickens. Yet, he has very rarely been regarded in the context of his profession. William Holdsworth does not even include him in his list of lawyers in Dickens.[82] There can be no doubt for any reader of the novel that Uriah is a lawyer, yet David's narrative emphasis on his depravity is almost always related to Uriah's social and not his professional position.

David Copperfield is not the first text that bears the suggestion that the legal profession may resonate with immoral tendencies in the human being, but Uriah Heep is the first fully developed character, who is also a lawyer. Moreover, Uriah has an unprecedented power in the novel as David's alter ego and nemesis, his doppelganger and his worst enemy. It is all the more interesting what strategy Dickens develops to overcome Uriah as the narrative's villain and who conditions Heep's demise. As it turns out, Uriah's most dangerous enemy is not Copperfield himself, but the underdog Mr Micawber, who not only finds employment in the law of all places, but also uses his position in the profession to bring about the victory of true justice. Micawber is an unlikely hero – he is clearly written more in the vein of funny ne'er-do-wells such as Dick Swiveller or Tip Dorrit. However, considering how close Uriah is to David's heart, one should keep in mind how close Micawber is to Dickens's heart – considering that he has so often been viewed as an allusion to, if not model after, John Dickens. Within this most personal of his novels, Dickens uses the lawyer's clerk to bring down the lawyer: the father figure wins against the sinister dealings of the law. Where David fails to

81 Jordan, "Social Sub-text," 79.
82 Holdsworth mentions Uriah only briefly as a clerk. See *Dickens as Legal Historian*, 47.

overcome his antagonist, the paternal Mr Micawber is his rescue. Ironically, while John Dickens obviously endangered Dickens's own social station through his chronic pecuniary difficulties, Mr Micawber clears David forever of his arbitrary social station. Uriah is purged from the narrative, which leads to the financial restoration of all fortune and David's union with Agnes. As David has established himself as a successful author and thereby has manifested his middle-class status, the embodiment of his bourgeois fears can disappear from the text to safe repression: since Uriah is overcome, one can see that David feels he has won a secure social identity and it is Mr Micawber, who has saved him.

Micawber bears a striking resemblance to Mr Skimpole, but lacks the sinister aspects of his nature. Micawber is a melodramatic man, who serves a great amount of the novel's comedy through his "manic plunges from elation to despair and back again":

> In him, the emotions, rather than being mingled, are laid out linearly, one after another, and, as often happens, the 'mechanisation' of a complex experience makes the business comic. It is allied also to the fact that Micawber enjoys, indeed revels in, his own despair, even to the extent of threatening self-violence by 'making motions at himself with the razor' from an upstairs window for the benefit of a pressing creditor in the street below . . .[83]

Micawber's entries and exits are usually timed for comic relief, although he has the air of causing trouble and David never conceals his fear that he or others may be drawn into Micawber's pecuniary difficulties. Micawber is not only representative of David's most embarrassing secret, but he also oozes the constant threat of social degradation. Micawber is clearly a minor and in many ways a flat character, endowed by his creator with very distinct physical and discursive markings, and the vignettes he livens up seem to follow a simple pattern: entry, mirth, misery, exit and epistle. Almost all of his occurrences in the novel can be broken down into these particular elements, which make him easily recognisable and stereotypically funny. To paraphrase Maria DiBattista, to know Mr Micawber at all, is to know him well.[84] However, adhering to Natalie McKnight's caveat that to rely on such stereotypes in Dickens makes one easily ignorant of their subversive potential,[85] one must take a closer look at Micawber, for his temporary alliance with Uriah and hence with the law is significant. At the same time, it is important to note that Micawber's entries are not exclusively

83 Wright, "Caresses that Comfort," 13.
84 See DiBattista, *Novel Characters*, 12.
85 McKnight, "Dickens and Gender", 197.

timed for comic relief, but are in fact more often than not moments of rescue. And thirdly, it is Micawber's understanding of justice as opposed to law that saves the day and brings down Uriah Heep. Understanding Micawber as a merely funny, flat and minor character is to grossly underestimate him. In fact, one can argue that Micawber embodies equity itself.

It is easy to underestimate Micawber not only due to the comic construction of the character, but also because David necessarily pushes him towards the margins of his narrative. After all, Micawber is too closely related to David's existence as a street-child. He does not only remind David of his most shameful experience in life, but he also bears the very real threat of relating the hero's temporary fall in life to those who shall be kept ignorant. The fact that this is not an illusion on David's part is clear when Uriah confronts David with his knowledge of the time he most wishes to forget. The narrator therefore has a considerable interest in keeping Micawber at bay and the character's often surprising entries are not necessarily presented as happy occasions, which clouds the fact that Micawber is at the same time an equally important source of rescue and relief. After David has quite forgotten about his acquaintance when trying to build a life for himself in Canterbury, Micawber surprisingly reappears in very significant circumstances, for he rescues David from the cross-examination of the Heeps. As David begins to feel highly uncomfortable in this mock trial scene under the penetrating eyes of both Uriah and his mother, it is Micawber who rescues him by entering the scene:

> I had begun to feel a little uncomfortable, and to wish myself well out of the visit, when a figure coming down the street passed the door – it stood open to air the room, which was warm, the weather being close for the time of year – came back again, looked in, and walked in, exclaiming loudly, 'Copperfield! Is it possible!' (*DC*, ch. 17, p. 288)

Micawber appears like a *deus ex machina* in exactly the right moment of David's increasing discomfort, bringing a refreshing air of freedom into the stuffy carceral space, but David's fear of his revealing the truth of their connection diverts the reader from recognising this as a moment of rescue: "I cannot say – I really cannot say – that I was glad to see Mr Micawber there . . ." (*DC*, ch. 17, p. 288/289) However, the moment clearly foreshadows the second time Micawber will rescue David from Uriah Heep and turn the novel.

David's need to avoid Micawber reduces him to a seemingly minor character, but whether or not he is also flat is a much more difficult question. While he is typically clearly marked both in outward appearance and discursive mannerisms, most famously his verbose and pretentious monologues, his psychology both is and is not complex. He is a type of character famous for his wish to avoid responsibility, yet he is the only one of these types who manages to overcome his personal desires for the greater good. The melodramatic dynamic that shapes his life creates comedy, but reveals at the same time that Micawber constructs an existence for himself that relieves him of other obligations. Consequently, he typically refers to himself in the third person as if his personal business were in fact someone else's. Thus, Micawber is an earlier version of the type that frequently occurs in the later Dickens, most notably in Harold Skimpole and William Dorrit. He represents a growing interest in the theme of responsibility, or, more precisely, the avoidance thereof, which is so common in the character type that is reminiscent of John Dickens. Dickens has Micawber seek forever for his good fortune, but presents him as most comfortably himself, when he has been able to declare that all is lost. David's narrative presents a pattern between Micawber's epistles announcing various forms of demise and his subsequent appearances that always ends on a high note, for once he has admitted to the world that he has failed, Micawber can enjoy his fate free of responsibility:

> I was so shocked by the contents of this heart-rending letter, that I ran off directly towards the little hotel [. . .], [b]ut, half-way there, I met the London coach with Mr and Mrs Micawber up behind; Mr Micawber, the very picture of tranquil enjoyment, smiling at Mrs Micawber's conversation, eating walnuts out of a paper bag, with a bottle sticking out of his breast pocket. (*DC*, ch. 17, p. 297)

Micawber's most distinct characteristic as a type in the novel therefore does not lie in his verbosity or baldness, but rather in his carefree existence on the brink of ruin, always relying on the hope that something will 'turn up':

> The compromise represented by Micawber encompasses nearly abject obeisance to fate and defiance of fate at the same time. The behaviour of the man is truly passive, his expression everlastingly hopeful. We have to credit more than words alone in this man of words, for he sees the world in such ineluctable colors of despair that hope itself is heroic.[86]

No one who is acquainted with the later Dickens can therefore be surprised at all that Micawber temporarily ends up in the law – after all, it is one of Dickens's major points of critique that those in the law shirk their personal responsibility for the systemic relief provided by the profession. Significantly, Micawber notes that the language of the law presses him into a rigid framework devoid of alternatives: "To a man possessed of the higher imaginative powers, the objection to legal studies is the amount of detail which they involve. Even in our professional correspondence [. . .] the mind is not at liberty to soar to any exalted form of expression." (*DC*, ch. 39, pp. 630/631)

86 Welsh, *Copyright to Copperfield*, 151.

Micawber's position as Uriah's legal clerk also changes his character towards a hitherto unimaginable professionalism, which brings about a quite uncharacteristic discretion in the character. Micawber frequently creates comedy and proves his amiability as a character because of his *in*discretion: both he and his wife share both their pecuniary and conjugal happiness or misery so freely that David repeatedly implies embarrassment at their lack of discretion:

> I never can quite understand whether my precocious self-dependence confused Mrs Micawber in reference to my age, or whether she was so full of the subject that she would have talked about it to the very twins if there had been nobody else to communicate with, but this was the strain in which she began, and she went on accordingly all the time I knew her. (*DC*, ch. 11, p. 179)

When Micawber learns discretion in the hands of the law, therefore, this is not a good sign as David means the reader to understand when he observes "an uneasy change" upon Micawber's announcement of his new professionalism: "I am here, in a capacity of confidence. I am here, in a position of trust. The discussion of some topics, even with Mrs Micawber herself [. . .], is, I am led to consider, incompatible with the functions now devolving on me." (*DC*, ch. 39, pp. 631/631) Even though David frequently expresses embarrassment at the openness of Mr Micawber, it is indubitably one of his most amiable characteristics and the turn towards secrecy forebodes trouble. Micawber ends up in the law to avoid responsibility and has to learn immediately that the profession bears the danger of corruption. His presence in the novel is therefore inextricably linked to Uriah and the juxtaposition of the two revolves around the covert discourse of the law and the question of whether Uriah will succeed in corrupting Micawber or not.

While Micawber's affinity for the law is often an element of comedy, such as in his frequent epistles, whose language echoes a particularly hyperbolic legalese, his position in it quickly becomes more serious. On the one hand, Micawber's ending up in the law is an anticipation of a theme frequently recurring in the later Dickens of the law as the logical ultimate end for ne'er-do-wells. If they prove unfit for everything else, they might still try the law, like Tip Dorrit:

> Tip tired of everything. [. . .] [Amy] got him into a warehouse, into a market garden, into the hop trade, into the law again, into an auctioneer's, into a brewery, into a stockbroker's, into the law again, into a coach office, into a waggon office, into the law again, into a general dealer's, into a distillery, into the law again, into a wool house, into a dry goods house, into the Billingsgate trade, into the foreign fruit trade, and into the docks. But whatever Tip went into, he came out of tired, announcing that he had cut it.
> (*LD*, ch. 7, p. 91)

Placing Micawber, who is melodramatically thrown out and into professions, out and into debt and out and into different accommodations, in the position as

Uriah's legal clerk, seems to be an anticipation of this theme: if he cannot succeed anywhere, he might still find a place in the law. On the other hand, Micawber is quickly confronted with the choice between giving in to Uriah's attempt to corrupt him and the unwanted option to finally take responsibility in defiance of the passivity the system of the law enables. This choice drastically increases the complexity of the character, for he is confronted with a moral dilemma that is quite out of keeping with the cheerful carelessness inscribed into his appearances in the novel up to this point. In fact, this flat and minor character learns something that is quite in parallel with David's own *bildungsroman*-maturation, for Micawber learns to take responsibility.

As an involuntary ally in Uriah Heep's embezzlement, legally possibly even liable as an accessory after the fact, Micawber cunningly subverts the system in favour of his integrity. He is posited as a counterpoint to Uriah's moral depravity: not quite the knight in shining armour, but nevertheless the representative of conscience and the embodiment of justice that causes the downfall of the villain. It is highly significant, therefore, that Dickens presents Micawber's moral victory as the result of a struggle with his own conscience:

> My object, when the contest within myself between stipend and no stipend, baker and no baker, existence and non-existence, ceased, was to take advantage of my opportunities to discover and expose the major malpractices committed, to [Mr Wickfield's] grievous wrong and injury, by – HEEP. Stimulated by the silent monitor within, and by a no less touching and appealing monitor without [. . .] I entered on a not unlaborious task of clandestine investigation, protracted now, to the best of my knowledge, information, and belief, over a period exceeding twelve calendar months. (*DC*, ch. 52, p. 841)

The humour caused by Micawber in the whole narrative sequence that ends in the defeat of Uriah aside, one can clearly see that Micawber is supposed to represent conscience against law, personal responsibility against the system. The choice between his own personal profit conditioned on Uriah's patronage and the morally right thing to do is the defining moment of this otherwise flat and funny character. He represents everything that Uriah is not – not least in his loving and literally fruitful union with his wife that counters Heep's violent misogyny. In this sense, Micawber becomes an unexpected moral signpost for David himself – having formerly expressed his bemusement quite openly, David finally has to admit that Micawber's moral integrity overshadows the shame he feels in knowing him: "I felt devoutly thankful for the miseries of my younger days which had brought me to the knowledge of Mr Micawber." (*DC*, ch. 52, p. 851) Micawber proves invulnerable towards the corruptive forces of the law – "the silent monitor within" cannot be suppressed by the language of the law – even when it comes in the powerful figure of Uriah Heep.

David Thiele has remarked that it is "now commonplace to observe that Uriah Heep is a dark double of the narrator"[87] and that was twenty years ago. The parallel between the two is certainly clear when it comes to David's class-consciousness and even the sexual desires and misogyny may be regarded as fairly overt, but it is only when we remind ourselves that technically, Uriah is Dickens's first elaborate lawyer figure that we realise what this implies about David's (!) attitude towards the law. Given the traumatically bad association with the word that David develops in his childhood – after all, the nineteenth-century expression for stepfather is father-in-law – there is no need to be surprised that the narrator of his novel might carry within him a deep-rooted fear of the law and all of its representatives to the point that he shies away from the profession.[88] The interesting aspect about this momentous turning-point in Dickens's works is that the text also still allows positive connotations: Tommy Traddles, for instance, is a lawyer too, after all, and David is most impressed with his close friend and willing to express a new degree of respect for him he has hitherto withheld, when Traddles proves his merits *as a lawyer*: "I cannot help avowing that this was the first occasion on which I really did justice to the clear head, and the plain, patient, practical good sense, of my old schoolfellow." (*DC*, ch. 52, p. 848) Similarly, Mr Wickfield is a very benign, if flawed, figure, who has "a very agreeable face" (*DC*, ch. 15, p. 247) that is clearly contrasted with the cadaverous face of the viper in his bosom. Thus, at a closer look, the text is fraught with ambivalent feelings towards the law and those who work in it. On the one hand, they can be extremely competent, clear-headed and astute; on the other hand, they may just be personified evil. In any case, what has seemed to many to be Dickens's profound disgust of the law as expressed in many novels after *David Copperfield*, offers itself here as a more ambiguous and less systematic condemnation. For the first time, the law plays a truly major role in a Dickens novel, but its significance is covert and hidden in the construction of characters and the narrator's subconscious. What we seem to have here is a blueprint both for the theme of the law and the construction of the lawyer figure, for a close focus on the significance of the law in the novel reveals aspects in Uriah and David, their attitude towards others and especially women, that return in all of Dickens's other lawyer figures.

It seems that Uriah is a kind of *ur*-lawyer, the first experiment towards a construction of such a character and almost all who follow can rightfully be regarded his infamous successors: his scheme to appropriate Agnes as an object of triumph

---

87 Thiele, "Gothic in *David Copperfield*," 201.

88 Beth F. Herst has argued that there is an evident parallelism between Mr Murdstone and Uriah Heep, for they both invade David's two childhood homes: See Beth F. Herst, *The Dickens Hero. Selfhood and Alienation in the Dickens World*. London: Weidenfeld and Nicolson, 1990: 58.

foreshadows Tulkinghorn's struggle with Lady Dedlock; his suspicions towards Annie Strong both anticipate Tulkinghorn's inquiries into Lady Dedlock's past and Inspector Bucket's criminal investigation. The fact that Uriah seems to ruin David's guardian angel Betsey Trotwood financially recurs in the twisted triangle of Miss Havisham, Pip and Jaggers; his wish to keep a woman captive recurs in Jaggers; David's own conflict with Uriah, his attraction in repulsion, is echoed in the relation between Pip and Jaggers. There are many more parallels that will hopefully become clear over the following chapters. In general, one can observe that it is absolutely remarkable that once Uriah Heep has been born and has wreaked havoc in this central novel in Dickens's career, the number of lawyers to appear subsequently drastically increases. It seems as if once the blueprint for the despicable lawyer character has been created in Heep, who has so much in common with the novel's hero, this duplicity carries on through many of Dickens's later works. On the grounds of *David Copperfield*, it is therefore not unequivocally possible to attest that Dickens 'detests' lawyers – in fact, there seems to be a great degree of that often mentioned attraction of repulsion, a covert admiration for the profession and a strong awareness for the social implications of what it means to be a lawyer. Can they ever be considered gentlemen? David clearly thinks no – in his pursuit of a gentlemanly status, he cannot stop at the law – Steerforth's condemnation makes this obvious. Uriah's position is too closely associated with everything David represses and hence is desperate to avoid. It is only when we regard this 'middle' novel from the perspective of law and literature and uncover the grave importance the theme of the law has for the construction of character that we see that there is a profound duplicity towards the lawyer in Dickens's fiction.

3 The Vulture

Uriah Heep is a character that got away from Dickens. He far exceeds his obvious function in the plot as villain and rival, his complexity takes on a prominence in the novel that is quite unnecessary. Uriah is an unintended Double that reveals crucial elements about the novel's subconscious underbelly. Careful readings of David's complexity as a character have brought forth that Uriah Heep is not only his nemesis, but another version of himself. As Claire Rosenfield writes in her ground-breaking essay on the subject, risen to unexpected fame through Gilbert and Gubar's appropriation for *Jane Eyre*, the Double is crucial for a comprehensive reading of the intended protagonist:

> The novelist who consciously or unconsciously exploits psychological Doubles may either juxtapose or duplicate two characters; the one representing the socially acceptable or conventional personality, the other externalizing the free, uninhibited, often criminal self.[89]

Dickens does both: he juxtaposes David and Uriah for the plot strategies discussed and he also duplicates them, since Uriah acts out David's true desires. Uriah is therefore not only villain or nemesis, but shares much more with the hero than the text wishes to admit. His complexity as a character thus exceeds the blueprint of the novel and the covert context of the law plays a major role. In the following chapters I would like to demonstrate that the creation of Uriah has henceforth a major influence on Dickens's conception of the lawyer figure and it is certainly no coincidence that one of the two most interesting lawyers Dickens has to offer in subsequent novels follows so soon after the publication of *David Copperfield*.

The first instalment of *Bleak House* appears only two years later and Mr Tulkinghorn is introduced among the major characters, which might come as a surprise, considering that he seems so clearly minor. After all, Dickens kills him off about halfway through the novel for technical purposes. Until then, however, Tulkinghorn is one of the most important characters in *Bleak House*, overshadowing others: "One of Dickens' most consistently undervalued achievements in *Bleak House* is the rich complexity in the characterization of the lawyer Tulkinghorn."[90] In order to demonstrate Uriah's legacy, however, it is worthwhile to begin with Vholes, who seems an almost identical copy of the earlier villain.

---

89 Claire Rosenfield, "The Shadow Within: The Conscious and Unconscious Use of the Double" in *Stories of the Double*, ed. Albert J. Guerard. Philadelphia and New York: J. B. Lippincott Company, 1967: 311–331, 314.
90 Eugene F. Quirk, "Tulkinghorn's Buried Life: A Study of Character in *Bleak House*," *The Journal of English and Germanic Philology* 72.4 (1973): 526–535, 526.

https://doi.org/10.1515/9783110754506-003

It certainly seems to have suited Dickens's purposes that the historically customary dress worn by lawyers of all different branches was black.[91] Not only is black the colour of death, so often associated with the lawyer in Dickens, but it also provides ample opportunity for metaphorically steering the negative image of the figure in general. One of the most pertinent images Dickens creates is that of the crow or vulture. The crow he uses for the picture of Tulkinghorn, the vulture is more clearly associated with Vholes, as the alliteration indicates already. Dickens returns to the image of the huge bird of prey that feeds off carcasses and threatens death and destruction – an image he already used with reference to Uriah Heep: "At the coach-window, as at the dinner-party, he hovered about us without a moment's intermission, like a great vulture: gorging himself on every syllable that I said to Agnes or that Agnes said to me." (*DC*, ch. 26, p. 430) The image of the vulture is disturbing not only through its association with death, but also due to its superiority: flying through the air with superhuman vision, it suggests that there is no escape, which is exactly the feeling David describes frequently when it comes to Uriah. Dickens repeats this vulture-like characteristic of Heep in Vholes, while he leaves the truly threatening power to Tulkinghorn. In the novel following *David Copperfield*, Uriah Heep is split in two, his most heinous characteristics distributed on two different creatures that are both uncanny representatives of the law. Vholes is the vulture, Tulkinghorn is the crow and they mirror different aspects of Uriah's personality.[92] This is especially apparent in their relationships with other characters and their attitudes towards women.

Vholes is in every way the death-like figure whose ugly exterior represents his depraved interior: "a sallow man with pinched lips that looked as if they were cold, a red eruption here and there upon his face, tall and thin, about fifty years of age, high-shouldered, and stooping." (*BH*, ch. 37, p. 455) He radiates both physical and emotional coldness, like a carcass, and his stooped shoulders resemble the vulture's posture. He is of course dressed in black, "black-gloved, and buttoned to the chin," his gloves covertly arousing the image of the undertaker. Accordingly, "there was nothing so remarkable in him as a lifeless manner" (*BH*, ch. 37, p. 455). The most disturbing aspect of his appearance, however, is "a slow fixed way he had of looking at Richard" (*BH*, ch. 37, p. 455). Like the large deadly

91 See Birks, *Gentlemen of the Law*, 240.

92 Louis Crompton has pointed out that the name Vholes also echoes 'vole': "A 'vole' is a field mouse, and Vholes's name consequently evokes the image of a parasite that destroys crops. 'Voling' also means making a clean sweep of the board at cards, an action suggestive of the thoroughness with which he mulcts his clients." Louis Crompton, "Satire and Symbolism in Bleak House," Nineteenth-Century Fiction 12.4 (1958): 284–303, 300. Garrett Stewart notes that the name "also suggests vortex and hole . . ." "The New Mortality of *Bleak House*," *ELH* 45.3 (1978): 443–487, 471.

bird of prey, he has his eyes on his next victim, observing the 'body' with anticipatory determination, lying in wait for the right moment to descend on him and do his damage. Esther gives us an image of Vholes that is an almost exact replica of Uriah hovering over Agnes and once again the lawyer's power of observation, his sleepless eyes that detect human weakness, are his most threatening asset.

From his first appearance onwards, Vholes speaks of Richard in the third person in his presence. He has already singled out his victim and objectifies him safely, secure in the knowledge that his lifelessness elevates him to a level of superiority towards Richard's passion, which is perceived by Esther: "Richard, all flush and fire and laughter, with the reins in his hand; Mr Vholes, quite still, black-gloved, and buttoned up, looking at him as if he were looking at his prey and charming it" (*BH*, ch. 37, p. 457). This is one of those tableaus Dickens creates in the mind to foreshadow Richard's tragic end, for his lively passions of "flush and fire and laughter" will succumb to death while Vholes lies in wait for the carcass: "Everything about Vholes, in fact – his appearance, his voice, his office in Symond's Inn – suggests death: death in himself and death for the client on whom he preys."[93] Like Uriah, Vholes turns his male victim into a puppet. Heep serves Wickfield alcohol to intensify his addiction and thereby weaken his will – Vholes serves Richard Jarndyce and Jarndyce, thereby consciously enabling what the novel presents as an addiction far worse than alcohol. Officially 'dealing' in the law, Vholes provides Richard with the drug that will cause the latter's demise. Like Uriah, Vholes humbles himself to disguise his destructive tendencies, reiterating "I am quite at your service" (*BH*, ch. 37, p. 455) as a similarly repetitive discursive mannerism as Heep's insistence on his humbleness. The myth that he merely 'serves' his client in fact serves the lawyer – both in the sense that it disguises his position of power and provides a legitimation for his profit. The service myth is employed as part of the character's deception like the humbleness myth of his predecessor; both mean to conceal their power over others which is a result of their manipulative cunning.

It is easy to mistake Vholes's hideousness both inside and outside as emblematic of Dickens's scathing critique of the law for there seems to be no other dimension to the character. Thus, Taylor Stoehr has reasonably pointed out that in "the characterization of Vholes, that '*most* respectable man,' Dickens gives us a living example of the abuses of the law . . ."[94] Vholes is a solicitor

---

93 Graham Storey, *Charles Dickens. Bleak House*. Landmarks of World Literature. Cambridge: CUP, 1987: 51/52.

94 Taylor Stoehr, *Dickens: The Dreamer's Stance*. Ithaca, N.Y.: Cornell University Press, 1965: 158.

and in *Bleak House* this seems to mean that he is merely an extended hand of the destructive power of Jarndyce and Jarndyce:

> Jarndyce and Jarndyce may possess a grasping and unwholesome hand [. . .], but this ostensibly invisible hand belongs collectively to the lawyers who profit from it; the novel's discourse of 'law-hand,' featureless or otherwise, thus becomes a killing joke about the agency and accountability of Chancery solicitors from Tulkinghorn, who sits at the pinnacle of his profession but does so under the pointing hand of Allegory, to the bottom-feeding Vholes, whose claw-like, black-gloved hands augment a demeanour equally funereal and predatory.[95]

It seems therefore that the insistence on the character's gloved hands not only brings to mind the undertaker, but also suggests that he tries to hide the hand that he puts out for profit as all representatives of the law eventually do. They are devils, whose only excuse for their deadly sin, greed, is their profession. Considering the stereotypical villainy and biblical condemnation, it comes as no surprise that Dickens also returns to the formulaic repetition of three as if trying to bring forth the real devil when he paints Vholes at his profession:

> Mr Vholes is a very respectable man. He has not a large business, but he is a very respectable man. He is allowed by the greater attorneys who have made good fortunes, or are making them, to be a most respectable man. He never misses a chance in his practice; which is a mark of respectability. He never takes any pleasure; which is another mark of respectability. He is reserved and serious; which is another mark of respectability.
>
> (*BH*, ch. 39, p. 467)

Both 'respectable' and 'respectability' are each reiterated thrice; not only suggesting that the narrator is trying to provoke a devil, calling him out three times to appear, but also reminiscent of David's three prophecies for Uriah's future as a lawyer. In *Bleak House*, the devil hides under the cloak of respectability: the profession itself is demonic and Vholes seems little more than a *diabolus ex machina*: "the devil figure on hand to snatch Richard's soul at the appropriate time."[96]

It seems that Dickens does not attempt to paint this symbolic lawyer type in anything but a hideous light and the satire on the legal profession that has brought *Bleak House* such fame is anything but subtle. However, to dismiss Vholes as merely representative is to miss the part he plays in the novel's perversions of power and thus his role in Dickens's conception of the lawyer figure. Vholes stands in direct succession to Uriah in his relationship to Richard. Feeding him just the

95 Daly, "Belligerent Instruments," 28.

96 Marilyn Georgas, "Dickens, Defoe, the Devil and the Dedlocks: The 'Faust Motif' in *Bleak House*," *Dickens Studies Annual* 10 (1982): 23–44, 39.

right amount of information as suggestive of progress in the suit, Richard is as dependent on Vholes as Wickfield is on Uriah. Moreover, as Richard begins to echo Vholes's discursive mannerisms, the young man seems to disappear before the reader's eyes. Vholes seems to drag him gradually off the face of the earth by sowing discord between him and Mr Jarndyce: the resulting antagonism between the two characters increases Richard's minority in the novel, preparing the reader for his disappearance.

Dickens is not covert about this lawyer's culpability and openly mocks Vholes's manipulation in prejudicial satire of the stereotype:

> Mr Vholes, after glancing at the official cat who is patiently watching a mouse's hole, fixes his charmed gaze again on his young client, and proceeds in his buttoned-up half-audible voice, as if there were an unclean spirit in him that will neither come out nor speak out . . . (*BH*, ch. 39, p. 470)

The dry, lifeless, methodical lawyer is also a supernatural spirit, a demon with magical powers. Like Uriah, who breathes into the pony's nostrils upon his first appearance, "as if he were putting some spell on him" (*DC*, ch. 15, p. 246), Vholes seems to be doing something similar to Richard. The young man's trust in the treacherous lawyer consequently comes off almost as tragicomic: "'I am perfectly aware, Mr Vholes,' says Richard, more familiarly and good-humouredly, 'that you are the most reliable fellow in the world; and that to have to do with you, is to have to do with a man of business who is not hoodwinked.'" (*BH*, ch. 39, p. 471) Dickens does not employ dramatic irony here: there is no unexpected twist, there is no underbelly. Richard is presented as the victim of a con artist and his gullibility is partly his own fault for not employing himself better in life and learning the earnestness David insists on as the source of all his successes.

Presumably, this is why many critics have preferred to read Vholes as systemic and not personable. Richard is certainly no hero, but having earned the love of Ada Clare, he is no character the novel dispenses with lightly and to read him as a victim of an omnipotent system that gradually wastes away so many likeable characters is perhaps less uncomfortable than to focus on the treachery that makes him a more complex victim of the narrative. It seems that Vholes may be a more digestible villain, if he is merely symbolic: ". . . all the forces of darkness, death, and destruction have been concentrated in one symbolic figure."[97] Dickens does not shy away from painting Vholes in the bleakest image, going as far as openly suggesting what accompanies almost every one of the lawyer's appearances in the novel: "So slow, so eager, so bloodless and

97 Crompton, "Satire and Symbolism," 299.

gaunt, I felt as if Richard were wasting away beneath the eyes of this adviser, and there was something of the Vampire in him" (*BH*, ch. 60, p. 692). Much earlier, the narrator has already suggested that Vholes wishes to devour Richard even literally: "always looking at the client, as if he were making a lingering meal of him with his eyes as well as with his professional appetite" (*BH*, ch. 39, p. 470). Vholes feeds off Richard both literally and metaphorically, since the money he receives for his 'service' literally sustains him and his oft-mentioned family. The vampire sucks Richard dry while he is still alive, which exceeds even the ghoulish nature of the vulture. Vholes is therefore in all respects likened to non-humanity: either as an animal, as a supernatural being or merely as a walking corpse. In contrast to this lack of human life in the figure, his watchful, active, dangerous eyes that penetrate Richard's well-being are even more uncanny. Dickens continues his emphasis on the lawyer's power of observation in both Tulkinghorn and Vholes, whose eyes are life-threatening for all involved. What they see, they keep and devour, the text implies – whether in the currency of secrets or the currency of human life is all the same to the lawyer.

Richard Carstone is the victim of the vulture that David is determined not to be; this later version of the young man, who has to prove himself in life, fails through a lack of earnestness. His often-mentioned good humour and laughing nature make him vulnerable to the manipulative power of others: "He was a handsome youth, with an ingenuous face, and a most engaging laugh; and after she had called him up to where we sat, he stood by us, in the light of the fire too, talking gaily, like a light-hearted boy" (*BH*, ch. 3, p. 27). Richard's light-heartedness and unwillingness to take his own existence and obligations seriously enough, the text suggests, drive him into the hands of the law. He shies away from the responsibility for himself and others, leaving Ada a young widow, who falls back into the care of Esther, who has claimed possession of her from the first. Richard is an unwanted rival for the first-person narrator and lacks her earnestness and sense of duty, which is why she triumphs over him in the end. His vulnerability to the manipulation of Vholes drives him away from his loved ones and his character flaw is to point his suspicions in the wrong direction. He is certainly presented as an easy target for the professional perpetrator, but Dickens once more suggests that the representative of the law is endowed with a sadistic nature.

Vholes not only brings Richard into his control, but consequently also Ada and to a certain degree Esther herself. As a minor character, he proves a considerable disturbance for the social structure of the novel, pitting characters against each other that should be united in domestic happiness. Vholes thus manages to invade the metaphorical space of the patchwork family and disrupts the natural course of human affection. His frequent excuse that his 'service' is supposed to sustain his own family therefore creates a tragic irony: Richard's own little family has to fall back on the real father figure after his death, while Vholes's own father in the village of Taunton is well provided for. In this sense, Vholes's theft of Richard from the rightful place in the family structure, which endangers Ada's well-being as his wife, echoes Uriah's disintegration of Mr Wickfield that endangers Agnes's well-being as his daughter. Significantly, through the interference of the lawyer, Agnes is driven into David's, Ada into Esther's arms. Both first-person narrators eventually gain their heart's desire at the depraved actions of those lawyers they proclaim to detest.

Underneath all the heavy symbolic investment in the character of Vholes therefore also lies the potential of duplicity, for his actions secure Esther's own desires. It is Vholes, who drives Richard to the brink, thereby destroys him and enables Esther to reclaim 'her' darling. Like David, Esther is a difficult narrator, coming across as almost omniscient and then revealing herself presumably unwittingly as unreliable. I argued that David emphasises Uriah Heep's sleepless eyes in order to insist on his own subjective blindness and keep the reader from recognising that he observes his fellow beings equally malevolently, or at least critically. Esther Summerson also shirks her responsibility as a narrator by frequently stressing her fabricated insignificance, thereby secretly constructing her narration as it suits her best. As Audrey Jaffe has shown in her excellent *Vanishing Points*, both Esther and David seek to avoid the responsibility of knowing:

> [A]s David Copperfield shows, the subject who presents him or herself as not knowing is not the same as the subject who doesn't know. [. . .] Insisting upon her status as one who does not know, who does not even occupy the subject's position in her narrative, Esther works to efface her own knowledge. And her self-effacing narration serves both a narrative and a characterological purpose, enabling her to structure her narrative and her character without appearing deliberately to do so.[98]

Both narrators proclaim innocence, especially when it comes to the ability of observation, in order to shield themselves from the suspicion they could share such lowly tendencies as other characters: "Like David Copperfield, Esther locates in other characters what she does not want to acknowledge in herself."[99] Thus, while Esther is never short on the subject of her love for Ada, she cannot acknowledge, of course, that she desires her as her property in replacement of her childhood

98 Jaffe, Audrey, *Vanishing Points. Dickens, Narrative, and the Subject of Omniscience*. Berkeley: University of California Press, 1991: 131.
99 Jaffe, *Vanishing Points*, 131.

doll,[100] which is a substitute for her wish to make Ada both mother and daughter for the satisfaction of her desire for female love.

The narrator's doll has an obvious function for the child to provide motherly comfort. Esther describes their 'relationship' as that between mother and child:

> My dear old doll! [. . .] It almost makes me cry to think what a relief it used to be to me, when I came home from school of a day, to run upstairs to my room, and say, 'O you dear faithful Dolly, I knew you would be expecting me!' and then to sit down on the floor, leaning on the elbow of her great chair, and tell her all I had noticed since we parted.
> (*BH*, ch. 3, p. 14)

The image of the child coming home from school to sit at the feet of a loving mother and tell her about their day is perfectly drawn with the eerie exception that this scene does not take place with a live mother, but an artificial child's toy, which is only a material possession. Esther tries to infuse her doll with life in order to compensate for the maternal affection she sorely misses and her devotion to the inanimate object creates an intended feeling of discomfort:

> That there is something uncanny is immediately established by Dickens, both by the ontological linkage developed and sustained between the two and Dolly's emergence in the text as human. Esther wishes Dolly to come to life and, through her narration, Esther does bring Dolly to life . . .[101]

Esther brings Dolly to life in the first chapter of the narrative in an uncanny foreshadowing of her subsequent relationship with Ada: "[S]he used to sit propped up in a great armchair, with her beautiful complexion and rosy lips, staring at me [. . .] while I busily stitched away, and told her every one of my secrets" (*BH*, ch. 3, p. 14). While the more or less unconsciously professed wish to come home after school to a mother never materialises itself for Esther, the wish to sit with a beautiful confidante, stitching away, will characterise a good proportion of her later life as she relates it to the reader. In Ada, Esther's doll finally comes alive, which is why she takes to her clearly uncommonly fast upon their first acquaintance:

> She came to meet me with a smile of welcome and her hand extended, but seemed to change her mind in a moment, and kissed me. In short, she had such a natural, captivating, winning manner, that in a few minutes we were sitting in the window-seat, with the light of the fire upon us, talking together, as free and happy as could be. (*BH*, ch. 3, p. 26)

100 Christine Van Boheemen-Saaf has argued in her brilliant essay on *Bleak House* that Ada is a reincarnation of the doll: "'The Universe Makes an Indifferent Parent': *Bleak House* and the Victorian Family Romance" in *Bleak House. Contemporary Critical Essays*, ed. Jeremy Tambling. Basingstoke: Macmillan, 1999: 54–64, 57.

101 Robyn L. Schiffman, "Wax-Work, Clock-Work, and Puppet-Shews: *Bleak House* and the Uncanny," *Dickens Studies Annual* 30 (2001): 159–171, 164.

Esther's freeness and happiness with Ada from the first moment echoes the comfort the lifeless doll has provided in the solitude of her childhood room and it shows that she immediately appropriates the beautiful girl as her new possession in substitution for the doll. Consequently, her mode of reference to Ada is exclusively marked by an owner's pride in the material qualities of her property and it sets in immaturely fast even during the meeting with the Lord Chancellor: "That he admired her, and was interested by her, even *I* could see in a moment" (*BH*, ch. 3, p. 27). *Even I*: Esther positions herself as authoritative of Ada's perception in the world and does not yield this self-proclaimed dominance for the rest of the novel. Within the same early chapter, she already refers to her as "my pet" (*BH*, ch. 3, p. 28), evidently a most telling name, and henceforth accentuates Ada's quality as her more or less animate object of comfort. Consequently, Ada only comes alive for Esther, but not for the reader. Trapped in an existence as Esther's doll, surrogate mother and daughter, the character clearly can never develop psychological depth and remains blatantly uninteresting for the reader. Her only function, apart from being taken legal possession of by Richard, losing all of her little fortune in the event, is to prove a source of unconditional love for Esther.

Esther's infantile desire to be loved as she has imagined her doll has loved her, comes to a climax in her reunion with Ada after her illness. Scarred and disfigured, by all Victorian standards no longer lovable as Mr Guppy will give her so wonderfully comically to understand, Esther finds in Ada the true substitution for her doll, for the moment is one of truly unconditional love:

> Ah, my angel girl! the old dear look, all love, all fondness, all affection. Nothing else in it – no, nothing, nothing!
>
> O how happy I was, down upon the floor, with my sweet beautiful girl down upon the floor too, holding my scarred face to her lovely cheek, bathing it with tears and kisses, rocking me to and fro like a child, calling me by every tender name that she could think of, and pressing me to her faithful heart. (*BH*, ch. 36, p. 442)

In the mute acceptance of her changed appearance, Esther finds in Ada a mother's love, something she has craved all her life. As a child, she projects such feelings onto her doll; as an adult, she seeks the same emotional gratification from Ada: "[I]t is only in Ada's embrace, at last and for a moment, that Esther can cease to be the comforter and caregiver and receive the loving ministrations of a mother."[102] Like Agnes does for David, Ada comes to substitute a mother's

102 Timothy Peltason, "Esther's Will" in *Bleak House. Contemporary Critical Essays*, ed. Jeremy Tambling. Basingstoke: Macmillan, 1999: 205–227, 216.

love for Esther as her doll has finally come alive. Moreover, Ada comes to compensate the unsatisfying reunion of Esther with her actual mother, Lady Dedlock, which has not coincidentally happened just before, as John O. Jordan has observed. Since the supposed reunion of biological mother and child constitutes no beginning, but an end of the relationship, the factual reunion with Ada serves as a placeholder: "the main significance of the scene lies in its juxtaposition to the preceding scene of failed reunion between Esther and her mother."[103] Esther finally finds the unconditional love she has sought and been deprived of both through the absence of an unknown mother and the forced rejection from her biological mother in the flesh: "Ada here takes the part of Lady Dedlock, providing Esther with the unconditional acceptance and love that her mother has been unable or unwilling to give."[104] Psychologically speaking, it is perfectly comprehensible that Esther is determined not to give Ada up: 'over my dead body' becomes 'over Richard's dead body.'

Like Agnes, Ada is of course a minor and a flat character, whose sole purpose is to exist as the narrator's object of affection. The love both Esther and David feel for these women is thus supposed to tell the reader a lot more about the protagonists than their loved ones. Ada is not, in Alexander Welsh's words, "a character in her own right":

> Dickens will not develop and make understandable the psychology of several characters as they interact but rather reveal the psychology of his protagonist as it is projected upon, or aimed against, some other invented figure. Therefore the more interesting Esther Summerson becomes for a thoughtful reader, the less interesting will be Ada Clare.[105]

Ada's sole purpose, therefore, is to fill Esther's desire for unconditional love, which is why Richard is an unwanted rival throughout the whole secondary love plot. His existence is, of course, necessary: both Esther and Ada first have to find and fulfil heterosexual love in order that Esther can finally take possession of Ada, so Richard is a necessary evil for the narrator. Eventually, however, in order for her to achieve her desires, Richard must disappear.

In this sense, Vholes acts as a *diabolus ex machina* too, for he creates the desired outcome for Esther. She expresses her anxiety at seeing him take possession

---

103 John O. Jordan, *Supposing Bleak House*. Charlottesville and London: University of Virginia Press, 2011: 54. See also Boheemen-Saaf, "Indifferent Parent," 58: "[I]t is highly significant that the chapter that has as its central event the relatively restrained recognition of the kinship between Esther and her mother should end in a climax of much greater emotional intensity with the reunion of Esther and Ada."

104 Jordan, *Supposing Bleak House*, 55.

105 Alexander Welsh, *Dickens Redressed. The Art of Bleak House and Hard Times*. New Haven and London: Yale University Press, 2000: 40.

of Richard, which diverts us from seeing that she wishes to take possession of Ada – a relationship that Richard seems to prevent from the start. There is no moment in the novel until Richard's death in which Esther has no reason to regard him as a rival in her affection for Ada, which is possibly why she alludes to their love plot uncharacteristically early. The two young people are paired off from the start, marginalising Esther as a somewhat androgynous, or at least asexual, fifth wheel that can at best be a mother, but never a lover. Esther's own desire for Ada as a replacement of the doll as the only other 'being' that she believes ever loved her is confronted with Richard as the most obvious 'natural' destination for Ada. Richard's death thus accomplishes a happiness for Esther that the text could not otherwise achieve: Esther can claim Ada for herself only as a heterosexual widow with a son. 'Her' darling is evermore her doll at the close of the novel; a success that the despicable Vholes has brought about. Since he has sucked the life-blood out of Richard, Esther is free to claim Ada as her own: "as erotic descriptions of Ada and her repeated identification of her as 'my darling' suggest, Esther is reproducing the role which Richard is too weak to undertake . . ."[106]

Both Virginia Blain and Taylor Stoehr have noted how significantly unempathetically Esther seems to relate Richard's fate: "Esther's narration gives no glow of feminine (or sentimental) sympathy to Richard's story; [. . .] she in fact makes a less than sympathetic narrator of this tale of failure and suffering."[107] Blain and Stoehr's observation relates to the somewhat counterintuitive fact that Richard's fate is split between the two narratives – he appears in both the omniscient heterodiegetic, as well as the subjective homodiegetic portions of the novel and Stoehr has convincingly argued that the two narrative strands give us almost two different versions of Richard:

> [W]hen Dickens wants to examine Richard's feelings and motives most closely, and to compare them with those of his ideal (Woodcourt), he finds it necessary for the first and only time in the novel to have Esther recount an interview at which she was not present. [. . .] This scene is remarkable for the relatively favorable light in which it places Richard – frank, manly, even responsible – and when Esther finally resumes the narrative again with her own voice, we suddenly become aware of how much her condescension and moralizing temper have conditioned our reaction to Richard . . .[108]

106 Helen Michie, "'Who Is This in Pain?': Scarring, Disfigurement, and Female Identity in *Bleak House* and *Our Mutual Friend*," *Novel: A Forum on Fiction* 22.2 (1989): 199–212, 203.
107 Virginia Blain, "Double Vision and the Double Standard in *Bleak House*: A Feminist Perspective" in *Bleak House. Contemporary Critical Essays*, ed. Jeremy Tambling. Basingstoke: Macmillan, 1998: 65–86, 69. See also Stoehr, *Dreamer's Stance*, 158–160.
108 Stoehr, *Dreamer's Stance*, 159.

Richard stands in Esther's way, because she desires Ada for herself. Richard therefore has to die, because "Dickens [. . .] moves behind his heroine and makes her win, he backs Summerson as willingly as he backed Copperfield, with similarly fatal results to those who come in her path."[109] Once Richard is eliminated, Esther can rightfully claim Ada as her possession, for the young widow has no other place in her society anyway. Esther can have both, therefore: marry Woodcourt for the desired heterosexual union and keep Ada as a reincarnation of her doll to be unconditionally loved by her.

Vholes is more than just "the quintessential lawyer" of *Bleak House*.[110] He serves as a covert executor of Esther's repressed desire for Richard's death. He is part of her subconscious as Uriah is of David's, bearing the narrator's abject wishes that allow no expression. Consequently, it comes as no surprise that both Esther and Dickens are as verbose on the subject of Vholes' hideous nature inside and out. As John O. Jordan has remarked about Uriah, the hatred and disgust the narrative of *Bleak House* expresses at the figure of Vholes is also quite excessive. The accentuation of the vampiric qualities he radiates is so pointed that it almost seems trite. Dickens harps on this particular villain with an intensity that the character's function in the novel hardly justifies. After all, he is simply one of several lawyers and that the system is bad the novel has repeated very loudly since chapter 1. Here is a minor and flat character who has an amount of animosity heaped upon him that is so out of proportion with his function in the novel that we can only understand his position if we see his place in Esther's subconscious. It is quite unreasonable to assume that Vholes is merely symbolic, no matter how much he resembles the grim reaper, who comes to carry Richard away.[111] After all, it becomes very clear that it is Esther's heart's desire that he be carried away. She simply cannot admit that Vholes acts according to her wishes, not least since this causes her 'pet' considerable pain.

Like David, who inflicts considerable unhappiness on Agnes for the majority of his life's story, Esther subconsciously also contributes to Ada's many sufferings. Like Agnes, Ada suffers mostly in silence, which is of course partly due to the fact that both can only express anything at all if the narrator lets their voice through. David conveniently suggests that Agnes never complains – Esther occasionally admits into her narrative Ada's rational and wise voice that makes one question whether her perceived flatness is not simply the result of the narrator's oppression of the character. In conclusion of the reader's first

109 Welsh, *Dickens Redressed*, 40.
110 H. M. Daleski, *Dickens and the Art of Analogy*. London: Faber and Faber, 1970: 165.
111 See Crompton, "Satire and Symbolism," 301.

acquaintance with Vholes, who grimly rides off with Richard as mentioned above, Ada quite clearly foresees the consequences for her own life with a clarity that even Esther cannot conceal:

> My dear girl told me, that night, how Richard's being thereafter prosperous or ruined, befriended or deserted, could only make this difference to her, that the more he needed love from one unchanging heart, the more love that unchanging heart would have to give him; how he thought of her through his present errors, and she would think of him at all times: never of herself, if she could devote herself to him: never of her own delights, if she could minister to his. (*BH*, ch. 37, ch. 457)

Like Dora Copperfield, née Spenlow, who obediently dies when required to make way for David's happiness with Agnes, Ada perceives her fictional fate with utmost clarity. Esther attempts to frame her doll's wise prophecy of what will happen by the additional "And she kept her word!" in order to make it seem like her own premonition of Richard's fate, but Ada not only hints at the inevitability of Richard's failure, but also almost candidly criticises him for his "errors."

Ada is no inanimate doll unless Esther forces her to be. Every now and then, the perceptive reader is offered a glance of Ada's strength and intelligence that Esther egotistically tries to oppress – after all, she needs Ada as a source of comfort for herself and not a woman in her own right. The only moment that suggests potential discord rising to the surface occurs when Ada chooses Richard over Esther. When she has realised that Richard has taken legal possession of Ada through their clandestine marriage, Esther literally describes her difficulties with yielding her claim on Ada as property:

> I had given my darling to him now, and I meant to go; but I lingered for one more look of the precious face, which it seemed to rive my heart to turn from. [. . .] And when I got downstairs, O how I cried! It almost seemed to me that I had lost my Ada for ever. I was so lonely, and so blank without her, and it was so desolate to be going home with no hope of seeing her there, that I could get no comfort for a little while, as I walked up and down in a dim corner, sobbing and crying. (*BH*, ch. 51, p. 593)

The passage is a momentous one as it reveals that Esther still regards Ada as a substitute for her doll and Richard has taken her away. Moreover, Esther's professed dislike of Vholes seems legitimated. After all, the choice Ada makes has only become necessary *because* of Vholes. The lawyer's power over Richard has caused the rift in the domestic harmony that would have otherwise allowed Ada to be married from *Bleak House* and remain with her husband under the patchwork family's roof. By siding with Richard, Ada runs the risk of delivering herself into the power of Vholes as Agnes temporarily finds herself defenceless against Uriah's control of her. Both David and Esther are more or less helplessly excluded from the lawyer-controlled sphere and it is worthwhile to note that neither prove the means of rescuing their professed angels. In both stories, intervention comes from outside in the shape of Mr Micawber and Richard's death.

On the surface, Esther does not only fear Richard's influence over Ada, but by extension also Vholes's. Since Vholes controls Richard, he potentially comes to control Ada and therefore proves dangerous for Esther. The rivalry between them is hardly as evident as the one between David and Uriah over Agnes, but the triangle that forms on the back of Mr Wickfield respectively Richard Carstone is almost exactly the same. Esther comes to fear Vholes not only in reference to Richard, in which instance she can be more or less open about the legitimate fear of losing Richard to the fangs of the law, but she comes to fear him as a power over Ada and that is far less easy to admit to. Esther engages in a duplicitous power struggle with Vholes: on the one hand, he does the evil which she wants to bring about herself, which is to get rid of Richard. Since she can never confess that, she makes him out as her enemy. On the other hand, he threatens to gain a position of power over Ada via Richard that Esther seeks herself. So, when Ada chooses Richard, it seems as if Vholes has won and Esther sees him as a vulture lying in wait for 'her' darling when she possessively guards the young couple's home: "I thought of the youth and love and beauty of my dear girl, shut up in such an ill-assorted refuge, almost as if it were a cruel place" (*BH*, ch. 51, p. 594).

Given the power struggle with Vholes that the text tries to suppress, it is no coincidence that Esther's alter ego, Lady Dedlock, is paired with the other powerful lawyer figure in the novel. The lawyers in *Bleak House* cause serious trouble for the novel's central women, because they invade their conventional domestic space, although the oppressive power of the law is predominantly associated with the male characters in the text. The Chancery suit functions in the male-dominated public sphere as a source of grievance for the men, who are most expressive about their plight. Gridley and Jarndyce, Boythorn and Richard Carstone, all constantly reiterate the failures of the system, the lack of responsibility on behalf of the representatives of the system and the difference between law and justice. The text thus evokes the impression that the overbearing disciplinary power of the law afflicts only the hegemonic males, but at a closer look, it is the women who suffer more. Pairing Esther with Vholes and Lady Dedlock with Tulkinghorn, the novel's most painful inflictions of the law happen beyond its own sphere.

The text is so extremely outspoken about the subject that it has turned itself into the most famous critique of nineteenth-century English law. There are hundreds of studies on the subject of the law in *Bleak House* from both disciplines involved. Whatever one would wish to say about *Bleak House*, a novel that has many Dickens critics in its grasp for most of their careers,[112] it is safe to say that *Bleak House* contributes to all debates on law reform and makes a case for justice and personal responsibility over statutes and systems. This is why Dickens's lawyer figures are almost exclusively regarded as representatives of the system and this is especially true for Mr Tulkinghorn, who certainly stands out as one of the most elaborate creations in the profession and maintains quite a prominent role in the plot until his mysterious death. Consequently, there seems to be a significant difference between Vholes and Tulkinghorn, although they represent the same profession: "While Vholes' motivations are to keep the system going and receive his own fees, Tulkinghorn's sins are far worse for the profession of law. Serving no one's best interest but his own, he destroys the foundation of the lawyer-client relationship."[113] The two characters differ considerably in their conception: while Vholes seems one-dimensional with regard to his sinister nature and vampiric appearance, Tulkinghorn is deliberately created more as an enigma that defies such obvious insight into his character. Consequently, his motives for exercising his sadistic power over Lady Dedlock have often been questioned. Thus, Boasberg has suggested that "Tulkinghorn's motives are one of the book's unsolved mysteries"[114] – unsolved, that is, unless he merely serves Dickens to expose the cruelty of the system, which was Robert Garis's premise: "In his patient explication of his thinking, as he tries to arrive at a 'decision', we hear the true action of System in process."[115]

All this is true, but there is more. Dickens certainly goes to great lengths in painting Tulkinghorn in the bleakest, most stereotypical and prejudicial colours by use of both metaphor and what Juliet McMaster has called his "language of appearance."[116] Tulkinghorn is as lifeless and dusty as the morgue itself:

> He is of what is called the old school – a phrase generally meaning any school that seems never to have been young – and wears knee breeches tied with ribbons, and gaiters or stockings. One peculiarity of his black clothes, and of his black stockings, be they silk or worsted, is, that they never shine. Mute, close, irresponsive to any glancing light, his dress is like himself. (*BH*, ch. 2, p. 11)

Like Vholes and Uriah Heep, Tulkinghorn is of course only dressed in black for professional, not personal reasons, but the custom serves Dickens in creating the most morbid associations around the figure of the lawyer. Like Vholes,

112 See John O. Jordan's wonderful introduction to *Supposing Bleak House*, for instance.
113 Boasberg, "Chancery as Megalosaurus," 50.
114 Boasberg, "Chancery as Megalosaurus," 50.
115 Garis, *Dickens Theatre*, 137.
116 Juliet McMaster, *Dickens the Designer*. Basingstoke: Macmillan, 1987: 10.

Tulkinghorn seems like the grim reaper, too deadly, too serious, too *observant* to be comfortable society for anyone. Critics generally refer to him as lifeless or heartless;[117] Marilyn Georgas identifies him as a reincarnation of the devil himself.[118] In an early review of *Bleak House*, George Brimley suspected that while Tulkinghorn's sole purpose might have been supposed to be the biased representation of despicable lawyers in general, the character somewhat got away from Dickens:

> Mr Tulkinghorn, the Dedlock confidential solicitor, is an admirable study of mere outward characteristics of a class; but his motives and his character are quite incomprehensible, and we strongly suspect that Mr Dickens had him shot out of the way as the only possible method of avoiding an enigma of his own setting which he could not solve . . .[119]

The question of Tulkinghorn's motive is the crux, of course. After all, one can only regard him as more than a type if his motive is psychologically comprehensible, so this lawyer also evokes this most difficult question: is he a type or a character? Does he or does he not have a motive? What are we supposed to see in Tulkinghorn other than his role as a particularly heinous embodiment of the profession? I will try to show in this chapter that, in fact, Tulkinghorn is both type and character. He is a type, but he got away from Dickens and his motive is psychologically far more interesting than it might seem. After all, he is a descendant of Uriah Heep too. Robert Donovan, like so many other critics, has claimed that Tulkinghorn has no "lively human sympathies,"[120] but what Brimley perceived so early on is quite true: Tulkinghorn grows into an enigma beyond his function in the plot and quite escapes Dickens's control until he can finally kill him.

Mr Tulkinghorn's pursuit of Lady Dedlock seems somewhat arbitrary the more determined he becomes to torture her with her secret. He seems to be following the customary rules of blackmail, but this conventional strategy never transpires. When she finally confronts him with the fact that he knows her most dangerous secret, he does not even know what he wants himself, it seems. He vaguely insists that he acts in Sir Leicester's interest and therefore needs to be in control of the wife's secret:

> 'When I speak of Sir Leicester being the sole consideration, he and the family credit are one. Sir Leicester and the baronetcy, Sir Leicester and Chesney Wold, Sir Leicester and his

117 See Stewart, "New Mortality," 471.
118 Georgas, "Devil and the Dedlocks."
119 Collins, *Critical Heritage*, 285.
120 Donovan, "Structure and Idea," 195.

> ancestors and his patrimony'; Mr Tulkinghorn very dry here; 'are, I need not say to you, Lady Dedlock, inseparable.' (*BH*, ch. 41, p. 494)

In this vein, Tulkinghorn's only other statement to how one should proceed in this case is that "[t]his is to be hushed up, if it can be" (*BH*, ch. 41, p. 494). Once again, a logical analysis of the character could only come to the conclusion that if this were true, the whole matter could be put to rest. Tulkinghorn is the only one in the know and therefore 'hushing it up' would prove to be no difficulty. Within the logic of the plot, however, this can be no solution. The fact that Tulkinghorn knows now has to bring about a twist. Lady Dedlock's actions have to be determined by the power he has over her and their secret 'misalliance' needs to be a considerable factor in his murder, for it is clear that Dickens needs both Tulkinghorn and Lady Dedlock dead before he can achieve the novel's denouement.

Consequently, those critics who do *not* read Tulkinghorn as a mere representative of the system have often wondered what his true motive might be. No one believes that his sole interest lies with his client and no one believes that Dickens wants to make him seem as the embodiment of the trustworthy family lawyer – if anything, Tulkinghorn is the opposite when one reads him as a representative of his profession, as Brenda Welch has done: "Tulkinghorn neither knows clearly who his client is nor feels any particular compunction to behave in a responsible manner even assuming that he knows whom he represents."[121] Welch has argued like Bruce Robbins that Dickens's critique of Tulkinghorn focuses closely on his unwillingness to take responsibility for his own actions and to rely on the rigidity of the law to relieve him from feeling any moral responsibility: "Tulkinghorn's failures as a solicitor arise from his fundamental failure to understand and appreciate this first principle of lawyering . . ."[122] It is this focus on Tulkinghorn's 'failures,' however, that very clearly distinguishes him from a scathing critique of lawyers in general, for it is completely uncertain whether he truly fails. The lawyer may not act in his client's interest when he drives his beloved wife to despair, but this seems more a failure on the personal, not on the professional level. Robert Garis has pointed out that, strictly speaking, Tulkinghorn is not loyal to Sir Leicester here,[123] so if he is neither merely systemic nor a 'good' lawyer, one can only attempt to read other personal interests into his behaviour. In contrast to Vholes, whose surface function in the text is to be a bloodsucking lawyer in the tradition of the prejudice against him, Tulkinghorn is

121 Welch, "Professional Responsibility," 60.
122 Welch, "Professional Responsibility," 60. See also Robbins, "Telescopic Philanthropy" and chapter 1.
123 See Garis, *Dickens Theatre*, 136–137.

conceived from the first with more depth and more complexity. The most dangerous assets the author has endowed the character with, which is clearly borrowed from Uriah Heep, are his eyes, which are often forcefully recalled in the reader's mind.

The first introduction of the character mentions his spectacles. The fact that he wears them is not significant per se: Mr Jellyby, Krook, Mrs Pardiggle and, most importantly, Mr Bucket are also drawn as bespectacled characters. There are considerable parallels between Krook, Bucket and Tulkinghorn, which I will come back to, and none of the characters in this list are particularly likeable, but it seems that the accessory's function is to keep Tulkinghorn present in the reader's subconscious, for after his death, the object is never mentioned again. Once Tulkinghorn is gone, it seems, there is no longer any need to remind the audience of the fact that spectacles allow their wearer superhuman vision. For the presentation of the lawyer, they seem indispensable: He "puts on his spectacles" (*BH*, ch. 2, p. 13) before he begins reading the papers that cause Lady Dedlock's pivotal reaction; he "glances over his spectacles" (*BH*, ch. 2, p. 13) to emphasise the significance of that moment; and he "adjusts his spectacles" (*BH*, ch. 10, p. 115), before he goes out for the first time in pursuit of Lady Dedlock's secret. While other characters may be wearing the same device, it is most emphatically associated with Tulkinghorn's penetrating gaze, which is not only, but also, an indication of his intellectual superiority. Here he is bespectacled in intellectual 'contest' with Snagsby on the first clues to the mystery: "Mr Tulkinghorn has seen the entry, found it before the Law-stationer, read it while the forefinger was coming down the hill" (*BH*, ch. 10, p. 116). He is not only inquisitive, a characteristic that likens his spectacles to Bucket's, but he is also intellectually superior to others. The spectacles sharpen his inquisitive glance that is clearly dangerous for its objects. He is surveillance embodied in a novel in which everyone is being watched. Tulkinghorn makes sure that discipline is being maintained. As a representative of Chancery, Tulkinghorn's panoptical power permeates the whole novel, as D. A. Miller has argued in his famous analysis of *Bleak House*.[124] In this sense, Tulkinghorn is of course the perfect and the only person to spot Lady Dedlock's transgression. Dickens shows us how he 'sniffs' out her secret, but it is his eyes that prove so dangerous for her: "[I]t may be that my Lady had better have five thousand pairs of fashionable eyes upon her, in distrustful vigilance, than the two eyes of the rusty lawyer, with his wisp of neckcloth and his dull black breeches tied with ribbons at the knees" (*BH*, ch. 29, p. 344). Dickens carefully juxtaposes the lawyer's seemingly harmless outward appearance with his invigilating glance: he sees everything that

---

124 Miller, *The Novel and the Police*, 58ff.

runs counter to the order he seeks to maintain. This juxtaposition suggests that there is much more to Tulkinghorn than the eye can see. The author has endowed him with a complexity that far exceeds a mere caricature of the stereotypical lawyer.

Tulkinghorn's surveillance of his world is a spitting image of Uriah's sleepless eyes that observe everything with potentially dreadful consequences for those who find themselves under his penetrating gaze. It is no coincidence, therefore, that the encounters between Tulkinghorn and Lady Dedlock are characterised by silent looks rather than language. In fact, both are "mute, close, irresponsive" (*BH*, ch. 2, p. 11) in each other's presence. Until the showdown in Mr Tulkinghorn's chamber, verbal exchange between the two opponents is conspicuously rare and the power struggle between them hovers unspoken in the air above them: "Mr Tulkinghorn comes and goes pretty often; there being estate business to do, leases to be renewed, and so on. He sees my Lady pretty often, too; and he and she are as composed, and as indifferent, and take as little heed of one another, as ever" (*BH*, ch. 29, p. 344). From the first moment the relationship between them is marked with animosity and suspicion and Lady Dedlock's seemingly inviolable hauteur is already penetrated by the lawyer: "[W]hile Mr Tulkinghorn may not know what is passing in the Dedlock mind at present, it is very possible that he may" (*BH*, ch. 2, p. 12). The paradox paints him in a position of power over her that is from henceforth frequently recalled to the reader's mind. Thus, their first actual exchange in the story is fraught with aggression and it is clearly foreshadowed that this extraordinary relationship will bring forth something unwanted:

> 'It would be useless to ask,' says my Lady, with the dreariness of the place in Lincolnshire still upon her, 'whether anything has been done.'
>
> 'Nothing that *you* would call anything, has been done today,' replies Mr Tulkinghorn.
>
> 'Nor ever will be,' says my Lady (*BH*, ch. 2, p. 12)

In a seemingly mundane exchange about the eternally ongoing suit, they have both managed to insult each other. While she calls him useless, he calls her stupid. She belittles his profession, his reason for living; he belittles her comprehension – not only as a woman, but also as a member of a superficial class. There is an unnecessary and possibly inexplicable aggression between them that henceforth characterises their relationship and reveals Tulkinghorn as a sadistic oppressor. From the moment of her involuntary emotional reaction, he has the upper hand and enjoys it. Thus, the next move he makes in this game is especially cruel: having found Nemo and having found him dead, Tulkinghorn writes to Lady Dedlock via Sir Leicester, "I have seen him" (*BH*, ch. 12, p. 133). It is easy to focus on the letter as an important twist in the plot, which causes Lady Dedlock considerable emotional distress. However, one should not overlook the intricate nature of the message, for the elliptic 'I have seen him' without any further information, without any indication of what he has found out and without any hint at whether *she* will see him, all make it particularly cruel.

John Kucich has argued that to inquire into the minds of great Dickensian villains is to destroy their artful construction. He sees them in the tradition of Iago as "absolute villains," villains, who are not driven by material motives or economic gain, villains who are committed to "violation for its own sake": "these are irredeemable, confirmed villains."[125] Tulkinghorn is one of them. He is of a kind of evil that is certainly of a different class than Dickens's more perfunctory villains and therefore it might be in vain to inquire into his motive. As Kucich writes, "if we could psychologize these villains, [. . .] these figures would lose the malevolent hold they exercise over the reader."[126] To a certain extent, this is probably true. After all, Dickens *wants* the reader to be stupefied as to what Tulkinghorn's true motive is:

> Whether he be cold and cruel, whether immovable in what he has made his duty, whether absorbed in love of power, whether determined to have nothing hidden from him in ground where he has burrowed among secrets all his life, whether he in his heart despises the splendour of which he is a distant beam, whether he is always treasuring up slights and offences in the affability of his gorgeous clients – whether he be any of this, or all of this, it may be that my Lady had better have five thousand pairs of fashionable eyes upon her, in distrustful vigilance, than the two eyes of this rusty lawyer . . . (*BH*, ch. 29, p. 344)

On the surface, the passage suggests many different motives that are supposed to emphasise that Tulkinhorn's villainy is idiosyncratic and incalculable. The juxtaposition of these different 'psychological' explanations only seem to emphasise that there will be no conclusive explanation, which greatly enhances the threat Tulkinghorn poses as a presumably evil force in the narrative. Although there seems to be a stronger hint towards Tulinghorn's resentment of the upper classes – the narrator suggests that his actions are motivated by spite towards the oppressive classes he leeches off and yet despises – the idea behind the passage evidently is to provide possible reasons that compete with each other and thus totally obfuscate the 'real' one:

> Flirtation with Tulinghorn's possible motives is not just coyness on Dickens' part; this list of motives, all of them plausible, are trivialized almost to the point of irrelevance by the bland equivalence drawn among them by the narrator. The very clutter of this list of motives takes away their grandeur from the reader who thinks he has privately guessed what

125 Kucich, *Excess and Restraint*, 62.
126 Kucich, *Excess and Restraint*, 63.

> really motivates Tulkinghorn, and it emphasizes instead their inadequacy as explanations, which, of course, is attested to by the frequent complaints among Dickens' early readers that Tulkinghorn could not exist.[127]

While all of this is probably true, Tulkinghorn is better than his own design. He is supposed to be a good villain, but in fact he is a great villain – a villain who is out to destroy Lady Dedlock for the sheer sexual pleasure of it.

Tulkinghorn seeks to exercise the kind of power over Lady Dedlock that Uriah exercises over Agnes. He is already in a more convenient position, however, for he has the full trust of Sir Leicester, which leaves him almost unrestricted access to his wife. There is a certain parallel between the way both Uriah and Tulkinghorn manage to implement their employers as mere puppets for their purposes, but the trust that Sir Leicester puts in Tulkinghorn is of the more dogged kind. When Sir Leicester acts as messenger, for instance, Tulkinghorn manages to use Lady Dedlock's own husband as a pawn in his torturous game, invading her home and sphere of trust. He has already made the transgression into her domestic space at the wilful condescension of Sir Leicester himself:

> It is Mr Tulkinghorn's room, and is never bestowed on anybody else, for he may come at any time. He is not come yet. It is his quiet habit to walk across the park from the village, in fine weather; to drop into his room, as if he had never been out of it since he was last seen there; to request a servant to inform Sir Leicester that he is arrived, in case he should be wanted; and to appear ten minutes before dinner, in the shadow of the library door.
>
> (*BH*, ch. 12, p. 139)

There is a deliberate paradox between the picture of the dusty, lifeless lawyer and the fact that his appearance is completely unpredictable. This uncanny unpredictability contradicts the conception of the character as methodical and steady, rigid and monotonous, so the reader can sense Lady Dedlock's fear of his arrival. She has no control over his unwanted presence, because her husband allows her enemy unlimited access. Like Uriah, who goes in and out of the Wickfields' home or Vholes, who is allowed to see Richard at all hours and therefore even invades the country, the lawyer becomes a harassing presence in the woman's domestic space that would so rightfully be her last resort in terms of Victorian gender ideology.

Instead, Lady Dedlock, as much as Agnes Wickfield before her, is made to feel unsafe in her own home. She has no control over Tulkinghorn's violent penetration of her sphere and feels the need to brace herself against the threat to her person he carries. There is no escape available for her, for convention dictates that she can never fully avoid his presence as her husband's guest. It is no

---

127 Kucich, *Excess and Restraint*, 63.

coincidence, therefore, that Tulkinghorn appears always at dusk and in the shadow: while he sees everything, he cannot be made out in the twilight in his dark apparel. He appears like a ghost, an embodiment of her guilt as in Shakespeare, but also as a real demon that threatens her life.[128] Thus, she awaits the arrival of her ghost in unbearable suspense:

> Every day before dinner, my Lady looks for him in the dusk of the library, but he is not there. Every day at dinner, my Lady glances down the table for the vacant place, that would be waiting to receive him if he had just arrived; but there is no vacant place. Every night, my lady casually asks her maid: 'Is Mr Tulkinghorn come?' (*BH*, ch. 12, p. 139)

Again, Dickens resorts to a triple structure: the devil will come when called three times and Lady Dedlock calls him forth "every day," "every day," "every night." In a different mystical interpretation of how to deal with ghosts, she tries to call him forth, acknowledge his presence and then release him, as superstition would have it.[129] In any event, Tulkinghorn is treated by the text almost like a supernatural being, which conflicts almost comically with the picture otherwise invoked of the rusty, mundane, boring lawyer. She awaits him like an apparition, but he appears like a lawyer: "He comes towards them at his usual methodical pace, which is never quickened never slackened" (*BH*, ch. 12, p. 139). And yet, he carries a power that exceeds far the power over papers and Lady Dedlock knows it. Tulkinghorn haunts her and *he* knows it. Thus, they fight an almost exclusively non-verbal battle that brings with it a string of humiliations for both as each try to win the upper hand.

The covert power struggle that eludes all the other characters is too complex to be understood as a simple fight of good versus evil – especially in light of the fact that while the text may express a certain sympathy with Lady Dedlock, she is never not considered guilty. She is a sexually licentious woman and herein lies the key towards Tulkinghorn's behaviour towards her: he is not as passionless as the text would like him to be. He may appear like the devil, but his interest in the woman is quite human. Whether or not he suspects her sexual deviance from the first moment of her unusual emotional reaction, he certainly begins to see the woman behind her position in the social hierarchy. When he reveals to her what he has found out about her former lover, the narrator withdraws from the text for an unusually long passage,

---

128 Although the figure of the lawyer has seldom been regarded as having an ethereal aspect, I would like to add Tulkinghorn and also Guppy to the wonderful list of ghosts John O. Jordan has identified in *Supposing Bleak House*. See pp. 114–115.

129 See Allan Woodcourt's reference to the superstition in *Bleak House* when he refers to himself as a friendly ghost, "only waiting, as they say ghosts do, to be addressed." (ch. 51, p. 587)

leaving man and woman to a verbal exchange full of sexual tension: "During the utterance of every word of this short dialogue, Lady Dedlock and Mr Tulkinghorn, without any alteration in their customary deportment, have looked very steadily at one another – as was natural, perhaps, in the discussion of so unusual a subject." (*BH*, ch. 12, p. 142) The narratorial commentary, "perhaps," is ironic, of course – a reminder of the Victorian drawing-room propriety that seems violated by the lawyer's predatory observation of the socially superior woman. He has fixed her in his glance, objectifying and degrading her by the insinuation that the man they speak of has sexually possessed her. She tries to restore her superiority over him, "Have the kindness, Mr Tulkinghorn, to open the door for me" (*BH*, ch. 12, p. 142), but no pretence of protocol can conceal that he has taken a liberty by his looking at her without respectfully averting his eyes. He has taken the liberty, of course, because he believes that a woman without virtue has no right to be shielded from a desirous male gaze. Tulkinghorn has begun the pursuit of the fallen woman as a criminal, which Inspector Bucket will take over after the lawyer's death. From this moment on, Lady Dedlock and Mr Tulkinghorn exist in a perverted secret love affair with one another:

> They appear to take as little note of one another, as any two people, enclosed within the same walls, could. But whether each evermore watches and suspects the other, evermore mistrustful of some great reservation; whether each is evermore prepared at all points for the other, and never to be taken unawares; what each would give to know how much the other knows – all this is hidden, for the time, in their own hearts. (*BH*, ch. 12, p. 142)

If the discursive markers were only slightly changed towards more positively connoted verbs, the narrator may as well be describing two people who carry on a secret affair and try to hide from other eyes. Significantly, the text changes Tulkinghorn's image from the rusty, lifeless creature, for now, he has a heart.

It is remarkable that Tulkinghorn's descriptions change whenever he is engaged with Lady Dedlock; in other instances, the text suggests that he is empty inside, which is why it is so easy to see in him a hollow figure, "a living tomb," as Garrett Stewart has it: His "private interior is comprised entirely of the secret inner lives of others, without which entombed privacies he himself could be a hole or void. His is a living silence unto death, and negation is the essence of his public self . . ."[130] From his first appearance, the text goes to great lengths to paint exactly such a picture of Tulkinghorn and then we find that at a closer look, Lady Dedlock begins to fill this void – it is just not entirely clear with what. If Tulkinghorn is not a systemic law-representative and not vice nor evil

130 Stewart, "New Mortality," 471.

embodied,[131] then it has seemed safe to assume that it is his love of power that drives him; after all, the text suggests that too: "whether absorbed in love of power . . ." (*BH*, ch. 29, p. 344) is listed as a possible reason for his relentless pursuit and he certainly gains such power when he has finally brought Lady Dedlock into a position at his mercy: "In a word, Tulkinghorn is a monstrous embodiment of the will to power [. . .]. He maneuvers people as he maneuvers bits of wax."[132] One can clearly sense a difference, however, between how he manoeuvres Snagsby or Trooper George or even Sir Leicester himself, and his manipulation of Lady Dedlock. The different degrees of his own hauteur, of his open and arrogant display of his intellectual superiority over others, is not restricted to class. Sir Leicester is also just a puppet to him, a figure above him in station, but not in intellect, as Tulkinghorn makes fairly clear by exuding his power over the wife under the Baronet's very eyes.

In contrast to Tulkinghorn, who sees absolutely everything, Sir Leicester Dedlock sees absolutely nothing. Tulkinghorn manoeuvres all the men to his advantage easily and successfully, as methodically as the text would have him be in all his 'professional' relations. What the text cannot suppress, however, is that the lawyer deals with his two female opponents entirely differently; he is no longer methodical, he is emotional. Such contradictions in the portrayal of Tulkinghorn are spread throughout the whole novel: the text calls him "dry," for instance, in the introduction to his love of port – a contradiction in terms. The wine reveals the lawyer's sensual nature: "he pours a radiant nectar, two score and ten years old, that blushes in the glass to find itself so famous, and fills the whole room with the fragrance of southern grapes" (*BH*, ch. 22, p. 264). 'Nectar' has a sexual connotation, at the very least with kissing;[133] the "blush" recalls the maiden, of course, and the "fragrance of southern grapes" evokes a stereotypical Mediterranean leisure that is in full contradiction with his dusty chambers. John O. Jordan captures the implication exactly:

> The language of the passage is extraordinarily sensuous, Keatsian even, and begs to be read aloud so that the reader can savor, vicariously with Tulkinghorn, the sweetness he imbibes. We do not usually think of Tulkinghorn as a sensualist, but here, observing him alone, the narrator captures something essential in his nature.[134]

There is no point to this passage, unless one would like to suggest that Mr Tulkinghorn has a sensual side after all and when it is not the wine that brings it

---

131 See Watt, *Equity Stirring*, 167.
132 Fradin, "Will and Society," 103.
133 Cp. Shakespeare's *Venus and Adonis*: "Such nectar from his lips she had not suck'd."
134 Jordan, *Supposing*, 59.

forth, it is the newly acquired knowledge of the sexual deviance of an important woman in his life.[135]

Once Tulkinghorn gets wind of Lady Dedlock's past, he is after her in a pursuit that differs very little from the enamoured chase Guppy performs to win the fallen woman's daughter. On the one hand, Guppy is just another one of those characters who seeks to sniff out a secret and in this he does not differ from Krook, Smallweed, Mrs Snagsby, Mr Bucket or Mr Tulkinghorn himself, as Robert Donovan has pointed out: "[A] great many characters are at work throughout the novel at unravelling some private and vexing problem of their own: Mr. Tulkinghorn, stalking Lady Dedlock's secret with fearful persistency, or Mr. Guppy approaching the same mystery from Esther's side . . ."[136] And yet, Guppy and Tulkinghorn have too much in common when one considers who they have literally set their eyes on. Both lawyers pursue 'criminal' women on different metaphorical levels, for both women have a mark on their reputation. The parallel between Lady Dedlock and Esther Summerson has often been remarked upon,[137] but the fact that both become the object of a lawyer's painful gaze has not drawn the same attention. Esther is placed under Guppy's surveillance, which is as penetrating as Tulkinghorn's of her mother and it is only the comedy of the destitute romantic lover that clouds the parallel. Nevertheless, Esther describes his unwanted and steadfast attention as torturing her too:

> I really cannot express how uneasy this made me. [. . .] to know that that absurd figure was always gazing at me, and always in that demonstrative state of despondency, put such a constraint upon me that I did not like to laugh at the play, or to cry at it, or to move or to speak. I seemed able to do nothing naturally. (*BH*, ch. 13, p. 148)

In her terror that is induced by Guppy's constant observation, Esther becomes the spitting image of her outwardly immoveable mother, who has learnt never to betray an emotion or even let on that she has any. Ironically, given her past sexual transgression, Lady Dedlock is a model of emotional self-control in the novel – admired especially by Tulkinghorn because of it – and Esther is forced by Guppy into the same rigidity that to her seems unnatural.

Guppy's sexual desire for the narrator haunts her as he leans in the shadows outside her window, the lawyer in black hiding in the dark. Dickens infuses Guppy's pursuit with a good amount of comic caricature, but considering that Esther also has a secret, it is easily imaginable that his observant pursuit of her

135 Joseph Fradin has put this more strongly in suggesting that the wine might serve as an actual surrogate for women in the material sense: "Will and Society," 104.

136 Donovan, "Structure and Idea," 190.

137 See above all Hilary Schor's chapter in *Dickens and the Daughter of the House*.

makes her uncomfortable beyond embarrassment. Mother and daughter are linked in their 'social illegitimacy,' adamant to hide their true identities from penetrating eyes. It should come as no surprise, therefore, that the subject of Tulkinghorn even comes up in the one moment in the novel mother and daughter share: "He is always vigilant, and always near me. I may keep him at a standstill, but I can never shake him off" (*BH*, ch. 36, p. 437). The statement is equally reflective of Guppy's behaviour towards Esther. Thus, beyond the taint of sexual deviance that lies on both mother and daughter, they share the fate of being pursued by a lawyer they cannot control. Through the parallel that is created by Guppy's presumably 'romantic' pursuit of Esther, the text therefore suggests that Tulkinghorn's interest in her mother is not of an asexual nature either. The fact that mother and daughter speak in the moment of their reunion about something as mundane as a lawyer might seem counterintuitive, but it is a technically necessary moment. On the one hand, it is the only account in direct speech of Lady Dedlock's fear of him, which is necessary for the reader to hear in order to suspect her, at least briefly, to be the murderess. On the other hand, Esther has to know about this figure in her mother's life in order to be able to express in her first-person narrative the relief she feels once he is dead. This relief is expressed by her not only as a substitute of her mother's feelings, inaudible in the heterodiegetic part of the narrative, but also as indicative of her own wish to be rid of all the lawyers. While Vholes and Guppy have a more direct bearing in her own life, the death of Tulkinghorn as one of a group of transgressive, invading, violent men, comes as a relief to Esther personally too. The brief interview with her mother has told her that she suffers from Tulkinghorn's aggression as much as Esther herself suffers from Vholes and Guppy, so she seems to conclude that only a dead lawyer is a good lawyer:

> This unforeseen and violent removal of one whom she had long watched and distrusted, and who had long watched and distrusted her; one for whom she could have had few intervals of kindness, always dreading in him a dangerous and secret enemy, appeared so awful, that my first thoughts were of her. How appalling to hear of such a death, and be able to feel no pity! How dreadful to remember, perhaps, that she had sometimes even wished the old man away, who was so swiftly hurried out of life! (*BH*, ch. 52, p. 595)

While Esther pretends to be shocked according to convention and female propriety, the suggestion that the lawyer's death is a relief not only temporarily frames her mother for the murder, but also expresses great relief that his pursuit of her is over.

Tulkinghorn's desire for Lady Dedlock expresses itself in animosity and aggression towards her, which he acts out instead in his encounters with her Double, Mademoiselle Hortense. Like Uriah Heep, Tulkinghorn is a master puppeteer and the text cannot conceal a certain admiration for his cool, calculated manner that allows him to unravel the mystery surrounding Lady Dedlock. He manages to obtain all the information he needs without even bringing this to the notice of those he uses. The fact that Jo never understands his function in Tulkinghorn's scheme is not surprising, given the text's presentation of the waif as an animal, yet Snagsby, Smallweed and even Trooper George experience their instrumentalisation at the hands of Tulkinghorn without a chance to understand what role they play in this particular game. Tulkinghorn acts superior and aloof, yet completely passionless towards the men. At times, he even disappears verbally from the dialogue, especially once he has implemented Bucket as his secondary. When Bucket interviews Snagsby on the whereabouts of Jo, Tulkinghorn withdraws from the surface of the text as if he were an actual puppeteer behind the curtain. He says nothing for a good portion of the interview, virtually disappearing from the reader's imagination. Such behaviour is supposed to be typical of the lawyer figure, the hollow shell that Dickens is supposed to have created. He instigates, coolly and passionlessly, so when Bucket and Snagsby move on as his puppets, they leave him "without a ruffle on the surface of his unfathomable depths" (*BH*, ch. 22, p. 267). This is the villain we are supposed to see, the villain who seems to have no motive but "irrational, violent danger."[138] This is the Tulkinghorn who is supposedly an empty shell, "an agent of an impersonal system."[139] However, this Tulkinghorn can only interact this coolly with men – women bring out quite a different character, for with women, Tulkinghorn is less of a lawyer and more of a man. His unperturbed looking at Lady Dedlock suggests his transgression from very early on in the novel; his aggression towards Mademoiselle Hortense anticipates his conduct at the climax of the conflict with the woman he desires.

It is of course indisputable that Hortense is a Double for Lady Dedlock, as many critics have pointed out. Virginia Blain has called the French maid Lady Dedlock's "surrogate."[140] Hortense, not Lady Dedlock, is the figure, who, "unleashing her innate violence,"[141] turns against Tulkinghorn in a justified reply to his covert aggression: "[S]he carries out what amounts to a political assassination against the most detested figure in the book, performing an act that both Lady Dedlock and Esther have imagined committing and thereby relieving them of the responsibility and the punishment."[142] Hortense serves as more than an execution of Lady Dedlock's anger against and fear of the lawyer, however. She also

---

138 Kucich, *Excess and Restraint*, 62.
139 Arnold Kettle, "Dickens and the Popular Tradition" in *Marxists on Literature. An Anthology*, ed. David Craig. London: Penguin, 1975: 214–244, 231.
140 Blain, "Double Vision," 79.
141 Blain, "Double Vision," 76.
142 Jordan, *Supposing*, 132.

exposes his behaviour towards women when it is not checked by his hierarchical subordination. While his unabashed observation of his social superior suggests his desire to violate her as a woman, it is only in verbal intercourse with her maid that one can glimpse his disdain of the female sex. Hortense is closely associated with Lady Dedlock's sexual deviance, a connection which is subconsciously made by Esther herself. When she witnesses the conflict between the two powerful women that leads to the splitting off of Hortense as an embodied Id, the maid is presented with two discursive markers of female sexuality:

> She remained perfectly still until the carriage had turned into the drive, and then, without the least discomposure of countenance, slipped off her shoes, left them on the ground, and walked deliberately in the same direction, through the wettest of the wet grass.
> 'Is that young woman mad?' said my guardian. (*BH*, ch. 18, p. 223)

Both her naked feet and the suggestion of mental disturbance are of course common nineteenth-century markers of female sexual deviance or transgression,[143] and not uncommon in Dickens. He has Alice Marwood return barefoot from transportation for prostitution several years earlier in *Dombey and Son*, an image that is mirrored in the same novel in little Florence who loses her shoes on the brink of the dangers of child prostitution.[144] In her obsession to appear virtuous to purge herself of her mother's taint, Esther embellishes the moment to create a greater distance between her and the dangerously sensual woman, but the moment also informs the reader of Hortense's propensity for violence. Her 'shocking' behaviour marks her as beyond the bounds of female propriety and in sexist ideology, her turning murderous is not far off. She is introduced not only as "[t]he embodiment of pure anger,"[145] but also as willing to dispense with the common rules for females: "her passion represents all that Lady Dedlock has suppressed."[146] The scene clearly prepares the reader to expect even more shocking behaviour from Hortense, but it also explains Tulkinghorn's subsequent conduct with her, which reveals more about him than her.

In their encounter, he faces the sexually illicit woman without the restraint the respect for his employer requires. While he has to hide his disrespect of Lady Dedlock when he suspects her past, he is free to express his contempt for

---

143 See Elaine Showalter, *The Female Malady. Women, Madness and English Culture, 1830–1980*. London: Virago Press, 1987.

144 See Dianne F. Sadoff, *Monsters of Affection. Dickens, Eliot & Brontë on Fatherhood*. Baltimore and London: The Johns Hopkins University Press, 1982: 63.

145 Jordan, *Supposing*, 132.

146 Robert Newsom, *Dickens on the Romantic Side of Familiar Things: Bleak House and the Novel Tradition*. New York: Columbia University Press, 1977: 89.

Hortense. His interaction therefore greatly contrasts with the image of the unmovable old lawyer. Instead of the unfathomable depths that he is supposed to display, he enacts more or less open aggression, calling her a "vixen" and a "wench," (*BH*, ch. 42, p. 500) which are of course both derogatory terms for females, but more importantly have strong sexual connotations. The difference in social station allows him to treat her condescendingly, but it is important to remember that this interaction with Hortense happens after he has had to control his behaviour in the open confrontation with Lady Dedlock in his chamber that will need in-depth discussion in the remainder of this chapter. After he has had to treat Lady Dedlock within the bounds of minimum propriety, it comes as no surprise that Tulkinghorn is as aggressive and offensive towards Hortense. He has to conceal both his contempt of and desire for the attractions of a deviant woman no longer and he threatens her quite openly with physical violence by means of his "key." The dialogue between the hostile woman and the restrained man is structured by the heterodiegetic narration's references to this key. Every pause in the quarrel is filled with his fumbling with the key: "tapping the key hastily upon the chimney-piece"; "rubbing his nose with the key"; "rubs his head with the key"; "examining the wards of the key"; "tapping his chin with the key" (*BH*, ch. 42, pp. 500/501). Considering the length of the dialogue, the number of times the narrative refers to the key seems excessive. On the surface, the key has symbolic meaning that Tulkinghorn himself means to emphasise:

> 'Look, mistress, this is the key of my wine-cellar. It is a large key, but the keys of prisons are larger. In this city, there are houses of correction (where the treadmills are for women) the gates of which are very strong and heavy, and no doubt the keys too. I am afraid a lady of your spirit and activity would find it an inconvenience to have one of those keys turned upon her for any length of time.' (*BH*, ch. 42, pp. 501/502)

Dickens means that Tulkinghorn deliberately draws attention to the key during their conversation as an implicit allusion to the open threat he concludes with. On the surface, the key means quite simply incarceration. Yet, it is impossible to overlook the phallic connotation, especially when he ends "to have one of those keys turned upon her . . ." He does not only threaten incarceration, he threatens rape, which springs from his sexual desire for the woman, who, in his eyes, is sexually depraved and therefore a 'legitimate' target: "[H]is male resentment of her insubordinate female energy is shown by his flourishing the phallic key."[147] Tulkinghorn suggests the use of his own 'key' as a means to shut her up. The key he openly uses is the key to his wine-cellar, in other words the key

147 Michael Steig and F. A. C. Wilson, "Hortense versus Bucket. The Ambiguity of Order in *Bleak House*," *Modern Language Quarterly* 33 (1972): 289–299, 291.

to his vault of sexual pleasure, and he imagines himself 'turning the key upon her' in order to possess and defeat this "most implacable and unmanageable of women." (*BH*, ch. 42, p. 502) He fantasises sexual violence against her as the woman he might possess in substitution for the woman he cannot possess. It is almost too obvious to note how much this picture of the lawyer differs from the image the text otherwise means to enforce. Tulkinghorn gets away from Dickens here, a vehicle of covert sexual aggression towards women, who, in the logic of the rapist, deserve no better since they are no longer seen as virtuous. When Hortense then shoots him *through the heart*, it must be felt as just retribution for the abuse Tulkinghorn has heaped on these women, who are quite unable to defend themselves, for they have to fear the condemnation of society that does not allow them to expose his harassment. They are confined to secrecy and it is this secrecy that Tulkinghorn uses as an excuse to violate them metaphorically.

The reason why Tulkinghorn is already aroused and thus has his key readily to hand, is that he has built up such desire in the open confrontation with Lady Dedlock. Critics who have attempted to psychologise Tulkinghorn have inevitably drawn on his more or less open misogyny, "the motive that Dickens openly supplies him with – his irrational hatred of the female sex . . ."[148] The text alludes to this quite openly:

> There are women enough in the world, Mr Tulkinghorn thinks – too many; they are at the bottom of all that goes wrong in it, though, for the matter of that, they create business for lawyers. What would it be to see a woman going by, even though she were going secretly? They are all secret. Mr Tulkinghorn knows that, very well. (*BH*, ch. 16, p. 193)

Tulkinghorn is "the enemy of womankind," as Alexander Welsh has it.[149] The fact that he believes them all to be "secret," of course, implies that he believes them all to be sexually corrupt, which serves as a rationale for his principal hatred. This hatred he shares with the devil, as Marylin Georgas has pointed out: "Hatred and suspicion of women in general is a trait universally attributed to the devil, [. . .] and is one of the most overtly-drawn traits of Tulkinghorn."[150] Tulkinghorn's misogyny is no secret, therefore, and it seems an explanation obvious enough for his treatment of Lady Dedlock. At the very least, the fact that he is said to believe that women are at the bottom of everything that goes wrong with this world would suggest that by unravelling her secret and then torturing her with it he means to put her in her place: "[H]is real purpose is [. . .] to humiliate Lady Dedlock by excluding her from a world of male, aristocratic privilege

148 Blain, "Double Vision," 76.
149 Welsh, *Dickens Redressed*, 62.
150 Georgas, "Devil and the Dedlocks," 27.

which he sees as his duty to protect . . ."[151] However, I would argue that Tulkinghorn is not *only* motivated by class resentment, he is not impersonally trying to bring her down from her high horse; in fact, he really seems to enjoy taking possession of her figuratively: "The special relish he takes in humbling Lady Dedlock is clear. Her pride and indifference – but also her beauty – enrage and stimulate him."[152] There is a reason why everything that is described as being said or done between the woman and the lawyer leads up to a climax, one of the most outstanding moments in the novel in its creation of suspense, but also in its creation of overt sexual tension. Tulkinghorn's aggression finally leads to his desired confrontation: the lady visits him at night in his room.

The lawyer's covert harassment of her coerces her to seek his presence. There can be no doubt that their final encounter has all the atmosphere of her offering herself to him in order to save her position and reputation. Their climactic private encounter is the inevitable conclusion of the almost public humiliation she has suffered from his telling a variant of her story in her own drawing-room, to her own extended family. He has threatened to expose her to the rest of society, for despite his lower social station, he has control over the peerage's perception of her – after all, he would expose a 'criminal' in society's eyes and he has made it abundantly clear to the 'fallen woman' on whose side society will stand – as if she did not know that already. Positioning himself in his employer's drawing-room as the embodiment of the condemnation society has for sexually deviant women, he hammers home what will happen to her, if she refuses to be controlled by him. His rendition of the story is the last straw – the ghost is a ghost no longer, he has come to claim her within her own home, surrounded by her own people, presumably protected by social superiority and yet, as a woman, completely helpless against his transgression:

> A story! O he is going to tell something at last! A ghost in it, Volumnia hopes!
>
> 'No. Real flesh and blood.' Mr Tulkinghorn stops for an instant, and repeats, with some little emphasis grafted upon his usual monotony, 'Real flesh and blood . . .'
>
> (*BH*, ch. 40, p. 488)

The ghost has finally materialised, Tulkinghorn poses a threat in the flesh to Lady Dedlock. His emphasis on flesh and blood is to be taken literally, of course, as he plans to allude to the sexual act between a man and a virginal woman. But the emphasis also changes his character, suggests his own blood pulsing through his veins in arousal as he can finally take possession of the woman. Tulkinghorn

---

151 Phoebe Poon, "Trust and Conscience in *Bleak House* and *Our Mutual Friend*," *Dickens Quarterly* 28.1 (2011): 3–21, 12.
152 Fradin, "Will and Society," 103.

becomes a human being, becomes real flesh and blood in his desire to act as a man with the woman he holds in his power. He knows he is about to inflict pain, "I hope Lady Dedlock will excuse its painful nature," (489) and he can only barely conceal his pleasure at doing so. What is painful about this moment for the reader is that the lawyer can openly abuse her in an environment that should technically protect her. After all, Chesney Wold is the home the man has given her who has unwittingly purged her shame through marriage. And yet, Tulkinghorn manages to sadistically enjoy his hold over her in plain sight, simply because the stain on her womanhood trumps all other considerations. The lawyer may be inferior in social station, but as a man, he can transcend class boundaries at least in secret in order to threaten, humiliate and essentially violate her: "Outwardly a misogynist who shuns and distrusts women, inhabiting a world only of men, Tulkinghorn is also a sadist who takes erotic pleasure in punishing women and keeping them under his control."[153]

Since Lady Dedlock understands that she is powerless against Tulkinghorn's hold on her, as he has all of society on his side, her visit in his room is an implicit offering, an attempt to buy his silence. I have already argued that a logical reading of the conflict does not allow the prolonged objectification of her that he seeks. He simply tries to possess her by the only means at his disposal, since the sexual act he desires is out of the question. The text betrays itself in Mr Tulkinghorn's room. There is no 'rusty' lawyer, no unfathomable depth, no passionless claim of the law. In his room, Mr Tulkinghorn is a man, aroused by the fact that he has a beautiful woman in his power: "Tulkinghorn's zest for dominance over Lady Dedlock is here obviously increased by the excitement of her beauty."[154] On the surface, the narrator tries to suppress the sadistic pleasure the lawyer finds in his pursuit: "To say of a man so severely and strictly self-repressed that he is triumphant, would be to do him as great an injustice as to suppose him troubled with love or sentiment, or any romantic weakness" (*BH*, ch. 41, p. 490). This introduction to the passionate climax between man and woman is both true and misleading. It is not love or romance that drives Tulkinghorn and the insinuation that he is triumphant despite his repressed character is of course accurate. Yet, this introduction tries to steer safely away from the sexual excitement he feels. As in all of his encounters with women, he is not at all as cold as the construction of the character otherwise requires:

> He stands before her, with one hand on a chair-back and the other in his old-fashioned waistcoat and shirt-frill, exactly as he stood before her at any time since her marriage.

---

153 Jordan, *Supposing*, 59.
154 Quirk, "Tulkinghorn's Buried Life," 533.

> The same formal politeness, the same composed deference that might as well be defiance; the whole man the same dark, cold object, at the same distance, which nothing has ever diminished. (*BH*, ch. 41, p. 491)

He is not the object, however; she is and he treats her as such. His previous, almost exclusively non-verbal and surveillant conduct has finally brought out the passion he has wanted to see. When she lets out all her anxiety, Tulkinghorn's satisfaction is audible: "So! Anger, and fear, and shame. All three contending" (*BH*, ch. 41, p. 491). He prides himself on having raised all of these feelings in an otherwise seemingly immoveable woman and his self-satisfaction is only superseded by the fact that he has before him the living proof of what he can do to a woman: "What power this woman has to keep these raging passions down!" (491) He admires her power mostly because it sweetens his victory. The more powerful she is in controlling her emotions while offering herself to him, the more powerful he is in having gained his hold over her, which she affirms. Her language of submission is unmissable. She refers to herself as "under his foot," freely offers him, "[i]s there anything that you require of me?" (492) and succumbs to his oppression: "Do what remains, now" (492). In her own home, at night in his room, all formal bounds of propriety dispensed with already, she gives in to his coercion – but of course he cannot seize what he wants her to offer. Dickens cannot tell the story that the subtext tells us. He can infuse the narrative with "the struggle in her breast" (491), "her lips"; the lawyer's obvious arousal at the despair of the woman in his power: "'I am ready to do it.' And she would do it! thinks the lawyer, watchful of the firm hand with which she takes the pen!" (*BH*, ch. 41, p. 492) These are the words that Dickens can use to tell us that at this moment, Tulkinghorn is closer to finally obtaining Lady Dedlock than ever before, that he has ground her into defeat, that he has taken at least metaphorical possession of her: "He has conquered her" (493).

Lady Dedlock's social superiority is now immaterial for Tulkinghorn. He thinks of her as a woman and for once, it seems, he thinks of himself as a man:

> 'I declare to you, Lady Dedlock, that with anything short of this case that I have, I would as soon have hoped to root up, by means of my own strength and my own hands, the oldest tree on this estate, as to shake your hold upon Sir Leicester, and Sir Leicester's trust and confidence in you.' (*BH*, ch. 41, p. 494)

This is not a professional statement. Why would an old, unpassionate lawyer not only express his wish to break up the marriage, but also refer to his own manly strength as a means to do so? The imagery, the reference to his own body, the emphasis on nature and most of all the fact that he has just admitted that he is jealous all fill this supposedly empty type with the complexity of a character; a character who feels passionate desire. He is not even concerned with her social station anymore, for her sexual deviance has put her in his reach. Significantly, the focalised narration does not refer to her as 'my lady' anymore, for Tulkinghorn thinks of her as a mere woman now:

> But, as he reflects when he is left alone, the woman has been putting no common constraint upon herself.
>
> He would know it all the better, if he saw the woman pacing her own rooms with her hair wildly thrown from her flung-back face, her hands clasped behind her head, her figure twisted as if by pain. He would think so all the more, if he saw the woman thus hurrying up and down for hours, without fatigue, without intermission, followed by the faithful step upon the Ghost's Walk. (*BH*, ch. 41, p. 496)

It is difficult to imagine that this passage is supposed to evoke the reader's sympathy. There is much too much pleasure in it to do so. The heterodiegetic narrative expresses exactly what Tulkinghorn wishes to see: the woman in pain. On the one hand, the narrative gives us the voyeuristic insight he would enjoy. Having observed her so closely with such sadistic pleasure, her private despair in her room with all the endowments of sexual license such as the loss of control over her hair, body and mind as if in the sexual act itself, is clearly what he would enjoy most. On the other hand, the narrative provides the other thing Tulkinghorn would like to see, which is the pain itself. After all, this is the only means he has left: if he cannot possess her, if he cannot truly conquer her physically, he can only do so mentally by inflicting pain. This is why he holds her in suspense, this is why he neither reveals her secret nor promises to keep it, this is why he enjoys her 'under his foot.' Causing her pain is the only means of penetrating her and it *cannot* be a coincidence that Dickens does not forget to tell us that Tulkinghorn falls asleep immediately afterwards.

It is a part of Tulkinghorn's sadistic pleasure at his moment of triumph that he has the power to be almost mute about what he wants their 'relationship' to be – he leaves the painful truth to be spoken out loud by Lady Dedlock herself. As John Kucich has pointed out, "[w]hat is most repellent about Tulkinghorn, in fact, is the unstated lubricity in his violation of Lady Dedlock, not just the recognition he tries to take away from her. Lady Dedlock herself supplies the sexual terms that Tulkinghorn never articulates."[155] His victory is complete when she has to paint the picture he so delights in:

> 'I am to drag my present life on, holding its pains at your pleasure, day by day?' she asks, still looking at the distant sky.
>
> 'Yes, I am afraid so, Lady Dedlock.'

155 Kucich, *Excess and Restraint*, 98.

> 'It is necessary, you think, that I should be so tied to the stake?'
>
> 'I am sure that what I recommend is necessary.' (*BH*, ch. 41, p. 495)

From hereon, she actually is in his captivity: "Always at hand. Haunting every place. No relief or security from him for a moment" (*BH*, ch. 48, p. 545). Lady Dedlock has to endure what John Kucich calls "psychological rape."[156] Once he has her fully in his control, Tulkinghorn is less careful to act a part, which reveals the depths of his character. After Lady Dedlock has let herself be overcome by him in his room, the text fully admits that his unfathomable depths are merely a role he plays: ". . . he can act a part too" (*BH*, ch. 48, p. 559). From now on, he is less eager to play this part with his victim, however, and takes liberties with her formerly unthinkable. He is confident, he has his object firmly in his grasp: "Imperturbable and unchangeable as he is, there is still an indefinable freedom in his manner, which is new, and which does not escape this woman's observation" (*BH*, ch. 48, p. 559). Lady Dedlock herself can only act against Tulkinghorn within very limited means: dismissing Rosa and fleeing from her own home and marriage. Therefore, Hortense has to come forth and act out the aggression shared by the crucial women of the principal plot. Esther and Lady Dedlock both wish the lawyer dead and so their female avenger fulfils the promise of deviance her naked feet have suggested.

Jan-Melissa Schramm has argued that the fact that Dickens "chooses Tulkinghorn to bear the burden of narrative guilt [. . .] confirms the discomfort the author of fiction feels at the industry of the legal profession."[157] It is not simply the case, however, that the representatives of the legal profession in Dickens are despicable, *because* they are in the profession. They find themselves in the law, because they have despicable personalities. The lawyers in *Bleak House*, be they Guppy, Vholes or Tulkinghorn, are far more than representatives of an evil system. They are sadists who enjoy the suffering of women in particular. Guppy is certainly the most harmless of the three, but the parody of the forlorn lover, so prominent in Dickens, possibly for personal reasons as Rosemarie Bodenheimer has argued,[158] can hardly conceal the pain the object of his 'affection' has to suffer. From his unwanted advances, an asset he shares with both of the other lawyers, to his awkward rejection of the blemished convalescent, he is a source of suffering for the first-person narrator and thus falls fully into the category of people who subject the women of the novel. Naturally, there is a metonymical dimension

156 Kucich, *Excess and Restraint*, 98.
157 Schramm, "Dickens and the Law," 290.
158 See Rosemarie Bodenheimer, *Knowing Dickens*. Ithaca, N.Y.: Cornell University Press, 2007: 25.

as these women are not only oppressed by the personified lawyers, but also by the law itself. Marked as illegitimate, the law denies them an identity. As Hilary Schor has shown, the seemingly separate spheres of the novel that are formally split through the narration, namely the 'public' plot that revolves around the law and the 'private' plot that revolves around domestic happiness, are not separate from each other at all: "Both parts of the narration, however circuitously, are 'In Chancery,' and it is female curiosity about property that brings the connection to light."[159]

Alongside this insight into the novel, one can see that the law invades the domestic plot at all levels to the women's considerable unease. In fact, they become victims in the one sphere that their contemporary ideology would grant them, so that they are bereft of all possible spaces. The lawyers transgress not only into their homes, but into their psyches, leaving them helplessly exposed to metaphorical penetration. They appear in the dark or twilight, they hover silently and observantly, and they wander in and out of all the houses women seek refuge in. More than once, the text emphasises that Tulkinghorn walks in and out of Chesney Wold as well as the house in town, as if he owned them, thereby constituting a general menace for Lady Dedlock everywhere. Vholes always appears unexpectedly at Bleak House and holds Richard and Ada so firmly in his grasp that they end up living in his space as if he had literally imprisoned them. Guppy's persistence in seeing Chesney Wold leads to his investigation into Esther's origins, which grants him the unlimited access to Lady Dedlock that supports Tulkinghorn's suspicion. Although apart from a brief encounter between Guppy and Tulkinghorn, none of these lawyers meet in either hetero- or homodiegetic narration, yet it seems that they all work together in mutual agreement to bring these women down. They are sources of misogynistic aggression with a propensity for sadism and psychological violence, that makes them the true heirs of Uriah Heep. It can never be said that they do not honour his legacy and they all have something in common: whatever they are, they are certainly no gentlemen.

159 Schor, *Daughter of the House*, 103.

4 The Bully

Mr Jaggers is no gentleman either – in fact, his moral duplicity is one of the central points in a duplicitous novel. Pip's relationship with Jaggers is overshadowed by his position between the horns of a dilemma: as the plot of the novel requires him to turn away both literally and metaphorically from Joe and the forge to Miss Havisham and London, the complicated relationship with Jaggers is sometimes pushed to the margin of the narrative, but the constellation of Pip and Jaggers echoes very closely David's relationship with Uriah. It is no secret that *Great Expectations* is a mature version of *David Copperfield*, so the rebirth of Uriah Heep is not surprising. It is, however, very telling how the late Dickens constructs the lawyer figure. Jaggers is even more ambiguous than Tulkinghorn, for he is not at all an object of the narrator's scorn or derision. In fact, the text expresses even more admiration and attraction towards the lawyer than the previous novels have. He is an extremely powerful figure, representing a measure of control over his environment that the narrator desperately seeks and he is a key figure in both Pip's idea of the gentleman and his relationship with women. Mr Jaggers is quite literally the key to Pip's fortune and he is a master puppeteer, who never shows his hand. He has mastered money and women, which are both central goals of Pip's. He is a father figure, an alter ego and one of the most crucial minor characters in all of Dickens. He is the most elaborately drawn of all of Dickens's lawyers: he combines the stereotypical assets of the despicable lawyer and yet frequently appears in the text as an object of admiration. Dickens's conflicted view of the law and its representatives has never been more intricate, duplicitous, or enlightened than in his construction of the Jaggers character.

Pip's first encounter with Jaggers at Satis House makes him one of the ghosts that haunt the narrator's childhood. He is a demonic figure that is mixed in with the likes of Miss Havisham and Magwitch, the Young Man and Mrs Joe, another threat for a child that lives in a state of constant terror. Deviating from Dickens's representations of Vholes or Tulkinghorn, Jaggers is a more overtly powerful figure, who is perceived as anything but dry, or rusty, or death-like. In fact, he brims with aggression that is mistaken for vitality; yet his eyes are as dangerous as Uriah's or Tulkinghorn's:

> He was a burly man of an exceedingly dark complexion, with an exceedingly large head and a correspondingly large hand. He took my chin in his large hand and turned up my face to have a look at me by the light of the candle. He was prematurely bald on the top of

https://doi.org/10.1515/9783110754506-004

> his head, and had bushy black eyebrows that wouldn't lie down but stood up bristling. His eyes were set very deep in his head, and were disagreeably sharp and suspicious.[160]
> (*GE*, ch. 11, p. 68)

In short, Jaggers looks like a dog about to attack, hairs standing on end as a sign of aggression and his first motion towards Pip is one of transgression for he freely handles the child's head and face: "The gesture here is but a premonitory instance of the [. . .] impulse to enslave others . . ."[161] Jaggers is physically intrusive where his predecessors are spatially intrusive, but he shares their most unsettling gift of omnipotent surveillance. It is remarkable that Dickens never spends time on Jaggers's outward appearance in terms of dress. The black colour that features in the clothes of lawyers in earlier works is completely transformed to Jaggers's face: his psychological interior is not mirrored in his apparel, but in his physiognomy. He is a more advanced villain, as it were, for Dickens delves deeper into his moral character. It is less easy to see in Jaggers a representative of an evil system, therefore, especially in view of the fact that Dickens seems to dispense more or less entirely with his systematic concerns so prominent in the earlier novels. Jaggers is introduced from the first as a man very much in his own right and not a signpost for more important matters on a grander scale. He has a physical power that the novel almost overemphasises by the repeated insistence on the largeness of his limbs, most importantly his hands; and he has intellectual power reflected in his "disagreeably sharp and suspicious eyes."

Consequently, Jaggers's intrusion into Pip's and others' lives is often of a physical nature, reflected in a propensity to touch inappropriately, and his often-mentioned large hands. In terms of proportion, Jaggers differs from Dickens's earlier lawyers, for his largeness gives him a physical prominence that does not let him blend in with the shadows. His mental power over others is reflected in his physical dominance, which means that he poses a threat for Pip in both respects. The narrator relates a "repeated anxiety about size in general,"[162] as Hilary Schor has observed, thereby enforcing the image of the little boy who is easily physically assaulted by others, which happens uncommonly often in the novel. From Magwitch's turning the child literally upside down, to the masochistic mention of

---

160 All references to *Great Expectations* are to the following edition and will be given parenthetically: Charles Dickens, *Great Expectations*, ed. Edgar Rosenberg. Norton Critical Editions. New York and London: W. W. Norton & Company, 1999.

161 Charles R. Forker, "The Language of Hands in *Great Expectations*," *Texas Studies in Literature and Language* 3.2 (1961): 280–293, 286.

162 Schor, *Daughter of the House*, 156.

Tickler to his final confrontation with Orlick, Pip finds himself more than even Nicholas Nickleby in physical confrontation with others. The text is replete with references to physical violence and Jaggers's bullying power poses a threat much less subtle than Uriah's or Tulkinghorn's schemes. This lawyer has both the intellectual and physical strength that make him the most powerful figure in the whole novel. The text's heavy emphasis on the physical is, of course, highly significant in view of the fact that Pip's one desire in life is to leave the physical nature of his life at the forge behind him. The life of a gentleman is supposed to be a life of the mind and his association with the working class haunts him in the shape of hands that are used for force of a different nature.

Jaggers's strong physical presence represents everything Pip tries to get away from, yet, ironically, it is Jaggers, who provides the means to do so, for he keeps the money. Making Jaggers not a shadowy, half-invisible, sneaky creature therefore creates a contrast within the plot that is otherwise more ghostly than even *Bleak House*. As John O. Jordan has shown, *Great Expectations* is full of "phantom figures that emerge out of darkness into ambiguous half-light"[163] and Mr Jaggers proves a notable exception, which is clear from his first appearance: unlike a ghost, he makes immediate physical contact by seizing Pip's face in order to make his power felt. In his representation of this lawyer, then, Dickens turns the tables: he still makes him stand out drastically from the social community of the novel, however dysfunctional this community may be, by making him the opposite of the novel's hegemony. While Uriah, Vholes and Tulkinghorn are notable as Other through their secretive, misleadingly passive and shadowy appearance in novels that insist on the wholesome nature of the group, Jaggers stands out as a single man of physical and intellectual strength in a novel full of physically and mentally weak characters – to put the matter cruelly. He typically observes those from the side-line, but unlike the earlier lawyers who tend to vanish, he occasionally takes centre-stage.

His first appearance, a mock trial of Wopsle, reveals in one fell swoop his intellectual and logical superiority, his capability to argue in a court of law and his uncanny ability to influence, even shift, public opinion. During the cruel trial that fully reveals Jaggers as a bully, Pip also presents him as something else: three times, he inserts into his narrative how Jaggers manages to manipulate the crowd: "Mr Wopsle hesitated, and we all began to conceive rather a poor opinion of him"; "We all began to suspect that Mr Wopsle was not the man we had thought him, and that he was beginning to be found out"; "We were all

163 John O. Jordan, "The Medium of *Great Expectations*," *Dickens Studies Annual* 11 (1983): 73–88, 76.

deeply persuaded that the unfortunate Wopsle had gone too far, and had better stop in his reckless career while there was yet time" (*GE*, ch. 18, p. 106/107). Clearly, the devil is at work again.[164] Pip's commentary is naturally funny in his satire of the gullibility of the public, but Jaggers's appearance out of nowhere, his merciless cross-examination of Wopsle and Pip's spellbound reiteration all demonstrate the devilish nature of the lawyer.

In addition, this second encounter between Jaggers and Pip also echoes David's first encounter with Uriah. Jaggers oozes omniscience in its worst form, "with a manner expressive of knowing something secret about every one of us that would effectually do for each individual if he chose to disclose it . . ." (*GE*, ch. 18, p. 107) The difference is that while Uriah pretends to conceal what he believes to be his intellectual superiority and Tulkinghorn 'respectfully' supresses it, Jaggers unashamedly condescends to the country community with "an expression of contempt on his face" (*GE*, ch. 18, p. 106). Despite the personality that comes forth much more frequently within this narrative than in the lawyer figure previously, Jaggers shares with his predecessors, especially Tulkinghorn, the alibi of acting for merely professional reasons. He professes to have no opinion and no judgement: "Understand that I express no opinion, one way or other, on the trust I undertake. I am paid for undertaking it, and I do so. Now, understand that, finally. Understand that!" (*GE*, ch. 18, p. 112) The fact of the matter is, of course, that Jaggers, like Tulkinghorn, is full of opinions and he does not even conceal them very well. His first appearance in the novel is overshadowed by mistrust, because of the lawyer's ability to manipulate people without their notice. When David finally strikes Uriah, he argues that it is the latter's responsibility and when Pip is drawn into Jaggers's circle, he feels the same effect on himself:

> Dinner went off gaily, and, although my guardian seemed to follow rather than originate subjects, I knew that he had wrenched the weakest part of our dispositions out of us. For myself, I found that I was expressing my tendency to lavish expenditure, and to patronise Herbert, and to boast of my great prospects, before I quite knew that I had opened my lips. (*GE*, ch. 26, p. 165)

Like Uriah, Jaggers lies in wait for people to embarrass themselves and unwittingly give out information that might be useful for him. His power is such that while Pip is aware of being this shrewdly observed, he is incapable of not being manipulated into the desired misconduct. Like all the lawyers, Jaggers is a puppet master, who turns the human beings around him into objects that serve his

164 See also Jack Rawlins, "Great Expiations: Dickens and the Betrayal of the Child" in *Great Expectations. Contemporary Critical Essays*, ed. Roger D. Sell. Basingstoke: Macmillan, 1994: 79–97, 85.

purposes. Pip's diagnosis fits all: he calls Jaggers's strategy "invisible agency" – the lawyer has inherited this from Uriah Heep and it is brought down to him through Vholes and Tulkinghorn. They all share the ability to completely fade into the background and hover over their victims like vultures until they crack. Although Jaggers differs in his physical presence and unabashed pride in his power, his methods are the same.

Dickens returns to the lawyer character in *Great Expectations* in its most fully developed form, giving him a position in the plot that quite mirrors his power over others. After all, he is the ombudsman for Pip in all his concerns, but particularly in his wish to become a gentleman. The narrator calls him "my guardian," in a twisted echo of Esther Summerson's relationship with John Jarndyce, which is indicative of the moral position Pip grants the lawyer. Hence, it is only with great difficulty that one can make out what Pip's, and hence the reader's, moral evaluation of Jaggers is supposed to be. His status is completely ambiguous and despite his manipulation of others, Pip never paints the picture of a villain. In fact, Jaggers is drawn as quite different from the real villains such as Orlick and Compeyson, as Peter Scheckner attests: "The remainder of the men, while not nice people, notably Uncle Pumblechook, Jaggers, and Abel Magwitch, are nonetheless more humane; certainly they are not in the same league with Orlick and company."[165] Yet, the fact that Pip calls him guardian is also deeply ironic, for Jaggers explicitly refuses to be a moral guide – in fact, he uses his professionalism, the professionalism that makes Wemmick separate his private and his professional life with almost neurotic vigour, in order to be exempt from moral evaluation. Obviously, Jaggers's position towards his own profession is telling, for he is heard expressing notions that only Uriah has openly announced; both Tulkinghorn and Vholes try to keep their cards more closely to their chest. In fact, Jaggers is a liar and a fabricator, which accounts for the narrative's unwitting profession of admiration for him. The narrator himself is deeply conflicted about this guardian, who seems an intellectual role-model, yet wears so many different faces that there is no 'person' for Pip to pin down: "It is typical of Pip's life, as a child and as an adult, that things are rarely what they seem, or that their aspect is always on the verge of changing from benign to menacing."[166] This is true for Jaggers also: he is a mentor and a devil, a role-model and a liar. Pip cannot make up his mind about how to present him, for the lawyer's fabrication of himself is too slippery for him to grasp. Jaggers is a

---

165 Peter Scheckner, "Gender and Class in Dickens: Making Connections," *Midwest Quarterly* 41.3 (2000): 236–250, 237.

166 Stoehr, *Dreamer's Stance*, 105.

father figure and complex character, but also an embodiment of the worst kind of legal practice and a vehicle for the novel's expression of contemporary prejudice.

Jaggers is a solicitor like all the other major lawyers in Dickens, but he notably transcends the position in the background that becomes the legal adviser. In fact, Jaggers is the only one out of all of Dickens's lawyers who is seen dealing with criminals and prospective defendants, forging alibis and witnesses' statements. Pip witnesses first-hand, how Jaggers prepares a case by examining a potential 'witness,' who is brought forth to fabricate a story: "What is he prepared to swear?" (*GE*, ch. 20, p. 133), he asks, and dismisses both the client and the proposed witness, as if they had insulted him: "'Tell him to take his witness away directly,' said my guardian to the clerk, in extreme disgust, 'and ask him what he means by bringing such a fellow as that'" (*GE*, ch. 20, p. 134). Jaggers's professional conduct thereby reveals how he forms the ethics of lawyering with his own hands. He is susceptible to bribery, he produces fake witnesses and he bullies his opponents with outright aggression that wins him his cases:

> [M]y guardian had a woman under examination or cross-examination [. . .] and was striking her, and the bench, and everybody present, with awe. [. . .] The magistrates shivered under a single bite of his fingers. Thieves and thief-takers hung in dread raptures on his words, and shrank when a hair of his eyebrows turned in their direction. *Which side he was one, I couldn't make out . . .* (*GE*, ch. 24, p. 158 [my emphasis])

Jaggers is a moral chameleon that represents more clearly than any of his peers in Dickens the moral duplicity of the law – the law is simply a matter of interpretation and Jaggers uses it to his best advantage. He is the typical stereotype of the mid-century lawyer, who achieves success through trickery, rather than truth.[167] Pip never pretends that Jaggers is not corrupt. In fact, he quite clearly taps into contemporary discourses on the corrupt lawyer, leaving no doubt that Jaggers is just such a one. The scene that he implicitly entitles as Jaggers "at it" resembles contemporary parodies of the barrister in *Punch* or *The Times*[168] and corresponds with the common prejudice against the Bar that had become prominent some twenty years earlier:

> Allegations against the Bar in the periodical presses and daily papers were to reach their peak in the 1840s, with fictional representation of the rhetorical excesses of the Bar continuing for a further twenty years as authors responded to, and experimented with, the example set by their storytelling counterparts in courts of law.[169]

---

167 See Birks, *Gentlemen of the Law*, 145ff.

168 See Cocks, *Foundations*, 90ff.

169 Jan-Melissa Schramm, "Is Literature More Ethical Than Law? Fitzjames Stephen and Literary Responses to the Advent of Full Legal Representation for Felons" in *Law and Literature.*

Pip's observation of Jaggers in court is more than satirical commentary, however, since it equally expresses Pip's admiration for the bully, liar and fabricator. After all, Pip is a fabricator himself, concerned with presenting his guilty self as morally upright. Hilary Schor has called him "one of Dickens's greatest fabulists"[170] and in the story he fabricates, Jaggers's moral duplicity serves an important function for Pip, since he needs to prepare the reader for his own re-evaluation of good and bad in the figure of Magwitch.

Therefore, Jaggers is also a different version of Magwitch and Magwitch is a different version of Pip in a novel in which almost all the male characters stand in relations of identity towards one another. Jaggers's simultaneous position within and outside of the law and his ability to adapt the moral or immoral stance most fruitful for the occasion and intended purpose, serve as an important excuse for Pip in his moral and immoral conduct towards others. Jaggers is presented as a storyteller, imaginatively constructing stories for his clients that best serve his own purposes and as a storyteller himself, Pip does exactly the same. In this sense, Jaggers is simply a part of Pip, a figure in his story that allows him to justify himself for the fabrication of events as best suits his purposes. Taylor Stoehr has pointed out that on an overall level, the novel is of course concerned with the major themes of "law, order, legitimacy versus crime, disorder, and illegitimacy,"[171] and Pip uses the figure of Jaggers to allow himself to switch just as easily from one category to another; suggesting that this is not corrupt or morally duplicitous, but rather the necessary skill of a good storyteller.

From his first appearance in the novel, Jaggers introduces himself as "the agent of another" (*GE*, ch. 18, p. 108) in order to absolve himself from the responsibility for his actions as much as Vholes insists that he has no personal motive, but only acts as a servant. Jagger's role as this 'agent' allows him to act more or less freely in the interest of his client without feeling personally responsible, which seems to constitute a moral vacuum Pip desires for himself. The narrator therefore sets Jaggers up in parallel to himself, but tries to direct the reader's attention away from their similarities. He emphasises the lawyer's intellectual and strategic superiority over his own naivety, the impressive physiognomy over his own self-proclaimed weakness and the violent nature as a complete opposite to his own allegedly gentle adoration of Estella. In actual fact, however, they have much more in common than the narrator lets on, for Pip is a bully too. His abuse of both Joe and Magwitch, his father figures, is obvious

Current Legal Issues 1999, Vol. 2, eds. Michael Freeman and Andrew D. E. Lewis. Oxford: OUP, 1999: 417–435, 418.

170 Schor, *Daughter of the House*, 154.

171 Stoehr, *Dreamer's Stance*, 109.

enough, but he also acts with condescension towards both Biddy and Herbert, unequivocally good characters by his own account. He treats them as accessories to his own story like Jaggers treats his clients. The two storytellers use others unscrupulously for their own purposes, which is why Pip insists on Jaggers's overwhelming presence in his own story in order to divert the attention away from his own conduct. Therefore, they stand in almost exactly the same relation towards one another as David and his lawyer. Both narrators comfortably displace the questionable aspects in their own natures onto the figure their audience is accustomed to see as morally ambiguous. They use the common prejudices about lawyers as a cover for their own sins, hiding behind those their society is used to condemning. Pip's desire to fabricate the idea that he is the complete opposite of Jaggers is most apparent in the one encounter between his proclaimed object of affection and his guardian. He presents the lawyer as soiling an innocent romance, as intruding into a sacred space. He is anxious to preserve the self-proclaimed purity of his feelings for Estella in view of the lawyer's contagious corruption:

> What I suffered from, was the incompatibility between his cold presence and my feelings towards Estella. It was not that I knew I could never bear to speak to him about her, that I knew I could never bear to hear him creak his boots at her, that I knew I could never bear to see him wash his hands of her; it was, that my admiration should be within a foot or two of him – it was, that my feelings should be in the same place with him – *that*, was the agonising circumstance. (*GE*, ch. 29, p. 187)

In order for Pip to keep up the myth of his untainted love for Estella, he sets up Jaggers as the symbol of corruption, as his moral opposite.

Jaggers does not belong in the sphere of domesticity Pip imagines for himself and Estella, he is an intruder in the love story, which is, after all, Pip's "favorite story."[172] Pip relates the discomfort caused by Jaggers's presence as evidence for the integrity of his own feelings, pretending to want to protect Estella and her environment from the corrupt forces embodied by the lawyer. This is why it is so manifestly difficult to determine the judgement the figure of Jaggers is accompanied with throughout the story, because Pip arbitrarily uses him for his own purposes. In the simplest terms, Jaggers is a vehicle of bad feelings for Pip, feelings he wishes to keep out of his own narrative, such as the question of his own guilt. The desire to place the responsibility for such feelings entirely with Jaggers is so strong in Pip that he even displaces it onto Herbert: "Jaggers made not me alone intensely melancholy, because, after he was gone, Herbert said of himself, with

172 Schor, *Daughter of the House*, 154.

his eyes fixed on the fire, that he thought he must have committed a felony and forgotten the details of it, he felt so dejected and guilty" (*GE*, ch. 36, p. 222).

It cannot be a coincidence that Jaggers has what all the other lawyers in Dickens desire: a woman in his literal possession. In her wonderful analysis of the novel, Lucy Frost attested long ago that "[o]ne need not be a student of psychoanalysis to perceive within *Great Expectations* a deep-seated fear of women."[173] It is Mr Jaggers, of all characters, who has not only conquered the fear, but has also conquered one of the many dangerous women in the novel. Jaggers confuses the boundaries between criminal and innocent behaviour, not only because he acts himself both within and beyond the bounds of the law, but also because he 'adjusts' people and their stories to press them into the norm of the law. His fabricated alibis and testimonies turn his clients into symbolic puppets, which is emphasised by the fact that they all willingly submit themselves to his hands to be given a shape that saves them. Due to the fact that Pip perceives his position in life to be solely based on the mercy of others – his sister, the convict, Estella, Miss Havisham and finally Joe – he clearly admires Jaggers's merciless ability to make others what he needs them to be. Jaggers does not depend on anyone's good will, he makes his world exactly what he wants it to be, which is an art Pip envies the most – after all, even his own narrative gets away from him and reveals desires he means to repress. His guardian represents what he most desires to learn, which is to control others in order to save himself from pain. It comes as no surprise, therefore, that the power Pip envies manifests itself most cruelly in Jaggers's domination of Estella's mother.

Although the lawyer of *Great Expectations* is a more ambiguous figure than his predecessors, he is nevertheless a source of pain for women: "This novel is haunted by shadowy women, half-women, victimized women, women whom Pip cannot see clearly, women who hide from the light."[174] Both Pip and Jaggers are fundamentally responsible for oppressing these women. Pip may hide behind the lawyer as his alter ego, but Jaggers openly exercises his hold on women. Both Molly and Estella suffer from his interference like Agnes, Annie Strong, Esther Summerson, Ada Clare and Lady Dedlock suffer from the earlier versions of the type. In Jaggers, the 'character,' in every sense of the word, fully breaks open and takes an unprecedented presence in the plot – no lawyer has been as important before in any of the novels. Jaggers pushes himself from minor to almost major character. In line with this fact, Jaggers's torture of 'his' woman is also out in the

---

173 Lucy Frost, "Taming to Improve. Dickens and the Women in *Great Expectations*" in *Great Expectations. Contemporary Critical Essays*, ed. Roger D. Sell. Basingstoke: Macmillan, 1994: 60–78, 70.

174 Schor, *Daughter of the House*, 177.

open. Mr Tulkinghorn seeks to disguise his desire, Mr Jaggers openly indulges in his lust.

Jaggers's domination of Molly is one of the most uncomfortable aspects of an uncomfortable novel, but critically, she is quite a neglected character. Her existence proves, as Jack Rawlins has pointed out, that Jaggers cannot be a positive character, no matter how strongly Pip lets his admiration shine through: "Jaggers cannot be benevolent, as the emotional truth of scenes like the brutalising of Molly attests."[175] However, her existence is also regarded by the novel as well as many critics as a matter of fact. Perhaps it is necessary to spell out what Jaggers harbours in his seemingly non-existent private life. In contrast to Wemmick's humorous double life, his severe separation of home and office, Jaggers is seen as devoid of such a private sphere, although Pip is a witness to his domesticity. One of the first questions Wemmick asks him is whether he has been to Jaggers's home for dinner. When Pip more or less involuntarily reveals to Jaggers that Wemmick has an elaborate private life, there is a profound emphasis on the fact that Jaggers does not. The contrast is such that Pip supposes this to be a source of conflict even: "I have never seen two men look more oddly at one another than Mr. Jaggers and Wemmick did after this apostrophe. At first, a misgiving crossed me that Wemmick would be instantly dismissed from his employment" (*GE*, ch. 51, p. 306). The secret of Wemmick's private life is of course an important plotline, but I would argue that it receives such enormous attention to pretend by contrast that Jaggers exists truly only in the professional realm. His own insistence that he is but the agent of another repeatedly draws attention to what seems to be a lack of personal identity and yet he is a most charismatic character, which is clear not least because of Pip's deeply ambivalent attitude towards him. On the surface, Jaggers is supposed to be a professional man and nothing more, he does not belong in domestic spheres.[176] And yet, the curious habit of washing his hands of his professional life confronts the reader with the fact that he does distinguish between different spheres. The reason why the text tries to divert attention away from Jaggers's home life is possibly that this home life harbours the character's most disgusting aspect. After all, he has a woman in captivity.

Molly's two appearances in the novel, which lie relatively far apart, provide a frame for Pip's level of understanding as he wants to present himself to the reader. In the narrator's version, Pip's first evening at Jaggers's house is one of

---

175 Rawlins, *Great Expiations*, 86.

176 See Anthony Winner, "Character and Knowledge in Dickens: The Enigma of Jaggers," *Dickens Studies Annual* 3 (1974): 100–121, 114.

youthful ignorance, the second one of mature understanding and disillusion. However, the element common to both vignettes, Molly, indicates that Pip has not developed at all. He is a witness to Molly's oppression twice, but only relates the relevance she has for him, in the sense that he finally realises that she is Estella's mother, which drastically decreases Estella's value. In a single moment, she becomes more easily attainable and simultaneously less desirable. Pip's egocentric narration thus remains almost indifferent towards Molly's existence, drawing due attention away from her, for he has no desire to question Jaggers's possession of her. He takes Jaggers's sadistic display of power over her for granted, withdrawing almost completely from his own narrative and giving no comment on what he is forced to witness. Jaggers does not even pretend that she is a regular servant, but ostentatiously treats her as a slave, praising her physiognomy as if he were selling her at market:

> "There's power here;" said Mr Jaggers, coolly tracing out the sinews with his forefinger. "Very few men have the power of wrist that this woman has. It's remarkable what mere force of grip there is in these hands. I have had occasion to notice many hands; but I never saw stronger in that respect, man's or woman's, than these." (*GE*, ch. 26, p. 166)

The moment is harsh: he both degrades her to an animal, emphasising her value for physical labour, and treats her as a sexual object by his perverted caress of her scars.

Technically, we are to understand that Molly is a kind of housekeeper, but Jaggers does not even pretend to be treating her like a professional servant. He exhibits her as an object he has complete control over, transgressing physical boundaries reminiscent of his first encounter with Pip. The difference is that his exhibition of Molly is clearly intended to demonstrate omnipotence and the blurring of lines between servant, slave and rape victim is intended. Significantly, Pip dispenses with narratorial commentary – in fact, his silence on the subject, as well as the silence of the other young men in attendance, makes them all complicit in Jaggers's abuse, which is subconsciously felt by the narrator. He relates that she pleads to be spared, that Jaggers ignores her suffering and that she silently accuses them: "While he said these words in a leisurely critical way, she continued to look at every one of us in regular succession as we sat" (*GE*, ch. 26, p. 166). Jaggers makes the men accessories in his domestic violence and they submit themselves to complicity – so much so that Pip never even questions Molly's role in Jaggers's private life. Moreover, Pip's narrative maintains until the end of the novel that Jaggers *has* no private life. This myth enables him to ignore Molly's role as a victim: if Jaggers has no private life, there can be no victim and the woman can be treated as a piece of the puzzle, since Pip insists that Jaggers is quite the enigma – despite all evidence to the contrary that he gives himself.

The novel provides a surprisingly elaborate rationale for Molly's objectification, which begs the question whether Dickens truly never read Brontë, as he claimed.[177] There is the factual backstory, but there is also a discursive marking of the character that is supposed to provide the real rationale for Jaggers's actions. As Wemmick relates, the official reason for Molly's presence in Jaggers's household is that she is a murderess, whom he has saved from execution. Unspoken is his attitude that since he has saved her life, he now believes that she is rightfully his. In nineteenth-century logic, Molly's crime has deprived her of rationality; as a criminal, she is considered beneath common humanity.[178] Thus, ideologically, she has forfeited her right to rational treatment because of the murder and it pairs her off nicely with the prominent criminal in the novel, Magwitch. Molly is thus clearly reminiscent of Mademoiselle Hortense, who is equally sensual and equally criminal, aspects which make her a target for Tulkinghorn's uninhibited humiliation of her. Their relationship is mirrored in the perverted love affair between Jaggers and Molly – while Tulkinghorn only wishes to turn the key on Mademoiselle Hortense, Jaggers has done so.

Pip's life-story is largely characterised by the fact that he learns to treat Magwitch humanely, whereas the novel denies Molly such treatment throughout. Hegemonically speaking, her position as Jaggers's subject is just, even presented as humane, for he prides himself in having saved her:

> Put the case, Pip, that passion and the terror of death had a little shaken the woman's intellects, and that when she was set at liberty, she was scared out of the ways of the world and went to him to be sheltered. Put the case that he took her in, and that he kept down the old wild violent nature whenever he saw an inkling of its breaking out, by asserting his power over her in the old way. (*GE*, ch. 31, p. 307)

In the novel's rationale for the objectification of the woman, Jaggers has saved Molly from herself and has created his very own madwoman in the attic. The parallels between Molly and Bertha Mason are unmistakable and possibly more than just a reiteration of the stereotypical nineteenth-century madwoman. Her deviant passion that leads her to the 'unnatural' attack of another *woman*, the subtext of sexual jealousy and consequently 'unnatural' sexual inclinations, her propensity for physical violence and her outward appearance, which is discursively marked as mad and hence sexually illicit, make Molly the spitting image of Bertha and Jaggers is as justified in keeping her as Rochester is of shutting up his first wife in the attic. As if to excuse himself pre-emptively for the

177 Cf. Schlicke, *Oxford Dickens*, 56.
178 Cf. Robin Gilmour, *The Idea of the Gentleman in the Victorian Novel*. London: George Allen & Unwin, 1981: 124ff.

horrifying scene at Jaggers's home, Pip presents Molly from his first introduction as a hybrid of beast and witch:

> Rather tall, of a lithe nimble figure, extremely pale, with large faded-blue eyes, and a quantity of streaming hair. I cannot say whether any diseased affection of the heart caused her lips to be parted as if she were panting, and her face to bear the curious expression of suddenness and flutter; but I know that I had been to see Macbeth at the theatre, a night or two before, and that her face looked to me as if it were all disturbed by fiery air, like the faces I had seen rise out of the Witches' caldron. (*GE*, ch. 26, p. 165)

Her panting speaks to her passions, her flowing hair to her madness and sexual licence. As Brian Cheadle observes, "[i]n every detail, [. . .] Molly is thus invested with all the energy and authority of that sexuality which Foucault sees Victorian texts as actively constructing."[179]

Molly is Bertha Mason's sister, equally confined by a male keeper in a perverted domestic ideal, punished for her sexual deviance, and a wild beast tamed. It is not unreasonable to assume that Brontë's madwoman had a direct effect on the creation of Molly. Even if Dickens truly did not read the novel, and we have ample reason to doubt that, according to Michael Slater,[180] the image of Brontë's madwoman acquired a life off the page: "Bertha's violence, dangerousness, and rage, her regression to an inhuman condition and her sequestration became such a powerful model for Victorian readers, including psychiatrists, that it influenced even medical accounts of female insanity."[181] Molly shares all the crucial characteristics to be discursively marked as a Victorian madwoman, which is the text's more or less explicit justification for Jaggers's control over her. He marks her as mad himself, when he refers to her "shaken" intellect and like Rochester, he suggests that he keeps her safe by hiding her from the outside world. Furthermore, both Molly and Bertha are marked not only by their sexually deviant behaviour, but by their race. Bertha is the aberrant creole, Wemmick mentions Molly's "gipsy blood" (*GE*, ch. 48, p. 293) almost in an afterthought. Their race and their sexual transgression – Molly has not only attacked out of jealousy, but was married over the broomstick;[182] Bertha, Rochester suggests, has an unnatural sexual appetite – are concomitant aspects of their unfemininity, which the respective men in these

---

179 Brian Cheadle, "The Late Novels: *Great Expectations* and *Our Mutual Friend*" in *The Cambridge Companion to Charles Dickens*, ed. John O. Jordan. Cambridge: CUP, 2001: 78–91, 84.
180 See Slater, *Charles Dickens*, 282: "Dickens was later reported as saying he had never read this book but that is hard to believe . . ."
181 Showalter, *Female Malady*, 68.
182 See Cheadle, "Late Novels," 84: "[I]f the reference is to an informal wedding marked by the young pair jumping over a broomstick, the metaphorical implication is that the woman is already pregnant, or about to be."

novels use as the justification to incarcerate them. At Molly's introduction over the dinner at Jaggers's house, the young men's complicit silence confirms a tacit agreement, which is echoed in the pact Pip, Wemmick and Jaggers make never to reveal to anyone the relation between Estella, Molly and Magwitch. At that moment, both Wemmick and Pip *agree* that Jaggers's captivity of Molly is the most desirous arrangement: Jaggers's justification that "she would be safer where she was," (*GE*, ch. 51, p. 308) is confirmed by the three men's fingers to their lips in complicit secrecy, using Jaggers's favourite instrument, the forefinger, to seal the woman's fate.

Despite the fact that Pip lets Jaggers present himself as the saviour of a damsel in distress, the text creates an unmistakable parallel between Molly and the other women in the novel, who are cruelly beaten into submission. Her second appearance in the novel is accompanied by Jaggers's suggestion that Estella's pride, her own deviant gender performance, will be beaten out of her by Drummle and Molly's existence as a madwoman shut up for all eternity in Jaggers's house is echoed by Miss Havisham's captivity in Satis House. Miss Havisham is another reincarnation of Bertha Mason. The madwoman of *Great Expectations* wastes away in her Gothic mansion like Bertha at Thornfield. Both are arrested in the role of forever bride, never wife. Both are rejected by the men they love. Both are 'mad' and both perish in the flames. Both Pip and Rochester injure their hands in the attempt to save them. Miss Havisham's existence is as fateful for Estella as Bertha's is for the young Jane Eyre. The parallels between these women are too obvious to be a coincidence. One might wonder whether Dickens compares Molly to the witches in *Macbeth* in Pip's imagination in order to divert the reader's attention from the similarities with Brontë's novel, but this is, of course, mere conjecture. The comparison certainly evokes Miss Havisham, who is clearly perceived as a witch by young Pip, who enters her house almost like Hansel. The fact that the adult associates Molly with Shakespeare's witches thus creates a necessary link between the women that explains their relation as Estella's surrogate and biological mother. The three women are fatally connected by their deviant femininity and subsequent torture of men. It is no coincidence that Jaggers, the lawyer, presides as master over them all – after all, he is the missing link that has brought them together. It is he, who defends Molly, thereby establishes his connection to Estella, whom he then delivers to Miss Havisham, a woman he represents in all legal matters. The triangle that causes so much pain for the first-person narrator is in existence because of the lawyer's interference, although Pip does not confront him with his role in the Bermuda triangle until he needs the revelation as an element in his plot. Pip's confrontation with Jaggers is an important moment in the solution of his story, but it has sometimes been overestimated in terms of the conflict.[183]

Although Pip's first and only 'honest' discussion with Jaggers, which reveals so much information that he needs to close his story, is built up to as a certain climax, it never questions Jaggers's moral character. While it seems that the child confronts an omnipotent father figure, Jaggers only reveals secrets otherwise unattainable for Pip, who seems quite content with sweeping all else under the carpet. The ambiguity of Jaggers is not resolved and the details of his private life not scrutinised, let alone criticised. In fact, Pip never questions Jaggers's oppression of Molly, nor his representation of Miss Havisham or the distribution of Estella as a child. He manages to convey the overt brutality Jaggers exerts over Molly only marginally by noting her 'training' when he witnesses her treatment:

> I observed that whenever she was in the room, she kept her eyes attentively on my guardian, and that she would remove her hands from any dish she put before him, hesitatingly, as if she dreaded his calling her back, and wanted him to speak when she was nigh, if he had anything to say. I fancied that I could detect in his manner a consciousness of this, and a purpose of always holding her in suspense. (*GE*, ch. 26, p. 165)

Similarly, in his second encounter with Estella's biological mother, Pip feels the need to mention not only that Jaggers is "sharp" with her, but also that she is reduced to a state of terror in his presence: "She stood looking at her master, not understanding whether she was free to go, or whether he had more to say to her and would call her back if she did go" (*GE*, ch. 48, pp. 291/292). Pip's egocentric narrative position has a double effect: first, although he imparts the information of the woman's suffrage at the hands (literally) of Jaggers, his own musings on the subject completely extinguish a sympathetic or even pitiful attitude from his tone. Second, his discovery of the biological relation to Estella and his fantasy of her suffrage as Drummle's wife places Jaggers on a par with the wife beater without judgement of the latter. In fact, while it is clear, as I argued above, that Jaggers cannot be a sympathetic character as all the evidence, even by Victorian standards, is against him, Pip cannot conceal his admiration for the powerful lawyer, which speaks volumes about his own relationship with women in general and Estella in particular.

When Jaggers muses in a self-satisfied tone whether his friend, the Spider, is going to abuse his wife, he openly expresses the desirability of 'taming' women as he has done to Molly. Pip pretends to be outraged by the suggestion, presumably

---

183 See Iain Crawford, "Pip and the Monster: The Joys of Bondage," *SEL* 28.4 (1988): 625–648, 644ff.

feeling protective of Estella, but he manages to be about as convincing as David is at Uriah's suggestion that Annie Strong may be an adulteress: "'Surely,' I interrupted, with a burning face and heart, 'you do not seriously think that he is scoundrel enough for that, Mr. Jaggers?'" (*GE*, ch. 48, p. 291) Clearly, Jaggers thinks exactly that, which is why he has just suggested it and Pip knows it. After all, he has witnessed that Jaggers himself considers the abuse of women into submission a highly laudable practice, as he insists on demonstrating in both exhibitions of Molly. Pip has known this even before he has seen Molly, since even Wemmick, the supposedly likeable neurotic, does not see anything wrong in announcing that at Jaggers's, Pip will see "a wild beast tamed": "It won't lower your opinion of Mr. Jaggers's powers" (*GE*, ch. 24, p. 157). It seems that too many grown men of Pip's acquaintance boast of the powers of breaking unruly women in both body and spirit, which necessarily reminds him uncomfortably of Joe's helplessness in the face of Mrs Joe and Tickler. The man Pip, who is really no different from the child Pip, not only desires dangerous women to be punished in an infantile wish for revenge, but he also lives in a world in which it seems perfectly acceptable to do so. Hence, it is not surprising that Pip only feigns outrage at the thought of Estella's abuse at the hands of her new husband, which he subconsciously sees as appropriate punishment for her treatment of him:

> Pip is 'burning' (always a significant word in this novel) because this is a 'painful' subject for him, but there is a weird excitement here – in Jaggers's telling of the story, in Pip's listening, in the certainty of the ostensibly vague 'putting a case.' The reader might ask, what, then, is Pip's 'case'? And will Pip, in turn, 'beat or cringe'?[184]

As an adult, Pip has found "a series of violent surrogates . . ."[185] and the lawyer Mr Jaggers is first among those. He does to Molly, what Pip wishes he could have done to his sister, what he will seemingly involuntarily do to Miss Havisham and what he desires to do to Estella.

Imagining women physically violated is highly satisfying for Pip as a revenge fantasy on his sister. Pip's trauma as a victim of domestic violence leads him down the tragic path from victim to perpetrator – at least subconsciously. A. L. French has argued that the characters in the novel can be grouped in two "distasteful categories": "One may beat because one has been beaten (Magwitch, Estella), or one may cringe for the same reason (Pip, Molly, Joe); or one may, because beaten, simultaneously beat *and* cringe (Miss Havisham) . . ."[186] Despite the astute analysis, it would be more precise to say that Pip belongs in category

184 Schor, *Daughter of the House*, 173.
185 Schor, *Daughter of the House*, 175.
186 French, "Beating and Cringing," 58.

three: he cringes, certainly, but he also beats, although he leaves this to the metaphor of Jaggers's large hands. It is now clear why one cannot shake the impression that Pip truly admires Jaggers and why he continues to harp on the physical dominance and large violating hands of the man: he represents the kind of totalitarian power over women that Pip wishes he had.

It is no secret that Pip longs for physical violence against women in a novel that seems obsessed with domestic battery. Excellent analyses by A. L. French, Lucy Frost or Hilary Schor have all shown how the text expresses the covert desire to revenge itself against dominant women: "The strong women are created vividly and unquestionably memorable, but because their strength is negative and is associated with the ability to inflict pain on men, they must be 'bent and broken' [. . .] before they can win approval."[187] What is possibly not so obvious, however, is the crucial role Jaggers plays in this scenario. The lawyer is a destroyer of women in a novel that wants to destroy women. He exerts that control over women that Pip dreams of and this goes beyond even his domestic violence against Molly. After all, Miss Havishman is virtually rendered legally incapacitated if it were not for her representative and Estella only finds herself in the traumatic position as Miss Havisham's guinea pig, because Jaggers has brought her there. The emphasis on Jaggers's treatment of others is clearly laid out when Pip observes how cruelly and yet indifferently he handles his clients, but there seems to be a missing link between Jaggers, the lawyer, and Jaggers, the tormentor of women. The link is obvious, however, when we place Jaggers in succession of Uriah and Tulkinghorn. Jaggers's open abuse of Molly in the presence of others, who look away from her harassment, is an imitation of Tulkinghorn's sadistic manoeuvres with Lady Dedlock; the possession of Molly fulfils what all of the previous lawyers dream of – whether in the shape of Agnes or Ada or Lady Dedlock herself. Like Tulkinghorn, Jaggers is a silent observer, manipulating people into unwittingly exposing themselves, a representative of omnipotent surveillance: "[H]e is like the unseen watcher in the central tower of the Panopticon, naming others, but not named himself [. . .], in the position, as criminal lawyer, of power, conferring identities, controlling destinies . . ."[188] Yet, he differs from Uriah and Tulkinghorn through the fact that the narrator of *Great Expectations* does not succeed in marginalising him. Jaggers's power exceeds the narrator's. He may have been intended as a minor character like all the other lawyers, but he gets away from the text. He does not hide in the shadows of either world or narrative, he

---

187 Frost, "Taming to Improve," 70/71.
188 Jeremy Tambling, "Prison-Bound: Dickens and Foucault," *Essays in Criticism* 36.1 (1986): 11–31, 20.

pushes himself to the forefront in all respects. This is why it is important to come back to the fact that there is a notable difference between his position in the legal profession and that of his predecessors. Involved in the execution of criminal law, Jaggers may be regarded as substantially more important, for he is literally involved in matters of life and death.

While in character construction Jaggers is an obvious successor of those sadistic lawyers before him, it is important to note that in terms of the legal profession, he is a different kind of lawyer. He is not in Chancery, nor does he prepare documents for cases in the equity court, he is a criminal lawyer in the sense that he both constructs witness accounts and argues in court. He is directly responsible for the lives of others, which is most obvious in Molly's case. His successful argumentation and forgery, which make her seem like a different person, create a new identity for her and prevent the death penalty, which is why he believes that her life is now his. If Jaggers represents a system, which all of Dickens's lawyers do, of course, to a certain extent, it is a very different system, for the shortcomings of the law here work to the characters' advantage, not disadvantage. Criminal law, the novel suggests, can be manipulated and corrupted against the system and hence it can serve the protagonists' purposes – *if* they are themselves corrupt enough to see this and *if* they are willing to take that responsibility. This is another reason why Pip cannot condemn Jaggers. After all, Jaggers takes a responsibility upon himself that the other lawyers deliberately shirk. He even undermines the system in order to achieve his intended result as his shady dealings with clients and the story of his triumph in Molly's prosecution make unmistakably clear.

Jaggers proclaims to be devoid of personal motives: coming back to his second appearance in the novel, when he insists that he is merely the "agent of another," one has to note that his insistence on a distinct detachment from his clients in dedication to the profession is one of his favourite stories: "What I have to do, as the confidential agent of another, I do. No less, no more" (*GE*, ch. 18, p. 108). Ironically, this sounds like Vholes, but in the case of Jaggers, it is a blatant lie. Any Dickens reader is used to such statements: all lawyers claim to be merely acting within the confines of their profession in order to make themselves immune to any kind of moral reproach. But in Jaggers's case, his ostentatious professionalism, underlined by his obsessive hand-washing, is a complete fabrication: as we have seen, he is a most active agent, who does much more than he is required to do. He bends the law and the professional limitations of his position considerably. He is not at all a representative of the system, for he works against the system. He is the most ingenious of all the puppeteers, for he is not only able to manipulate the other characters, but also the overbearing power of the law itself. In that sense, his defiance of the system seems to answer to a desire implicit in many Dickens novels, for Jaggers does not take it lying down. He is a liar and a fabricator, but through lying and fabricating, he achieves results! One of the most insistent narrative undercurrents of the novel is that "Jaggers would do it if it was to be done" (*GE*, ch. 20, p. 132). He is a figure of power not only in the negative, but also in the positive sense. His clients are certainly presented with little sympathy by Pip, but he nevertheless notices their admiration of and trust in the lawyer, who has an air about him like a miracle worker: "'Jaggers is for him, 'Melia, and what more could you have?'" (*GE*, ch. 20, p. 132) In reverse, if Jaggers is on the other side, the case is lost already. Observing his guardian in his natural habitat, surrounded by clients, Pip cannot help but notice that Jaggers is extremely successful at what he does. There is no apathy, no submission, no standstill as in Chancery; there is movement and progress and people who are saved from capital punishment.

Jaggers is no barrister, but he certainly comes closest to that branch of the profession. He is the only one of Dickens's lawyers whose actions are of consequence for the letter of the law and the overarching narrative of what he does revolves around the death penalty. We know that Dickens himself was conflicted about the subject and there has been discussion as to whether his disapproval extends to capital punishment *per se* or only public executions.[189] Therefore it might not be entirely irrelevant that his most effective and charismatic, if not especially likeable, lawyer figure is busy getting his clients off of death row, as it were. Given the fact that Magwitch's fate and therefore Pip's life will revolve around this very question towards the final climax of the story, one might argue that the whole thematic treatment of capital punishment is merely an analogical preparation for that conflict. Also, it is clear that Pip is particularly interested in this question as he carries his own alleged guilt, resulting from his childhood trauma that lets him identify with the convict. Pip's more or less explicable feelings of guilt have been the topic of much discussion,[190] so it is possibly natural that the first-person narrator focuses especially on the question of punishment and the idea of punishment is inseparable in every way from the construction of Jaggers. He is a punisher, a source of fear and terror for both Pip and Molly and all of his clients, but he is also the one person in the novel, who can prevent or, at least, divert punishment. Jaggers is effective in saving people from capital punishment, which makes him such an attractive figure for Pip and suggests him as a father figure, who would have been able to save him from Tickler and Mrs Joe. All of Jaggers's lies and questionable methods therefore find much less scorn in

189 See Slater, *Charles Dickens*, 247–250.
190 See above all Jordan, "The Medium" and Eiichi Hara, "Stories Absent and Present in *Great Expectations*," *ELH* 53.3 (1986): 593–614.

the text than other lawyers in Dickens would encounter. Jaggers's methods do not necessarily differ all that much from the practice of Dodson and Fogg in *The Pickwick Papers*, but in this late novel, the lawyer's power constitutes a source of admiration, not derision. Pip admires Jaggers as a lawyer, who works against the system, but he admires him more as a man who would have been able to save him from his childhood trauma.

Jaggers's attempts to keep up the appearance of professional integrity do contribute to the comic potential of the novel. When he is in the process of forging witness accounts, a fact his client does not feel the need to hide by admitting that the witness in question is prepared to swear "anythink," which is in itself a crime, of course, Jaggers's false outrage speaks to the duplicity of his actions: "Mr. Jaggers suddenly became most irate. 'Now, I warned you before,' said he, throwing his forefinger at the terrified client, 'that if you ever presumed to talk in that way here, I'd make an example of you. You infernal scoundrel, how dare you tell ME that?'" (*GE*, ch. 20, p. 134) While his clients are generally presented by the text as subpar, they nevertheless understand his outspoken instructions, taking his forgery to extremes. Any witness will do, if they are also prepared to swear "anythink":

> Mike looked at his cap, and looked at the floor, and looked at the ceiling, and looked at the clerk, and even looked at me, before beginning to reply in a nervous manner, "We've dressed him up like – " when my guardian blustered out:
>
> "What? You WILL, will you?" [. . .]
>
> After some helpless casting about, Mike brightened and began again:
>
> "He is dressed like a 'spectable pieman. A sort of pastrycook." [. . .]
>
> "Take him past that window, and let me see him."
>
> The window indicated was the office window. We all three went to it, behind the wire blind, and presently saw the client go by in an accidental manner, with a murderous-looking tall individual, in a short suit of white linen and a paper cap. This guileless confectioner was not by any means sober, and had a black eye in the green stage of recovery, which was painted over. (*GE*, ch. 20, p. 134)

Producing a witness is a charade in the world of *Great Expectations* and the fact that the witness in question here is himself "murderous-looking" certainly does not escape the reader's attention. Jaggers is a cheat, but the premise of the charade is that while he mutely instigates it, it has to come off as if he never had any part in it. Like all the other lawyers, he tries to evade responsibility, but unlike the others, he is so skilled at professional puppeteering that he nevertheless achieves the desired results. His strategy in Molly's defence is related by Wemmick as a great triumph:

> "Mr. Jaggers was for her," pursued Wemmick, with a look full of meaning, "and worked the case in a way quite astonishing. It was a desperate case, and it was comparatively early days with him then, and he worked it to general admiration; in fact, it may almost be said to have made him. He worked it himself at the police-office, day after day for many days, contending against even a committal; and at the trial where he couldn't work it himself, sat under Counsel, and – every one knew – put in all the salt and pepper."
> (*GE*, ch. 48, p. 293)

Jaggers gets things done. In the context of this book, one cannot help being reminded of the exchange between Tulkinghorn and Lady Dedlock: "Nothing that *you* would call anything, has been done today" (*BH*, ch. 2, p. 12). What Jaggers does, even Lady Dedlock would call something. The law simply takes on a completely different level of significance in this novel, for people's lives are not wasted, as they are in Chancery, but they are saved. Nevertheless, Jaggers's success requires an almost completely unscrupulous interpretation of the law itself and Pip never forgets this. Jaggers may express himself in legalese reminiscent of Mr Micawber and he may try to hide his person behind his profession, but by Pip's insinuation, there is a distant hint of mockery here too. Significantly, Pip urges Jaggers "to be more frank and manly" with him, when he is determined to ascertain the truth behind his expectations. The ensuing dialogue, in which Jaggers insists on "putting a case" (a phrase he repeats *thirteen* times) is therefore distinctly humorous despite Pip's palpable pain at these revelations, for Jaggers will neither be frank nor manly: he hides behind the legal curtain still: "Mind! I admit nothing" (*GE*, ch. 51, pp. 306–308).

On the surface, Jaggers is no less corrupt than Vholes, but he achieves a different outcome, because he works in a different branch of the law. His perceived superiority towards others, which he does not even attempt to hide, reveals that he also only acts for himself. He does not save people from capital punishment for the greater good, but for his own satisfaction. Jaggers is deeply self-interested, which is clearly epitomised in the fact that he uses Molly for his own pleasure. Having saved her from capital punishment, he takes her prolonged punishment into his own hands. On the one hand, Dickens simply repeats the story of the lawyer, who has problems with women. All powerful in the public world, they struggle in domesticity with their sadistic desire to dominate the female sex and Jaggers has what Tulkinghorn would envy. The lawyer figures thus portray a deeply ambivalent position towards women that may or may not reflect the author's own. On the other hand, Jaggers is even more complex than his heinous treatment of Molly suggests, for there is a hint at a backstory that might provide another line of explanation for what is clearly suggested is his misogyny.

Jaggers, "the unseen watcher,"[191] is always an uncomfortable presence for Pip, but possibly never more so than when Estella is present. He expresses almost extreme anxiety at the fact that Jaggers sees him with the unattainable object of his affection. I have argued above that the encounter serves Pip in constructing the myth that Jaggers is so completely different from himself, that his love for Estella is pure and not corrupt, that he detests the violence against women represented by the lawyer. In order to keep up his favourite story, Pip needs to pretend that his love for Estella is genuine and Jaggers provides him with the opportunity to do this by contrast. Thus, Pip freely explains the anxiety he feels in this particularly perverted moment of domestic harmony and goes untypically deeply into explaining his own emotions. Given that he is, of course, an unreliable narrator, this explanation is misleading as a closer look at the vignette proves. Pip later admits that at least, he never meant to *conceal* his feelings: "Mr. Jaggers had seen me with Estella, and was not likely to have missed the sentiments I had been at no pains to conceal" (*GE*, ch. 48, p. 292). However, the reason for his extreme discomfort in Mr Jaggers's presence is the fact that the lawyer seems to act so completely out of character at Satis House: "Anything to equal the determined reticence of Mr. Jaggers under that roof, I never saw elsewhere, even in him. He kept his very looks to himself . . ." (*GE*, ch. 30, p. 186) Jaggers stops observing, which is so unlike him that it scares Pip. The lawyer who otherwise sees everything, whose eyes are from the first described by Pip, has stopped looking about him and it is his cold presence that Pip gives as a reason for the fact that he finds the evening unbearable. This is not true – he quite consciously insinuates something else:

> He kept his very looks to himself, and scarcely directed his eyes to Estella's face once during dinner. When she spoke to him, he listened, and in due course answered, but never looked at her that I could see. On the other hand, she often looked at him, with interest and curiosity, if not distrust, but his face never showed the least consciousness.
> (*GE*, ch. 30, p. 186)

Pip is jealous. He reads into Jaggers's ignorance of Estella a love interest in her. He reads into her interest in him an offended vanity on the look-out for flattery. When he later explains to himself that "I knew I could never bear to hear him creak his boots at her, that I knew I could never bear to see him wash his hands of her," (*GE*, ch. 30, p. 186/187) he implies that he could not bear to see Jaggers make an object of Estella as he has seen him do of Molly. He has come to be so in awe of Jaggers's powers, powers he wishes to possess himself, that the lawyer is not just a role-model, but also a rival. Pip attests him the power to conquer what he finds himself helpless against, which is Estella's rejection of him. The

191 Tambling, "Prison-Bound," 20.

very fact that he describes her as taking an interest in Jaggers, which is also completely out of character, since we know that Estella never takes an interest in anything according to Pip, is enough to alarm him and make him imagine all kinds of sordid secrets in the pair's past.

It is difficult to determine whether Dickens means to insinuate that maybe Pip is jealous for a reason. Jaggers's behaviour towards Estella certainly resembles that of a rejected lover, for it borders on impropriety. Like Tulkinghorn, Jaggers pushes the boundaries of proper conduct, as she clearly notices too. His deliberate oversight of her is rude and possibly results from an offended or wounded ego. Furthermore, the story of the older man, who places a female orphan in another woman's care and waits for her to grow up to marry her obviously has a precedent in Dickens. It is perfectly possible that "[b]ehind the professional there flickers a man who may [. . .] have a 'gentle heart',"[192] like Mr Jarndyce, who 'acquires' Esther as a girl and simply waits for her to reach marriageable age. It is far from impossible that Dickens has the same in mind for his construction of Jaggers and Estella. Pip certainly suspects something and he receives one more hint. When he finally receives the last pieces of the puzzle as to who Estella really is, Jaggers addresses Pip's feelings for her for the first time by including it in his "cases": "But add the case that you had loved her, Pip, and had made her the subject of those 'poor dreams' which have, at one time or another, been in the heads of *more men than you think likely*" (*GE*, ch. 51, p. 308 [my emphasis]). Who are these men he refers to? As an adult, Estella has become part of a bidding war that Drummle has won, but those are not men Pip would have found *unlikely* to woo Estella. Jaggers clearly refers to a more distant past and then, Estella was shut up in Satis House, receiving only relatives such as the Pockets – and professionals, like Jaggers. It is quite reasonable to assume that Jaggers may be referring to himself as a man, whom Pip would not be likely to suspect as Estella's jilted lover.

The lawyer's insertion of this momentous sentence into his speech can be easily overlooked, but it provides insight into this construction of the lawyer, who brings to light many aspects that Tulkinghorn's text represses. Jaggers's ownership of Molly and his sadistic pleasure in presenting her like a slave to the young men who look up to him can now of course be seen as a compensation for the fact that Estella has rejected him. If Jaggers has had to learn that he is not omnipotent, for even he cannot break the novel's most celebrated woman, he has her mother under his thumb in her stead. This lawyer figure fulfils a fantasy both Uriah Heep and Tulkinghorn share: they both dream of complete domination

192 Winner, "Enigma of Jaggers," 116.

over Agnes and Lady Dedlock respectively and this late version of the same character is given an 'appropriate' female into his domination. Both Uriah and Tulkinghorn cannot succeed: the women they dream of possessing have to be saved from their predators by the text according to their social status. Agnes is an unequivocal heroine, so Uriah can safely be criminalised. Lady Dedlock is an ambivalent female, but while she may deserve a narrative death as a fallen woman, she does not deserve so harsh a degradation as actually falling into the lawyer's hands. The domination of women that these lawyers seek can only be realised in a lower class woman, who has forfeited her right to live through murder and who is not coincidentally racially marked. As mentioned above, the text does not refrain from emphasising Molly's "gipsy blood" (*GE*, ch. 48, p. 293) as a further justification for her position in Jaggers's hands. She is clearly worth less than her daughter, who is put on a pedestal by the narrator, so there is an immanent judgement of her as better off in the lawyer's possession. Like Bertha Mason, whose incarceration in the attic is presented as a 'natural' consequence of her deviance, Molly is punished for her deviance like all the other deviant women in this novel – only her fate needs no questioning. The text cannot imagine a reason why a "gipsy" murderess would not be enslaved by her male superior.

Lucy Frost has shown that all those proud women the novel contains have to be bent and broken into a submissive position at the hands of violent men. This dynamic culminates in the constellation of Jaggers and Molly. It is not surprising therefore that Pip can never decide whether he fears or admires Jaggers. Peter Brooks has noted Pip's own "perverse, sadistic eroticism,"[193] which the text cannot quite conceal. Jaggers's relationship with Molly is thus a manifestation of the narrator's repressed misogyny that finds relief and also pleasure in violence towards women. In that sense, Jaggers is a role-model for Pip, because he has achieved absolute domination of a female that, luckily, the story denies Pip: "Jaggers's obsessive disciplining of Molly has an intense erotic charge"[194] that is mirrored in Pip's relationships with both Estella and Miss Havisham. His deepest desires come to light in the figure of the lawyer. This desire is woven so deeply into the text that Jaggers also evades punishment. He is the only one of Dickens's lawyers who is never brought to justice. Jack Rawlins points out that Jaggers is clearly "beyond salvation,"[195] and yet the text curiously dispenses with punishing him. He is neither killed nor criminalised; in fact, the novel fails

---

193 Peter Brooks, "Repetition, Repression, and Return: *Great Expectations* and the Study of Plot" in *Great Expectations. Contemporary Critical Essays*, ed. Roger D. Sell. Basingstoke: Macmillan, 1994: 98–109, 102.

194 Cheadle, "Late Novels," 84.

195 Rawlins, "Great Expiations," 85.

to provide an ending for him *at all*. After his last appearance in Magwitch's trial, Jaggers simply vanishes. Like the devil he is, the novel seems to suggest, he evades moral judgement and simply exits – there is no trace of him afterwards, there is no resolution to his story, Pip never mentions his 'guardian' again. Neither ending of the novel resolves the relationship between Pip and the lawyer, who is so clearly a kind of alter ego.[196] This fact would suggest that there is something of the absolute villain in Jaggers as John Kucich defines them in Dickens. As an agent of the law, Kucich has Jaggers only as "morally ambiguous,"[197] but the fact that he disappears into thin air as Shakespeare suggests Iago does, evading the text's punishment, seems to class this lawyer in an unwanted, yet admired category of evil.

Many critics have noted that Pip is overcome by his sense of guilt. His conscience seems to provide an eternal obstacle towards happiness and while he can repent, he can never truly overcome his conscience. It seems only natural, therefore, that this narrator should admire the lawyer, who has no conscience. After all, in all his professional dealings, which are more or less the only dealings we witness, Jaggers is presented as anything but scrupulous. His idiosyncratic treatment of 'the truth,' his ruthless or at best indifferent behaviour towards his inferiors and his control of everyone around him show him to be a man without a conscience. It goes without saying, therefore, that Jaggers is not what might be referred to as a gentleman. And yet, he is the most powerful figure in a story, whose professed goal is to create a gentleman. This contrast creates an irony that cannot be overlooked. Pip's admiration for the man who cannot, by any means, be classed as a gentleman, although that is Pip's only immaterial goal, creates a tension in the text that is clearly reminiscent of *David Copperfield*.

Pip is equally attracted in repulsion to his own lawyer figure. As it turns out, Dickens makes a point when it comes to lawyers: none of them, as discussed so far, could unequivocally be classed as gentlemen. Even Tulkinghorn, who has worked himself up to serve among the aristocracy, is in his dealings quite clearly deemed beneath the idea of the gentleman. Historically, as we have seen, the question of the lawyer's social affiliation was difficult enough, since education was still the determining factor: "In general terms the title of the attorney to be ranked even among the middle classes was doubtful."[198] While Dickens gives no insight into the level of education in the construction of his lawyers, he clearly suggests that they are no gentlemen. After all, within

196 See also Rawlins, "Great Expiations," 85.
197 Kucich, *Excess and Restraint*, 74.
198 Kirk, *Portrait of a Profession*, 204.

their profession this would mean "acceptance of moral as well as legal obligations; it meant fair dealing with friend or foe; it meant a 'liberal' outlook and education."[199] As the previous chapters have tried to show, there is a greater deal of ambiguity in Dickens's creation of the lawyer character than one would think, but it seems safe to say that none of these lawyers are constructed as committed to "fair dealing with friend or foe." In fact, the opposite seems to be the case. While they are too powerful to be regarded with ease by any of the narrators, and both intellectually and strategically superior to many others in their respective worlds, they obviously do not distinguish sharply between friends or foes, just as much as the late novel *Great Expectations* seems unable to determine whether Jaggers is friend or foe. The ambiguity of the lawyer figure thus stretches through Dickens's whole career and the construction of the character acquires a great deal of complexity. From the early stereotypes to the *ur*-lawyer Uriah Heep to Jaggers the admirable monster, Dickens keeps returning to the question of whether a lawyer can ever be a gentleman.

199 Kirk, *Portrait of a Profession*, 204.

5 The Hero

It is one of the central arguments of this book that all of the lawyer figures that appear in Dickens and that are discussed here are descendants of Uriah Heep. His appearance on the scene provides a blueprint of a psychologically complex character that far supersedes the stereotypes of the early novels and shapes all subsequent lawyer characters. The inherent ambiguity in all of them, however, indicates that Dickens is never fully content with the image he creates. What is the relation between the legal profession and a person's moral integrity? How is the power that comes with the occupation best used? Those are frequently recurring questions. In his late novels especially, the questions of the lawyer's moral integrity and his social status gain increasing prominence. In these late works, it seems, Dickens splits the lawyer characters more consciously. Stryver is an evident replica of Jaggers and these two openly exercise the ruthlessness that earlier lawyers in Dickens attempt to conceal.

Systemic readings of Vholes and Tulkinghorn have emphasised their unethical strive for material gain and both Jaggers and Stryver are conceived by Dickens as carrying such interests on their sleeves. Like Jaggers, Stryver is a liar and fabricator, who uses his position as barrister for his profit and the truth is secondary to all the legal proceedings in *A Tale of Two Cities*. Once again, the law plays a major role in this novel and it is certainly no coincidence that it shares *Great Expectations*' interest in criminal, rather than civil proceedings. Dickens continues the idea that justice is a question of the most convincing narrative. This is represented by Stryver and Jaggers, who are both embodiments of the power of the lie. In that sense, the two novels seem inseparable from one another, for Jaggers is the more fully-fledged variant of the character of Stryver as Dickens had conceived of it several years before the serialisation of *Great Expectations*. However, *A Tale of Two Cities* also seems closely related to *Our Mutual Friend*, for Dickens writes Sydney Carton and Eugene Wrayburn almost as identical characters. These two novels thus generate a major change in the position towards the lawyer in Dickens's fiction, for the lawyer character moves from the periphery to the centre: he becomes a protagonist. Accordingly, Dickens increases the character's complexity by splitting them in two: both Sydney Carton and Eugene Wrayburn are only half a lawyer and they are both given a conscience.

The theme of duplicity in *A Tale of Two Cities* is hardly subtle. It is customary therefore to see that Sydney Carton as a character can only live through Charles Darnay, although critics have complained that even the two combined are insufficient to make a decent hero. Their position in the novel as Doubles of

https://doi.org/10.1515/9783110754506-005

one another hardly needs commentary, only perhaps in the sense that their identification is so strong that 'double' is the wrong term for it. After all, we are used to Dickens's Doubles as characters that stand more democratically next to each other, such as David and Uriah, for instance, and the equation of Carton and Darnay is such as to confuse the differences between them completely. Thus, Cates Baldridge has argued, "'doubling' is too pallid a word to describe adequately what goes on, for such a term still implies two separate identities, two discrete selves, whereas what actually occurs is more properly described as a veritable *merging* of two individuals into one."[200] Or, one could say with Albert Hutter, that Dickens "divides a single ego into two . . ."[201] Whichever way we approach this, it is customary to regard Darnay as a Double to Carton and not the other way around. This is because Charles Darnay's position in the novel and his success in winning the love of Lucie Manette seems to say something about Carton in turn, but in terms of the construction of character, Darnay needs Carton more than Carton needs Darnay. It is Charles Darnay who seems virtually empty and it is Sydney who provides emotional insight into the character. So, while no one would dispute that they are more than physical Doubles and Philip Collins has noted that they "say in dialogue what is usually an anxious monologue,"[202] the character of Carton could dispense with Darnay and still be the hero of this novel. After all, to say that Dickens "endows some depths of interiority"[203] upon him means to define the character only very mildly.

Dickens introduces Sydney Carton as an introspective character from his first appearance in the novel, thereby inviting the reader to focus his interiority. He could not put it more pointedly that this lawyer wishes himself somewhere and someone else, when his "whole attention, when Mr Cruncher looked at him then or afterwards, seemed to be concentrated on the ceiling of the court" (*TTC*, bk. II, ch. 2, p. 71).[204] During the first two chapters that mark Carton's entry in the novel, the fact that he looks persistently and doggedly at the ceiling of the

---

200 Cates Baldridge, "Alternatives to Bourgeois Individualism in *A Tale of Two Cities*," *SEL* 30.4 (1990): 633–654, 646/647.

201 Albert D. Hutter, "Nation and Generation in *A Tale of Two Cities*," *PMLA* 93.3 (1978): 448–462, 455.

202 Philip Collins, "A Tale of Two Novels: *A Tale of Two Cities* and *Great Expectations* in Dickens' Career," *Dickens Studies Annual* 2 (1972): 336–351, 345.

203 Jonathan Grossman, "*Two Cities* Networked: The Historical Novel and Form in French Revolutionary Politics," *Novel* 50.2 (2017): 176–196, 178.

204 All references to *A Tale of Two Cities* are to the following edition and will be given parenthetically: Charles Dickens, *A Tale of Two Cities*. Penguin English Library. London: Penguin Books Ltd., 2012.

court is mentioned six times in combination with the epithet "the wigged gentleman." This is an emphatic departure from Dickens's other introductions of lawyers, for he dispenses completely with the typical outward markings. Apart from the wig, Carton's appearance is hardly mentioned, there are no comparisons with crows or vultures, he is not marked as a devil-figure or a ghost. In fact, his blatant desire to be anywhere but in court during these important early trial scenes is supposed to reveal more about this character than about any other lawyer before him. It is obviously significant that Carton is the only lawyer introduced in court: all of the previous major lawyers enter in the domestic spheres. Carton is shown where he is supposed to belong, appropriate to his profession, and he is marked by his ardent wish *not* to belong there.

Carton is the opposite of the lawyer 'at it': he openly defies his profession, not the system. In this sense, it is more appropriate to see his Double not in Darnay, but in Stryver, as J. M. Rignall has pointed out: "[H]e has been marginalized, so to speak, by the energy and values embodied in Stryver who, more properly than Darnay, is his alter ego."[205] After all, Dickens makes the parallel unmistakably clear, for he introduces the two wigged gentlemen as exactly the same and yet completely different. While Stryver is 'at it,' Carton refuses to participate, his inaction and inattention expressing a silent protest against the court proceedings. Their professional costumes are supposed to render them indistinguishable representatives of justice, but Carton deliberately confuses the identification with his colleague through his ostentatious indifference to the proceedings in court. These proceedings are at length demonstrated by Dickens to be a fabrication, an arbitrary narration that is as highly ambiguous as the novel itself.

The court proceedings in *A Tale of Two Cities* are Dickens's most elaborate discussion of an actual trial since *The Pickwick Papers*. Even *Bleak House*, which goes to its famous lengths in its condemnation of the judicial system, is not this thorough on the professional execution of the law. Darnay's first trial constitutes a vivid dramatization of the actors and actions in law, but the manner in which the novel presents such is reminiscent of the Dodger's astute assessment that this is not the shop for justice. Consequently, the attorney-general is Mr Attorney-General, the personified enemy of the unjustly accused and the jury's preconceived notions determine a trial, which is without evidence. The satire is trenchant, the chapter title "A Disappointment," deeply cynical. The jury, the crowd, the highest representative in the legal order, all act on prejudice and are prone to manipulation. The

205 J. M. Rignall, "Dickens and the Catastrophic Continuum of History in *A Tale of Two Cities*," *ELH* 51.3 (1984): 575–587, 581.

case is fabricated, the witness is bought; the attorney-general 'spins' the case and bullies the jury:

> Mr Attorney-General had to inform the jury [. . .] [t]hat, for these reasons, the jury, being a loyal jury (as he knew they were), and being a responsible jury (as they knew they were), must positively find the prisoner Guilty, and make an end of him, whether they liked it or not. That, they never could lay their heads upon their pillows; that, they never could tolerate the idea of their wives laying their heads upon their pillows; that, they never could endure the notion of their children laying their heads upon their pillows; in short, that there never more could be, for them or theirs, any laying of heads upon pillows at all, unless the prisoner's head was taken off. (*TTC*, bk. II, ch. 3, pp. 77/78)

Dickens gives us legal practice at its worst, for now it is not only incompetent and formulaic on paper and the case does not simply end in heaps of discarded documents and massive financial costs, but here, for the first time, the life of an almost unequivocally good character is on the line. The whole system, it seems, rests on lies and fabrication. Accordingly, Carton's trick that introduces the reader to the physical resemblance between the two men that will resolve the novel's final conflict, is in itself highly ambiguous. Not only is it doubtful evidence, but it is also treated by Stryver as a fabrication: "'That was a rare point, Sydney, that you brought to bear upon the identification. How did you come by it? When did it strike you?'" (*TTC*, bk. II ch. 5, p. 102) Thus, even the one trick that resolves the whole conflict is not exempt from suspicion, as Frances Ferguson has pointed out. Dickens "treats this resemblance as one that waxes and wanes" and thereby "raises the possibility that even the observed resemblance is a lawyer's ploy."[206] Although the legal context in the novel is exclusively a sphere of life and death, the arbitrariness within the system is treated no less drastically by Dickens. There is no truth in the law, it seems. Thus, Sydney Carton can provide the ultimate twist in the case without seeming to be paying attention. His note, handed to Stryver as Darnay's legal counsel, saves a life, yet seems to be born of utter indifference: "[T]he wigged gentleman who had all this time been looking at the ceiling of the court, wrote a word or two on a little piece of paper, screwed it up, and tossed it to him" (*TTC*, bk. II, ch. 3, p. 85). The bare minimum of words and an utterly careless handling of them are enough to turn a case of capital punishment on its head.

In such a legal system, a 'striver' is of course a morally highly ambivalent character. Dickens anticipates Jaggers in his characterisation of the barrister, Stryver, who is his only representative of this branch of the profession. Stryver

---

206 Frances Ferguson, "On Terrorism and Morals: Dickens's *A Tale of Two Cities*," *Partial Answers* 3.2 (2005): 49–74, 67/68.

acts as defence counsel, but his success in court makes him a dishonest man, Dickens suggests with remarkably little restraint. Stryver is marked as professionally and socially oppressive and ungentlemanly, both a bully and a boar:

> Mr Stryver, a man of little more than thirty, but looking twenty years older than he was, stout, loud, red, bluff, and free from any drawback of delicacy, had a pushing way of shouldering himself (morally and physically) into companies and conversations, that argued well for his shouldering his way up in life. (*TTC*, bk. II, ch. 4, p. 93)

It seems blatantly obvious that Dickens uses the same character for Jaggers – the two have too much in common.[207] Significantly, Stryver clearly enjoys his position of dominance over Carton as Jaggers enjoys his over Pip. The successful criminal lawyer, Dickens seems to suggest, cannot switch into a private mode that would be devoid of the lust for power. Thus, Stryver exploits Carton in a relationship that also seems reminiscent of the dysfunctional bromance between Vholes and Carstone. Unabashedly profiting both financially and reputationally from Carton's extensive and strategically brilliant preparation of his cases, Stryver condescends to him in order to hide the fact that he is the latter's intellectual inferior. He thus emphasises what is suggested as Carton's excessive emotional nature: "[T]he old seesaw Sydney. Up one minute and down the next; now in spirits and now in despondency" (*TTC*, bk. II, ch. 5, p. 103).

On the surface, Stryver's assessment of Carton serves as evidence for what is supposed to appear as the latter's lack of moral fibre for the most part of the novel, so that he can prove his full, Christ-like merit with a flourish at the end. Until then, he must appear a scoundrel and ne'er-do-well, a relative of Richard Carstone and Henry Gowan, and the insight Dickens gives into his dealings with Stryver seems only designed for that purpose. Thus, Stryver the bully alerts the

---

207 I would like to add the relation between Stryver and Jaggers to Philip Collins's list of why the two novels seem to be inextricably linked: "It is clear that, different though they are in many respects, the consecutive novels *Little Dorrit*, *A Tale of Two Cities*, and *Great Expectations* belong together, more than to the novels immediately before and after them. Think of the themes and situations common to them: prisons; characters imprisoned in their own past (Mr. Dorrit, Mrs. Clennam, Dr. Manette, Miss Havisham), all bad cases of 'where we stopped growing,' the inability to pluck from the memory a rooted sorrow; the events of a generation ago having dire consequences in the present; heroes who lose or almost lose the girl they love (recall the original ending of *Great Expectations*); heroes, too, who are much less confident, cheerful, and generally praiseworthy than their predecessors; daughters who are their fathers' 'golden thread' (Amy Dorrit and Lucie Manette); various minor figures in common, such as the businessman who is more benevolent and tenderhearted than he appears (Pancks, Lorry, and Wemmick). All, whatever element of humor they contain, share a somber tone." Collins, "Two Novels," 345.

reader to Carton's unfulfilled potential: "'[Y]our way is, and always was, a lame way. You summon no energy and purpose" (*TTC*, bk. II, ch. 5, p. 104). Dickens also makes them school chums for the same effect. Stryver provides first-hand knowledge that Carton has always lacked what it needs, which is of course a variant of David's famous earnestness. Stryver functions as a mirror to the legal proceedings that overcast the novel, for he serves as a witness in the moral 'trial' of Sydney Carton and the question of his goodness. In order to bring about the final redemption most effectively, however, it must seem that Stryver is a witness for the narrative prosecution and so the relationship between the two lawyers creates the impression that Carton's aimlessness and moral depravity, represented in his constant inebriation, is beyond reform: "[N]othing in his past behaviour would lead anyone to imagine that he will be a force for good,"[208] and Stryver vitally contributes to exactly such an image. He literally brings out the worst in Carton – not in the sense that Pip describes Jaggers as able to bring forth inappropriate and embarrassing behaviour – but in the sense that he provides negative information about the character for the reader.

However, a look at Stryver beyond his narrative function also reveals a deep-seated rivalry between the two men that apparently derives from their school days. As part of the novel's overall theme of duplicity, the two lawyers are set up in parallel to compare the progress of each of them: "At last, it began to get about, among such as were interested in the matter, that although Sydney Carton would never be a lion, he was an amazingly good jackal, and that he rendered suit and service to Stryver in that humble capacity" (*TCC*, bk. II, ch. 5, p. 101). While their cognomens are supposed to evoke the impression that the power relations between them are strictly hierarchical, the text's emphasis of Stryver's dominance over Carton quite clearly suggests otherwise. As it turns out, to borrow loosely from Austen, one has got all the competence and the other all the appearance of it:

> It had once been noted at the Bar, that while Mr Stryver was a glib man, and an unscrupulous, and a ready, and a bold, he had not that faculty of extracting the essence from a heap of statements, which is among the most striking and necessary of the advocate's accomplishments. But, a remarkable improvement came upon him as to this. The more business he got, the greater his power seemed to grow of getting at its pith and marrow; and however late at night he sat carousing with Sydney Carton, he always had his points at his fingers' ends in the morning. (*TTC*, bk. II, ch. 5, p. 100)

In truth, Stryver is not a capable lawyer at all; in fact, he lacks the most crucial element of good legal practice, for he cannot discern the crux of the case. In

208 Ferguson, "Terrorism and Morals," 64.

this sense, he is certainly inferior to all of Dickens's other lawyers, for he lacks the competence in the law the others have. The fact that Dickens pairs the two lawyers in this novel thus becomes highly relevant for his later construction of this type. Stryver lacks the intellectual ability to be the lion the world sees in him and he derives his legal power solely from the learned ability of the jackal, who provides him with the logic to argue his case in court.

Although he is often overlooked as a character, the creation of Stryver may duly be considered a prejudicial jibe at the lack of education and intellect among the members of the Victorian Bar, which makes him the vulgar person he is. The rivalry Dickens creates between these two different types of lawyers thus emphasises their apparent difference in terms of class. This difference is also markedly imprinted on the discourse between the two that could be classified as a type of banter with a very serious competitive subtext pursued by Stryver. His insistence that Sydney is too emotional a character thus shines in a different light, for he attests an excessive sensibility that is of course a common prejudice against the upper classes – so is the idleness that is Stryver's most explicit reproach of Carton. On the surface, it seems that Carton lacks an ideal sense of professionalism and earnestness that makes him a worthy representative of the middle classes, but underneath, the text suggests that Carton cannot be a professional man, because of his socially superior station. The hero himself defines this exactly, when he claims that Stryver simply pushed himself into the front rank despite their equal upbringing:

> Before Shrewsbury, and at Shrewsbury, and ever since Shrewsbury, [. . .] you have fallen into your rank, and I have fallen into mine. Even when we were fellow-students in the Quartier Latin, picking up French, and French law, and other French crumbs that we didn't get much good of, you were always somewhere, and I was always – nowhere.
>
> (*TTC*, bk. II, ch. 5, p. 104)

'Nowhere' in this reading is a position clearly above Stryver's in terms of social rank and the novel makes a consistent point that Carton, unlike the lion, has not only received this education, but that it has also made him intellectually superior, which allows him to decipher legal proceedings that Stryver cannot master.[209] Carton's 'genteel' nature, however, forbids him from truly thriving in the profession, because it is socially and morally beneath him. As John Kucich has pointed out, Stryver is an example of "what success means"[210] and this is a

209 Much later, the novel points out that Carton has maintained his French in almost native quality.

210 John Kucich, "The Purity of Violence: *A Tale of Two Cities*," *Dickens Studies Annual* 8 (1980): 119–137, 122.

success that Carton cannot partake in because of his gentlemanly nature. In Sydney's own words, it sounds as if he was kept from a success that should be rightfully his: "You were always driving and riving and shouldering and pressing, to that restless degree that I had no chance for my life but in rust and repose" (*TTC*, bk. II, ch. 5, p. 104/105). Thus, Cates Baldridge accuses Stryver of unethically profiting from what "should rightly be the labor of a single person," which makes Carton a "victim of alienated labor."[211] While this is true, strictly speaking, the text suggests through Carton's status as a gentleman that such success as Stryver's is not open to him. It becomes his social station much better to spend his time in court seemingly indifferently staring at the ceiling.

Their difference in class is clearly a source of aggression for Stryver, who frequently attacks Carton in the attempt to diffuse that difference: "[Y]ou are such an insensible dog"; "I am a tenderer sort of fellow than *you*"; "I am a man, [. . .] who cares more to be agreeable, who knows better how to be agreeable, in a woman's society, than you do" (*TCC*, bk. II, ch. 11, p. 161). The novel's comedy is too subdued to make such dialogue between the two truly funny, but it is still impossible to overlook the irony of the bully who considers himself a man of feeling. More importantly, however, Stryver's frequent attacks of Sydney reveal his class struggle. He tries to create an image of himself as a gentleman, skilled in social intercourse and genteel towards women in contrast to Sydney. This contrast is a mere fabrication, however. As Stryver is a skilled liar in court, so he is in his social life. He uses Sydney to elevate himself in social station, harping on their allegedly different manners: "'Your manners have been of that silent and sullen and hang-dog kind, that, upon my life and soul, I have been ashamed of you, Sydney!'" (*TCC*, bk. II, ch. 11, p. 161) I do not mean to imply, of course, that Sydney is not all of those things, because the novel tries very persistently to create this kind of 'hero.' Stryver's derogatory remarks about Sydney also reveal something about the speaker, however, and I do think that this belongs to Dickens's picture of the successful lawyer.

The contrast between the two characters, who are inextricably linked, suggests that the legal profession allows either success for the vulgar, or failure for the genteel. One 'whole' lawyer is split into these two versions and there is no question with whom the novel sides. Thus, Sydney's retort, "It should be very beneficial to a man in your practice at the bar, to be ashamed of anything," (*TTC*, bk. II, ch. 11, p. 161) accentuates the ruthlessness and lack of delicacy that success in the profession requires. David Marcus has suggested that Sydney is

211 Baldridge, "Individualism," 644/645.

"too paralyzed to realise [. . .] his professional capabilities,"[212] but the juxtaposition with Stryver as his alter ego shows that Sydney cannot be a capable professional, if he is supposed to turn out a reformed hero. Thus, John Kucich has argued that "Carton appeals to us through his freedom from convention and from constraint,"[213] which is another way of saying that we like Carton, because he refuses to thrive in a profession that the novel again presents as dishonest, corrupt and vulgar. There is a lawyer in Carton, which is clear enough from his intellectual ability to discern the law and provide Stryver with his successful cases, but the narrative fate that awaits Sydney does not allow him to be identified with the profession. Thus, his talent, "his genius," as John Kucich has it, is far superior to that of a lawyer: "The mark of Carton's genius is this very ability to penetrate to the most important, the most essential levels – to see beyond the limited vision of others, or to say what others dare not say."[214] Carton's innate social station thus gives him an air of superiority over Stryver that is the privilege of the gentleman. All his idleness and indifference can therefore be read not as just characteristic of the typical Dickensian ne'er-do-well, but as discursive markers of the gentleman protagonist. It is easy to see in Carton the "guilty scoundrel,"[215] or the rogue,[216] or even a clown,[217] but since the novel pairs him with Stryver, it clearly suggests that Carton is too much of a gentleman to be a lawyer. Carton is not a dandy like Henry Gowan,[218] but he is not a professional man either, although his intellect would easily allow him to be. As the character says himself to his alter ego, he has too much shame to be a successful lawyer.

The competition between Stryver and Carton extends beyond the question of class. As all the other lawyers in Dickens, they have set their eyes on a woman, albeit with very different perspectives. In congruity with the conception of their characters, Stryver's material interest in Lucie Manette is juxtaposed with Carton's ideal love for her. In the logic of the novel, this means, of course, that neither can win her. Stryver's offer is beneath her, Carton's is

212 David Marcus, "The Carlylean Vision of *A Tale of Two Cities*," *Studies in the Novel* 8.1 (1976): 56–68, 65.

213 Kucich, "Purity of Violence," 123.

214 Kucich, "Purity of Violence," 123.

215 Hutter, "Nation and Generation," 451.

216 See Susan Cook, "Season of Light and Darkness: *A Tale of Two Cities* and the Daguerrean Imagination," *Dickens Studies Annual* 42 (2011): 237–260, 254.

217 Edwin M. Eigner, "Charles Darnay and Revolutionary Identity," *Dickens Studies Annual* 12 (1983): 147–159, 149.

218 See William R. Harvey, "Charles Dickens and the Byronic Hero," *Nineteenth-Century Fiction* 24.3 (1969): 305–316, 310.

beyond, for it is a love not designed for worldly desires. Since he is a Christ-figure on earth, he cannot propose that he take her as his legal property – this would clearly go against all the idea(l)s associated with the character.[219] More importantly, though, Stryver is after Lucie as Uriah is after Agnes and as Tulkinghorn is after Lady Dedlock: he wants to make her his possession. On the surface, Stryver reveals his interest in the only eligible woman in the novel only in order to alert the reader to Carton's love for her. When Stryver refers to "the pretty witness" as "the admiration of the whole Court," (*TTC*, bk. II, ch. 5, p. 105) the only narrative reason for the exchange is for the reader to realise that Carton loves her, which his gloom and his forced dismissal of her make clear. On the diegetic level, Stryver shows his competitive stance towards Carton, because he tries to draw a confession out of him:

> 'Do you know, Sydney,' said Mr Stryver, looking at him with sharp eyes, and slowly drawing a hand across his florid face: 'do you know, I rather thought, at the time, that you sympathised with the golden-haired doll, and were quick to see what happened to the golden-haired doll?' (*TTC*, bk. II, ch. 5, p. 105)

We tend to concentrate on Carton at this moment, as the rest of the chapter that closes with his desperate tears asks us to do, but Stryver reveals himself here as another sadist. His suspicion that Carton is in love with the pretty witness is of course well-founded, as the narrative means to imply, and his subsequent pursuit of Lucie is not so much directed at her than at Sydney. It seems that while he enjoys having the morally superior person under his thumb professionally, in a twisted shadow of Uriah's professional 'relationship' with Mr Wickfield, he also needs to make advances towards the woman the other one loves the most in order to torture them.

Both Sydney and Mr Wickfield douse themselves in alcohol to be able to ignore the predators that are after their ideal women. Both predators are not only after material gain in the possession of the ideal woman, but also show considerable pleasure in mental torture. Stryver's triumphant putting down of Sydney as a man, as a lawyer and as a lover, owes much to Uriah Heep's perverted boast of his having Mr Wickfield under his thumb. Consequently, when Stryver announces his designs on Lucie Manette, he does so towards Carton in the full knowledge that the latter is in love with her himself:

> 'Now, don't let my announcement of the name make you uncomfortable, Sydney,' said Mr Stryver, preparing him with ostentatious friendliness for the disclosure he was about to

219 See Robert Alter, "The Demons of History in Dickens' *Tale*," *Novel: A Forum on Fiction* 2.2 (1969): 135–142, 140.

> make, 'because I know you don't mean half you say; and if you meant it all, it would be of no importance. I make this little preface, because you once mentioned the young lady to me in slighting terms.' (*TTC*, bk. II, ch. 11, p. 162)

Dickens carefully creates the impression of the glee Stryver feels at revealing towards Carton what he believes is his right to do: "'She will have in me a man already pretty well off, and a rapidly rising man, and a man of some distinction: it is a piece of good fortune for her, but she is worthy of good fortune'" (*TTC*, bk. II, ch. 11, p. 163). The speech is disgusting, of course, because it is meant to be disgusting. Stryver sounds like Uriah underneath his presumed humility. For the purpose of the investigation of Dickens's creation of the lawyer figure, it is indispensable to note, therefore, that Stryver displays the same lust for power, the same sadism and the same wish for the possession of a woman. Significantly, he claims to have no financial motive: "'I don't care about fortune: she is a charming creature, and I have made up my mind to please myself: on the whole, I think I can afford to please myself" (*TTC*, bk. II, ch. 11, p. 163). He dreams of possessing for the sake of dominating her – it is no coincidence, of course, that in the first exchange between the two lawyers Lucie Manette is appropriated by materialistic terminology in excess: nine times in the short dialogue they refer to her as an object, calling her repeatedly "the pretty witness," "the picturesque doctor's daughter" and "the golden-haired doll" (*TTC*, bk. II, ch. 11, p. 105). Again, if Carton is to be a hero, he can only display the opposite of Stryver's designs, making her an ideal beyond worldly possession and thus, he can never win her. Instead, he is tortured by Stryver, who pretends that he seeks advice, only to gloat in what he believes to be his assured success in winning the woman his morally superior friend loves: "'[Y]ou take it more easily than I fancied you would, and are less mercenary on my behalf than I thought you would be; though, to be sure, you know well enough by this time that your ancient chum is a man of pretty strong will" (*TTC*, bk. II, ch. 11, p. 163). The whole conversation as Dickens presents it is little more than a pissing match that Stryver believes to be winning far and wide.

There is certainly no subtlety in the portrayal of the brute and his condescension towards Carton, which is possibly why Stryver has received relatively little critical commentary. He is too obviously pompous, too false, too condescending, too corrupt to be worthy of in-depth analysis. The narrative never holds back judgement: "The prosperous patronage with which he said it, made him look twice as big as he was, and four times as offensive" (*TTC*, bk. II, ch. 11, p. 163). Consequently, Stryver's actual courtship is a farce and reminiscent of Pecksniff's advances towards Mary Graham in *Martin Chuzzlewit*. Recalling Mary's terrible anguish at the violent advances made towards her, however, one can be relieved that Dickens spares both Lucie Manette and the reader the same treatment and confines himself with using Stryver's conceited self-assurance for comic effect only in indirect discourse, but the comedy is certainly not one of Dickens's greatest funny intervals. On the one hand, the satire of the man is too blunt to be creative and on the other hand, the humour seems slightly misplaced in a tale that certainly counts as one of the author's bleakest. Moreover, it is clearly discernible that Dickens invests very little in the plotline of Stryver's courtship. Once he has made all the jokes ("Mr Stryver having made up his mind to that magnanimous bestowal of good fortune on the doctor's daughter, resolved to make her happiness known to her . . ."; "whether he should give her his hand . . ." (*TTC*, bk. II, ch. 12, p. 165), he quickly wraps up the story in Mr Lorry's unequivocal assessment of the matter: "'[T]here really is so much too much of you!'" (*TTC*, bk. II, ch. 12, p. 167).

It is therefore completely consistent in the construction of Stryver that afterwards he pretends he never really wanted her; that eventually he does marry money, revealing his true object after all; and that he is reported as pretending towards his wife that the girl was after him. He backpedals when he has finally managed to understand the rejection ("I am glad the thing has dropped") and subsequently seeks his rescue in degrading the object: "[Y]ou cannot control the mincing vanities and giddinesses of empty-headed girls" (*TTC*, bk. II, ch. 12, p. 172). None of this is particularly unusual; he is simply one of many conceited Dickensian men, only less fully drawn out. He is never even shown in discourse with Lucie Manette, so the reader is spared an exhibition of dominance over the heroine. It is also consistent with the character's lack of complexity that Dickens dispenses with him more or less silently. He disappears sometime during Darnay's second trial and receives no ending and no final judgement. Like Jaggers, he vanishes into thin air, but the desire to be rid of such a character is more explicit in the *Tale*, which imagines "any such offender's being carried off to some suitably retired spot, and there hanged out of the way" (*TTC*, bk. II, ch. 21, p. 250). The violence the narration wishes on Stryver is a logical conclusion for a despicable character, who bears all the classic characteristics of the lawyer in Dickens – only in such rudimentary construction as to seem almost trite. The creation of Stryver is only of interest when we consider his function as Sydney Carton's alter ego.

The contrast between the two lawyers shines a light on Carton that foreshadows his self-sacrifice and ascent towards heaven, but he is nevertheless an ambiguous figure. The outwardly embodied despicable lawyer Stryver is, after all, part of Carton's interior too. Carton claims he has "no business" so that he will not be tainted by association, but his competence in the law is nevertheless an important aspect in the character and all of the preceding chapters have shown that almost all characters in that profession are also objects of admiration. In

Carton, Dickens tells the story of the reformed lawyer that dominates his later work and repeats itself in Eugene Wrayburn. Philip Collins argued that Sydney Carton is the product of Dickens's "evident desire at this period to create unconventional heroes or antiheroes."[220] Carton's idleness, his seeming indifference towards everything around him, his lack of purpose as attested by Stryver; his drinking and his opinion of himself, above all, create the image of a truly conflicted hero and an angry young man. The novel thus suggests that "we must disapprove of him."[221] Yet, he is also "one of Dickens's most loved and best-remembered characters"[222] and a "powerful and attractive figure."[223] He bears the novel's theme of duplicity within himself and thereby creates an ambivalent attitude in the reader.[224] William Harvey calls him a "half-hero" and his position in the novel as a morally equivocal figure approaching "the role of leading character" seems indicative of the late Dickens indeed.[225]

Sydney Carton, Pip and Eugene Wrayburn are all deeply conflicted characters. What unites the two lawyers in contrast to the first-person narrator of *Great Expectations*, however, is their freely expressed self-loathing and this self-loathing is brought forth in particular by the desire for a woman. These two lawyers as half-heroes do not simply wish to take possession as their predecessors and alter egos do, but they both express a distinct sense of their self as unworthy. Thus, the reader's ambivalent attitude towards them is inextricably linked to the ambiguous love plots that unite *A Tale of Two Cities* and *Our Mutual Friend* in similarity. I have argued that Carton cannot be successful in his profession if he is supposed to be a good character and therefore it is highly significant that the desire for Lucie Manette brings out his wish to be more successful: "Waste forces within him, and a desert all around, this man stood still on his way across a silent terrace, and saw for a moment, lying in the wilderness before him, a mirage of honourable ambition, self-denial, and perseverance" (*TTC*, bk. II, ch. 5, p. 106). This ending of the chapter that supposedly introduces "the jackal," is a confirmation of the suspicion about his love for Lucie that the text has introduced through Stryver. Again, less than subtly, Dickens tries to create sympathy for the man who could possibly be

---

220 Collins, "Two Novels," 347.
221 Kucich, "Purity of Violence," 124.
222 Daniel Stout, "Nothing Personal: The Decapitation of Character in *A Tale of Two Cities*," *Novel* 41.1 (2007): 29–52, 29.
223 Simon Petch, "The Business of the Barrister in *A Tale of Two Cities*," *Criticism* 44.1 (2002): 27–42, 31.
224 See Kucich, "Purity of Violence," 125.
225 Harvey, "Byronic Hero," 312.

saved by the love of a good woman, or so is the sexist assumption that fills the subtext here:

> Sadly, sadly, the sun rose; and it rose upon no sadder sight than the man of good abilities and good emotions, incapable of their directed exercise, incapable of his own help and his own happiness, sensible of the blight on him, and resigning himself to let it eat him away. (*TTC*, bk. II, ch. 5, p. 106)

The text foreshadows what Stryver will suggest for Sydney's salvation, which is a "good woman." Significantly, when he advises Carton to find himself a happy home as a solution for his 'wasted' life, the word he uses is "nurse" (*TTC*, bk. II, ch. 11, p. 163). The novel's direct and indirect suggestions that this unhappy bachelor simply needs a comfortable home, made comfortable by a woman who is half mother, half nurse, raises the expectation that Carton may be successful in his suit for Lucie. Otherwise, Dickens could well spare the highly uncomfortable scene that seems to be a narrative hybrid between a proposal and a suicide note.

It seems that Carton's love for Lucie has the potential to make him a better man, for this is the twist in the story and the somewhat artificial explanation for why one is supposed to support the hero's selfless death. In this sense, David Marcus has argued, "Carton's love for Lucie has aroused the sympathetic capacity within his nature, and by caring for another, he finally emerges from the self-imposed prison of indifference."[226] This is not an unreasonable assumption, for unrequited love in Dickens has made many a loveable character – with the exception of Pip, perhaps. Smike, Tom Pinch and Toots are wonderful in their hopeless love for women who are deemed by the text as too far above them and their love brings out selfless and devoted behaviour, especially towards the men who are worthy of becoming a partner. While Carton's attitude towards Darnay is a variant of this – he literally dies for him, after all – his relationship with Lucie is drastically different. The novel is so insistent on the tale that Carton suffers in silence that it is easy to overlook the fact that he does not. While his more pathetic predecessors never share their feelings, let alone dare express them to their object, Carton imposes his pain upon Lucie in a scene that anticipates the many conversations Eugene Wrayburn will have with Lizzie Hexam. Carton's declaration towards Lucie is deliberately paired with the "assertive, aggressive and vulgar Stryver,"[227] and therefore easily shines by comparison.

---

226 Marcus, "Carlylean Vision," 65.

227 Michal Peled Ginsburg, "Dickens and the Scene of Recognition," *Partial Answers* 3.2 (2005): 75–97, 93.

The respective chapter titles, the immediate succession of events and the explicit reference to Stryver's informing Carton that he will not marry Lucie, all place the two men's desires for the same woman in direct parallel, suggesting that where the one was refused to everyone's satisfaction, the other may be accepted.

Carton seeks out his potential nurse on a day "when the sight and scent of flowers in the City streets had some waifs of goodness in them for the worst, of health for the sickliest, and of youth for the oldest" (*TTC*, bk. II, ch. 13, p. 174). Carton hopes for such medicinal effect if he can make the flower, Lucie Manette, his own and this implicit announcement certainly garners the reader's support. It is not easy to see, therefore, that Carton embarks here on an endeavour not to charm, but to torture a woman. The scene that has all the conventional characteristics both within and beyond fiction of a proposal is in fact an imposition on the young woman's confidence that she finds unbearable. Carton burdens her with the idea that she could have saved his life, then asks her never to relieve herself by sharing this knowledge and leaves her in extreme distress. He forces her to listen, despite his frequent acknowledgement throughout the scene that this is painful to her, and then asks her to bury this source of pain within herself. This is coercion that is reminiscent of David's brutal demand of Agnes to love him and his other women in silence and this also evokes the image of Tulkinghorn, who drives Lady Dedlock to extreme distress, only to force her to bury these emotions within her.

Carton's abuse of Lucie Manette is just the same. It serves him to establish himself as a hero, whose self-sacrifice for her will move everyone to tears because of his self-tortured expressions of love and his proclaimed hopelessness, but the woman is here nothing more than a plot device. One need not always call such behaviour in fictional men metaphorical rape, but Carton's penetration of her confidence, which is completely and entirely unwelcome, and the use of such confession for the more pitiable image of a hero, is not far from it. This is even more obvious, when one recalls that Dickens's other unrequited lovers are never allowed to make such advances and declare their pain towards the woman who supposedly causes it. Carton is privileged, because this scene is crucial for the emotional impact of the ending Dickens has in mind, but one cannot help but notice that this wilful imposition of pain upon a woman is something we have seen in all of the lawyers. No matter how much Carton may pretend not to be a proper lawyer, through his use of the Stryver puppet, his behaviour towards the woman clearly suggests otherwise.

Carton is one of Dickens's most difficult creations, because he is not only merely a half-hero, but also a half-character in a sense. He serves too many aspects of the novel and the more he has to, the less he becomes a person. No matter how "disenchanted with life"[228] the text tries to make him out to be, his voluntary path to the guillotine is too much. Almost all readers and critics have found the *Tale*'s ending unconvincing at best. Most might agree with John Kucich's analysis of "Sydney Carton's Christ-like martyrdom" as "artificial, inadequate, and even embarrassing."[229] Even the reminder that Carton's last speech is nothing but a "theatrical curtain-line,"[230] because in the end he is only "a melodramatic scapegoat,"[231] helps very little, for the flattening of the character towards the end is inconsistent with the elaborate insight into his troubled soul for almost all of Book II. Albert Hutter's pithy diagnosis probably describes it best: "He suffers chronically from meaning too much in relation to too many other characters."[232] Carton has to do too many things at the same time: he has to be a troubled soul evoking sympathy; a man unlucky in love, who evokes pity; a plot device that provides a resolution and a figure that moves to tears in the end. It is not surprising, therefore, that Dickens gives Carton the scene with the beloved woman that he denies to all other hopeless lovers.

However, when we look at Carton as a lawyer character, which he indubitably is, it is highly interesting that he is too good a person to be a good lawyer, but as a lawyer too bad a person not to torture the woman he wants. His indifference towards her distress, which he frequently notes during their conversation, but happily treats as inconsequential, is in keeping with his general display of indifference and makes the woman little more than an object that promises a better future. Although Carton claims to have no actual design, his confession as such is of course a veiled proposal. His motives are therefore not necessarily any better than those of Stryver, the 'man of delicacy.' Dickens puts a lot of effort into making them seem opposite, but it is too obvious that while Stryver may be looking for a wealthy doll, Carton too is only looking for a motherly nurse. His sacrifice in the end is of course supposed to say different, but it is too unconvincing to absolve Carton from the suspicion of coercion towards Lucie Manette. The text cannot help but betray the objectification of women that seems to be in the Dickensian lawyer's nature.

Carton is such a different lawyer in Dickens, only half a lawyer in fact, because he is a gentleman. I have argued above that the text's repeated emphasis of his idleness is first and foremost a marker of class. Carton is not a successful

---

228 Harvey, "Byronic Hero," 310.
229 Kucich, "Purity of Violence," 119.
230 Collins, "Two Novels," 347.
231 Hutter, "Nation and Generation," 456.
232 Hutter, "Nation and Generation," 456.

lawyer, because essentially, it does not befit his station in life. Only a couple of years later, Dickens creates the exact same conundrum in another lawyer, whose status as a gentleman and his conscience as a human being, make him unfit for the profession. The common mark of successful lawyers such as Jaggers and Stryver seems to be, after all, that they do not have a conscience or at least do not act in accordance with it. As liars and fabricators, they demonstrate what the legal profession allows in terms of unethical license. This marks them ostentatiously as ungentlemanly both in social station and moral conduct. Carton is both a gentleman by birth and by conduct – or at least, it is his ambition to be such. The same is true for Eugene Wrayburn, who is another of Dickens's dandyesque creatures.

Sydney Carton and Eugene Wrayburn are both emblems of what happens to the character, when Dickens wants his lawyer to be a hero – or his hero to be a lawyer. The two notions conflict because of the arbitrary social status of the lawyer, so both protagonists need to prove that they are above that. In Eugene Wrayburn, such demonstration is almost obnoxious. The parallels between Carton and Wrayburn are obvious, but *Our Mutual Friend* is much more explicit about the lawyer's twisted desires. Eugene Wrayburn is the epitome of all of Dickens's conflicted lawyers and for the first time, the lawyer's sadistic desire towards women need not be wrought out of the subtext. In Eugene, Dickens tells the story of all of his lawyers as openly as possible. We have seen that the two crucial characteristics of the lawyer are his relationship to his profession and his relationship with women – Eugene Wrayburn is the one lawyer in Dickens who addresses both these characteristics with an almost unnatural degree of self-awareness. He is also the only one who can be duly considered a hero in novelistic terms – even more so than Sydney Carton. *Our Mutual Friend* invites a reading of John Harmon as protagonist,[233] but Eugene Wrayburn clearly runs a very close second and is just as frequently considered to be the actual hero of the novel as his interior seems to be developed with much greater care than Harmon's.[234] At the same time, he is also irritating as a potential protagonist, because his ostentatious passivity somewhat conflicts with the idea of the hero.[235] The novel is almost too explicit about the fact that Eugene is a peripheral observer,

233 See Catherine Gallagher, *The Body Economic: Life, Death, and Sensation in Political Economy and the Victorian Novel*. Princeton, N.J.: Princeton University Press; 2006: 83ff.
234 See Robert Baker, "Imagination and Literacy in Dickens' *Our Mutual Friend*," *Criticism* 18.1 (1976): 57–72.
235 See Michal Peled Ginsburg, "The Case Against Plot in *Bleak House* and *Our Mutual Friend*," *ELH* 59.1 (1992): 175–195, 187.

languid thinker and obviously a representative of the "Carlylean Dilettante."[236] As Sally Ledger has argued, Eugene seems almost completely "ill-adapted to the struggle for survival in modern London, lacking the force and energy associated with normative middle-class masculinity that is needed there."[237] Eugene is portrayed as indifferent to the point of obnoxiousness, demonstrating himself as not belonging to his social class and frequently voicing disgust for his peers. He "disagrees intensely with the shams of his class,"[238] he is a "prisoner of wealth";[239] he "has something in him of both Arthur Clennam and Henry Gowan";[240] he is "[p]assive and indifferent to the point of ineffectuality";[241] and he has "something of the glamour of the exceptional man, blessed with idleness, and with an aristocratic grace of ease . . ."[242]

Considering what Dickens plans to do with Eugene in the long run, the character's ostentatious display of privileged indifference does not only seem to serve an overt criticism of upper-class mentality, but also foreshadows the class-divide that prevents the love story. Thus, there might even be a degree of justice in his death by the hands of the earnest schoolmaster. However, Dickens's overall design need not divert attention from the fact that Eugene is a lawyer and as the dual conception of Stryver and Carton has shown, ambition in the law is detestable in Dickens's novels. Thus, both Eugene Wrayburn and his own Double, Mortimer Lightwood, also a lawyer, of course, openly emphasise their disgust for their own profession. They are the only lawyers in Dickens, who are not only aware of the prejudice that taints their profession, thereby echoing Uriah Heep, but also openly declare that while it is their profession, they still want no part in it. On the one hand, Eugene's refusal to be a lawyer in any way but in name is part of the humour the character creates as a comic dandy: "I protest against the tyrannical humbug of your friend the bee" (*OMF*, bk. I, ch. 8, p. 94). He refuses the Victorian moral discourse of earnestness David is so fond of to the extent that

236 Barry V. Qualls, "Savages in a 'Bran-New' World: Carlyle and *Our Mutual Friend*," *Studies in the Novel* 10.2 (1978): 199–217, 209.
237 Sally Ledger, "Dickens, Natural History, and *Our Mutual Friend*," *Partial Answers* 9.2 (2011): 363–378, 371.
238 Keith Easley, "Caught in Time: Performance and Spectatorship in *Our Mutual Friend*," *Dickens Studies Annual* 50.2 (2019): 295–362, 308.
239 Easley, "Caught in Time," 304.
240 Jennifer Gribble, "Depth and Surface in *Our Mutual Friend*," *Essays in Criticism* 25 (1975): 197–214, 198.
241 Anna Gibson, "*Our Mutual Friend* and Network Form," *Novel* 48.1 (2015): 63–84, 69.
242 Brian Cheadle, "Work in *Our Mutual Friend*," *Essays in Criticism* 51.3 (2001): 308–329, 324.

he sometimes even sounds like Skimpole.[243] In this vein it seems that Dickens once again employs the myth that the man without goal or orientation finds his purpose in life through the love of a good woman. The pursuit of Lizzie Hexam gives Eugene's life direction and even provides redemption, it seems. His path to righteousness is then the less dramatic version of Carton's, for although Dickens originally planned to kill him too,[244] Eugene's eventual survival leaves him "the bravest and most principled man in the book."[245] If this were true, Eugene Wrayburn would be a very unusual lawyer indeed.

In *Our Mutual Friend*, the law profession is a waiting game, a fiction within fiction. Mortimer Lightwood complains that he has been a solicitor for five years without any business; Eugene Wrayburn tells us that it has been seven years since he was called to the Bar and he has had no business; even Mortimer's clerk is allowed to mention that he has been in the profession for three years and if he did not keep a fictional appointment book, "his mind would have been shattered to pieces without this fiction of an occupation" (*OMF*, bk. I, ch. 8, p. 87). Nothing happens in the law in *Our Mutual Friend*, but this is a different nothing from the absurd standstill of things in *Bleak House*, because here, the lack of occupation is clearly ascribed to the lawyers' own responsibility. They do not strive to make business for themselves, which, as independent lawyers they would have to do as much as Stryver or Jaggers; they refuse to follow the prejudice so often evoked in *Bleak House* that the law makes business for itself. It seems that their central position in the novel, which makes them share the role of hero as two versions of the same character, requires that one cannot mistake them for successful lawyers or even ambitious lawyers. In order to come off as what could be considered the novel's hero, Eugene openly has to declare "I hate my profession" upon his first appearance. Similarly, Mortimer Lightwood has to respond with "I hate mine" (*OMF*, bk. I, ch. 3, p. 19/20). Both lawyers expressly do not identify with their profession, which proves a precondition for their goodness as characters. This is not to say that they are incompetent: like Sydney Carton, they both have the intellectual competence to deal very precisely with legal matters, as their treatment of Rogue Riderhood or their role in the Harmon plot effortlessly proves. They are both highly intelligent men, who could easily apply themselves in their profession, "if only they could

243 See Dominic Rainsford, "*Our Mutual Friend* and Victorian Moral Philosophy," *Dickens Quarterly* 27.4 (2010): 273–291, 279.

244 See Bodenheimer, *Knowing Dickens*, 120ff.

245 Peter Smith, "The Aestheticist Argument of *Our Mutual Friend*," *The Cambridge Quarterly* 18.4 (1989): 363–382, 380.

see the point."[246] It is a vital part of their construction as characters that they do not see the point. They are the first characters in Dickens who are *in* the law and complain *about* the law since Micawber and the reason for this is clearly shown in the fact that they have a conscience – or, to be more precise, one of them has a conscience that proves strong enough for both.

The two lawyers are set up as Doubles, who are united in their professed disgust for what they do. Eugene's upper-class idleness is only a marker of his superior social station, which prevents a bourgeois professionalism. He is given "Sydney Carton's indifference"[247] for the same reasons inherent in his association with a non-professional class, but this also evokes a certain unscrupulousness Dickens usually attests to such ranks in society and Eugene proves a case in point. His indifference is not only laudable indifference towards the law, but also conditions his reckless behaviour towards others that makes him a more ambivalent figure than a simple hero. His position as both hero and lawyer suggests a parallel to the popular lawyer figure in Victorian sensation fiction, but he must be considered a kind of "dark version" of the character: "Eugene represents an ambivalent and amoral figure to whom knowledge comes belatedly and unconvincingly."[248] His indifference and lack of purpose aside, which is hardly treated as a real character flaw considering the dubious nature of his profession, Eugene's most obvious aspect of duplicity shows in his treatment of Bradley Headstone, which is the more acceptable version of what he does to Lizzie. In his prolonged torture of the obsessed schoolmaster, Eugene becomes "darkly confused with criminality,"[249] but also shows his propensity for "sadistic amusement."[250]

Eugene's treatment of Bradley Headstone clearly shows that his indifference towards his surroundings is merely feigned and that when he is presented with the opportunity to exercise power over others, he does so with a master's pleasure. It does not make him less of an ambivalent figure that the emphasis is placed on the fact that Eugene is far superior to Headstone in society's ranking and that he bears himself towards the schoolmaster with all the arrogance his class allows him. It is indicative that Eugene refuses to learn the latter's name,

---

246 Rainsford, "Moral Philosophy," 278.

247 Rosemarie Bodenheimer, "Dickens and the Identical Man: *Our Mutual Friend* Doubled," *Dickens Studies Annual* 31 (2002): 159–174, 169.

248 Lisa Surridge, "'John Rokesmith's Secret': Sensation, Detection, and the Policing of the Feminine in *Our Mutual Friend*," *Dickens Studies Annual* 26 (1998): 265–284, 267/268.

249 Surridge, "Policing of the Feminine," 268.

250 John Kucich, "Dickens' Fantastic Rhetoric: The Semantics of Reality and Unreality in *Our Mutual Friend*," *Dickens Studies Annual* 14 (1985): 167–189, 178.

which is a display of power and discrimination he later shows in his antisemitic behaviour towards Riah, whom he renames Aaron in a discriminating christening and an uncanny allusion to the appropriation of a slave: "[I]t comes into my mind that – no doubt with an instinctive desire to receive him into the bosom of our church – I gave him the name of Aaron!'" (*OMF*, bk. III, ch. 10, p. 535). Both instances seem to echo Eugene's obnoxiously reiterated indifference towards anyone or anything, but they reveal that Eugene finds motivation, when he can cause pain to others. It seems like "decadent energy gone awry," in Ray Sherer's words, who argues that in the relationship between Bradley and Eugene, Dickens "contrasts love and destructiveness . . ."[251] As it turns out, however, Eugene cannot distinguish between the two, for in his interest in Lizzie both his 'love' for her and a desire to destroy her are inextricably intertwined.

Eugene's professed dislike for his own class easily diverts the reader from the fact that he nevertheless enjoys exercising his class privilege over others. It also serves him as a welcome stratagem in his attempt to capture Lizzie, for it is as the wealthy gentleman that he can set himself up in a twisted version of *Pygmalion* and provide her with education. His spurning of Lady Tippins and his other peers suggests that he is embarrassed to belong to their society, but when he acts outside of this society – in conduct with Lizzie Hexam, Jenny Wren, Bradley Headstone and Mr Riah – he is more than happy to imitate their privileged condescension; in this sense, he is a closer replica of Steerforth than Uriah Heep. He may look down on his own class, but this does not entail that he is any more sympathetic to those beneath him. The game he plays with Bradley Headstone is an unabashed exercise in humiliation of such groups. On the surface, one may understand Eugene's sudden ambition to taunt the schoolmaster merely as sexual jealousy, which is how his Double, Mortimer, reads the situation: "with a feeling of astonishment that so careless a man could be so wary, and that so idle man could take so much trouble" (*OMF*, bk. III, ch. 11, p. 544). Mortimer's observation means to suggest that Eugene has finally found a purpose in life in his love for Lizzie and that his treatment of Bradley Headstone merely serves to present himself as the superior mate for her, but the rivalry between the two goes far beyond sexual jealousy. There is a sadism at play here, which foreshadows Eugene's behaviour towards Lizzie as only that of a predator, never of lover. Even if we do not queer this hero's conduct as both Eve Kosofsky Sedgwick and Holly Furneaux have done in their wonderful readings of the novel, it is simply astounding how little Dickens tries to veil his

251 Ray J. Sherer, "Laughter in *Our Mutual Friend*," *Texas Studies in Literature and Language* 13.3 (1971): 509–521, 519.

protagonist's abusive behaviour towards others. His pleasure in the treatment of Headstone might still be classed as a point of the survival of the fittest that a text in the 1860s may condone, even though it has sexual undertones between males, but the unashamed echo in what Eugene does to Lizzie is a cruel reflection on what Sydney Carton does to Lucie Manette.

Both Mortimer and Eugene are lawyers without clients, so Eugene finds objects outside of the law to objectify. As if the lawyer's propensity to dominate others had to find an outlet elsewhere, he executes his power over all subjects he comes in contact with whether he maintains a romantic, a rivalrous or simply a disdainful attitude towards them. It is easy to underestimate the fact that Dickens made Eugene a lawyer, as it seems to have so little relevance for the plot. After all, in *Our Mutual Friend* the legal system is virtually invisible. Mortimer Lightwood describes the case of the missing John Harmon as his only case in five years; Eugene never even acts as the barrister he is. The only legal dealings the reader may witness are those revolving around Rogue Riderhood and they are mostly geared towards the question of Gaffer Hexam's guilt. Hence, for the story he means to tell, Dickens had absolutely no apparent need to make Eugene a lawyer – anything but, it seems. This is also visible in the character's relation to his predecessors such as Henry Gowan or even Skimpole, the indifferent dandies. Steerforth even openly frowns on the profession and so does Eugene – nevertheless, he is a lawyer character. The only value his profession has for him, however, seems to be that it puts him in the position to exercise power over others and it opens the door for his abuse of Lizzie Hexam. His profession becomes a tool for him that he uses to achieve his designs outside of the law. In this sense, he differs remarkably from the corrupt lawyer figure such as Vholes or Jaggers, for Eugene does not seek his profit within the law – he is too much of a gentleman for that. Instead, the only use that the reader can see him make of his profession is for the achievement of his highly personal desires.

The story of Eugene's pursuit of Lizzie, indigestible as it is, could be told with the use of any idle upper-class gentleman, but Dickens returns to the lawyer, despite the fact that he has a figure of higher social station in mind, as the novel makes clear enough. In order to make Eugene Wrayburn what he is, Dickens thus reverts to both class privilege and the sadism that seems to come with the profession. Eugene seeks domination over a woman so blatantly that what is supposed to be a love story is hard to stomach. It is hardly any wonder that no critic accepts the superficial myth that his 'love' for Lizzie gives his life purpose. As Jennifer Gribble points out, "Dickens cannot embody in Lizzie Hexam a sufficiently convincing source of Eugene Wrayburn's change of heart (hence the retreat to the simplest operation of the novel's symbolism which confers on him a watery regeneration)."[252] The fault lies not in the construction of Lizzie: it is simply implausible that "her love [. . .] can redeem Eugene Wrayburn from the monotony and aimlessness of his life."[253] It is no wonder therefore that Dickens originally planned to kill Eugene through the hands of Bradley Headstone, which would have been a more likely outcome. As it is, Eugene's redemption is about as likely as Sydney Carton's self-sacrifice.

While the plot of the questionable man's salvation at the hands of a 'good woman' is conventional enough to suggest to the reader that this is what happens in *Our Mutual Friend*, the novel is not shy about its perversion of the story. Eugene's abusive nature is right there at the surface of the text for the reader to pick up on. His conduct towards her is never not tainted by coercion, which is obvious from the first encounter, when he forces her to leave her own house, because she feels violated by his gaze: "'One of the gentlemen, the one who didn't speak while I was there, looked hard at me'" (*OMF*, bk. I, ch. 3, p. 27). Eugene's forceful observation of Lizzie, a trait he has inherited from Tulkinghorn's unperturbed gaze at Lady Dedlock, constitutes a foreshadowing of his violent conduct towards her and is repeated when he looks in on her as she grieves in the privacy of her home:

> He could see the light of the fire shining through the window. Perhaps it drew him on to look in. Perhaps he had come out with the express intention. [. . .] It was a little window of but four pieces of glass, and was not curtained; he chose it because the large window near it was. [. . .] [He] looked long and steadily at her. A deep rich piece of colour, with the brown flush of her cheek and the shining lustre of her hair, though sad and solitary, weeping by the rising and the falling of the fire. (*OMF*, bk. I, ch. 13, p. 164)

The rising and the falling of the fire also suggest the rising and the falling of her bosom, of course, and like all other lawyers before him, Eugene shows that he knows how to violate the domestic sphere that is supposed to be the female shelter. His observation is violently intrusive and demeaning as he thinks of her as a "piece" that is the object of his desire. It is crucial that his first transgression towards her happens while she is in her own home, for the uncanniest talent of the lawyer in Dickens is that they invade all spaces. Like Uriah Heep and Mr Tulkinghorn, Eugene keeps to the shadows, trying to see without being seen, thereby putting himself in a position of power over his object:

---

252 Gribble, "Depth and Surface," 197.

253 William J. Palmer, "The Movement of History in *Our Mutual Friend*," *PMLA* 89.3 (1974): 487–495, 490.

> His incipient will to possess, licensed by class and gender privilege, is strongly present both in the connoisseur's commodification of Lizzie as 'a deep rich piece', and in the way he brushes aside her right to her own feelings in the dismissive 'though sad and solitary'.[254]

Brian Cheadle has argued that "what makes the presentation of Eugene disconcerting [. . .] is the radical depth of his self-division."[255] Eugene's abuse of Lizzie Hexam is not only imminent from their first introduction, but he is also too highly aware of his misconduct not to be condemned for it. As Cathy Shuman points out, we are supposed to disapprove of Eugene,[256] almost as much as he disapproves of himself. The guilt he presumably feels for his behaviour towards the woman is comically expressed in his likening him and Mortimer to criminals and the pattern of his sentencing them to different kinds of future penance during their 'detective' work. Yet, these expressions of guilt or shame are also clearly hypocritical and used for Mortimer's frequent expressions of enjoyment at the lack of Eugene's earnestness. In fact, as long as Mortimer sees humour in Eugene's ways, the novel encourages the reader to do so too. The alliance between the two men therefore makes light of what Lizzie has to endure as the object of Eugene's designs.

In his perverted version of Pygmalion, Eugene uses his offer of education as a means to manipulate Lizzie emotionally and force her into feeling grateful enough to be able to reciprocate his advances. He implicates Jenny Wren in his offer in order to put further pressure on Lizzie, well aware of the fact that she will not deprive her friend of such a chance. He sees that she considers herself in his debt already for he has acted in defence of her dead father and he ruthlessly exploits her sense of obligation:

> I happen to be able to promise you that a watch shall be kept upon that false accuser, Riderhood. I happen to be able to give you some little consolation in the darkest hour of your distress, by assuring you that I don't believe him. On the same occasion I tell you that I am the idlest and least of lawyers, but that I am better than none, in a case I have noted down with my own hand, and that you may be always sure of my best help, and incidentally of Lightwood's too, in your effort to clear your father.
>
> (*OMF*, bk. II, ch. 2, p. 237)

It is no coincidence that Eugene speaks in full self-identification as a lawyer – the profession he otherwise despises puts him in the perfect position to torture

254 Brian Cheadle, "Improvising Character in *Our Mutual Friend*," *Essays in Criticism* 59.3 (2009): 211–233, 227.

255 Cheadle, "Improvising Character," 226.

256 See Cathy Shuman, "Invigilating *Our Mutual Friend* – Gender and the Legitimation of Professional Authority," *Novel* 28.2 (1995): 154–172, 158.

the woman. His speech is an echo of Tulkinghorn's insistence on what he is presumably professionally obliged to do, which is a fabrication to keep Lady Dedlock in his power longer. Eugene uses the same lie, feigning professional power, in order to force Lizzie into submission. His argument shows his inadvertent legal competence: it is skilful, concise, convincing and disgusting and the text makes no effort to hide the fact – on the contrary: "If he meant to follow home what was in Lizzie's thoughts, it was skilfully done. If he followed it by mere fortuitous coincidence, it was done by an evil chance" (*OMF*, bk. II, ch. 2, p. 237).

The openly exercised manipulation of the woman, or girl even, is truly disturbing and while completely in keeping with the behaviour of lawyers in Dickens otherwise, it is fully at odds with Eugene's social status as a gentleman. It is as if Dickens has turned the lawyer figure as embodied by Tulkinghorn completely on its head: the sadist of *Bleak House* never flaunts his pleasure, yet is mostly presented as unlikeable. The sadist of *Our Mutual Friend* is openly exposed as such, yet maintains a position as charmer in the text. The more the reader sees of Eugene's conduct, the more explicit the text becomes about his immoral, even unlawful, strategies. As he still contemplates how to satisfy his desire for Lizzie, his discussion with Jenny Wren about his wish to "set up a doll," is an ostentatious reference to prostitution. Lizzie has just agreed to accept his offer to educate her, so strictly speaking, he has already laid the groundwork for exploiting her for the gratitude he has imposed upon her. As he now suggests in her presence, "I think of setting up a doll, Miss Jenny," the implication that Lizzie is that doll is painful to her, to the reader, and obviously to Jenny Wren, who sharply tells him not to: "You are sure to break it" (*OMF*, bk. II, ch. 2, p. 238). As Stephen James points out, "this moment [. . .] is hard to reconcile with Eugene's repeated emphasis that he has no clear intentions regarding Lizzie."[257] In keeping with his silent observation of the "piece" he has seen through the window, Eugene is clearly incapable of thinking of Lizzie as anything other than an object he may or may not acquire as he pleases: "Eugene's condescending use of the doll image fetishises Lizzie as a commodity to be bought or passively 'set up', reducing her to a plaything, discardable when broken and outgrown."[258]

There can be no doubt about Eugene's intentions. Whether or not he repeatedly claims to have no design on her, the text says different and it does so right at the surface. So, when the subject of the doll Eugene wishes to possess comes up again between him and Jenny Wren, triggered by his sexual frustration because

257 Stephen James, "Repetition, Rumination, Superstition: The Rituals of *Our Mutual Friend*," *English* 61.234 (2012): 214–233, 220.
258 Cheadle, "Improvising Character," 223.

Lizzie has fled and he cannot find and possess her, the subject of prostitution is again painfully obvious. Eugene's question "I cannot persuade you to dress me a doll?" is an insufficiently coded way of asking whether she will reveal Lizzie's hiding place; her reply "if you want one, go and buy one at the shop," is an accurate suggestion for the sexually frustrated Victorian gentleman. As Brian Cheadle points out, her "snappish retort [. . .] comes as close as the Victorian novel will allow to implying that if Eugene wants no more than a well-dressed skirt he should pay for a girl in a brothel."[259] It is astounding with what little effort Dickens tries to hide the fact that his hero's intentions towards the woman are completely dishonourable. His behaviour towards her is reminiscent of Jaggers's possession of Molly, who is not an unrelated female predecessor, due to her criminal association. While perfectly innocent and virtuous herself, Lizzie is nevertheless tainted by her father's questionable occupation and her lack of education marks her as easily pushed across the demarcation towards prostitution.

The novel's physical description of Lizzie Hexam is remarkably similar to that of Alice Marwood and her easy relocation to another village alludes to a stereotypical gipsy image. Her uneasy position in society is one of the central aspects of the novel's plot, for it allows Dickens to make her the target for many different transgressions, culminating in Eugene's attempted rape. As Sally Ledger has pointed out, "Lizzie's inferior class position leaves her particularly vulnerable to the sexual advances of a social superior."[260] She is trapped at the intersection of class and gender, hopelessly exposed to the novel's various predators and like Lady Dedlock, she has to flee her own home even *before* she becomes a fallen woman. The danger she is in is symbolically emphasised in the novel through her association with the river: "The novel is haunted by the possibility that Lizzie, the girl of the river, could end up dead in the river like so many of London's so-called 'fallen women' in the nineteenth century."[261] Her retreat to the country, officially a strategy to save her from losing her virtue, is also an implicit admission of the fact that she is already too close to falling victim to Eugene's unscrupulous manoeuvres. Thus, her attempt to escape into anonymity provides her no rescue, for Eugene would not be a proper lawyer, if he were unable to find her. His use of the drunken Mr Dolls to sniff out Lizzie's whereabouts even Mortimer notes as ungentlemanly behaviour: "'Eugene, Eugene, [. . .] can you stoop to the use of such an instrument as this?'" (*OMF*, bk. III, ch. 10, p. 539)

259 Cheadle, "Improvising Character," 223.
260 Ledger, "Natural History," 371.
261 Ledger, "Natural History," 371.

The crucial characteristic of this lawyer, as Dickens has conceived of him, is that he will stoop to anything in his ruthless pursuit of the woman. While he "shows a sensitivity and moral consciousness that sets him apart from the other members"[262] of his own class when in their circle, he unashamedly exercises his class privilege in the attempt to possess the working-class girl. In a perverted pastoral setting, Eugene has not persuaded Lizzie to come with him and be his love, but has followed her into the green world to violate her there, unseen by the society that deems him to be of superior moral conduct. He hides from the eyes of such society with whose evaluation of the union he implicitly concurs: "Passively embedded in 'Society,' Eugene can only think of Lizzie in exploitative terms; he wishes to possess her as an object, but he is unable to act against a social system that would not facilitate his union with the penniless daughter of a river dredger."[263] While the novel condones his indifference towards the suffering of Bradley Headstone, who disqualifies himself through his resort to violence against himself and others conditioned by the fact that he is presumably supposed to be a villain,[264] Eugene's careless treatment of Lizzie is also a variant of his treatment of the schoolmaster.

The text does not even attempt to hide the fact that Eugene enjoys Lizzie's pain when he has finally found her and seeks to force her into submission – still exploiting the gratitude he imposes upon her, but also not shying away from physical force. Her desperate entreaty that he not touch her, he counters with his manipulative spell "don't be unhappy, don't be reproachful," and ignores forthwith (*OMF*, bk. IV, ch. 6, p. 691). Reverting to a common cliché, he excuses his physical and emotional transgression by accusing her of provoking him:

> You don't know what my state of mind towards you is. You don't know how you haunt and bewilder me. You don't know how the cursed carelessness that is over-officious in helping me at every other turning in my life, won't help me here. You have struck it dead, I think, and I sometimes wish you had struck me dead along with it.
>
> (*OMF*, bk. IV, ch. 6, p. 691)

The lawyer's argument is ancient: because she has bewitched him, he has lost his senses and is not liable for what he will do to her. If she does not release him, which she is of course unable to do, he will have to do what he wants to do and she can only blame herself. Eugene's speech is without a doubt and clear as day a recant of the rapist's rationale even in Victorian terms. Thus, it seems certainly questionable that Dickens suggests, the argument may carry

262 Palmer, "Movement of History," 492.
263 Anna Gibson, "*Our Mutual Friend* and Network Form," *Novel* 48.1 (2015): 63–84, 76/77.
264 See Ginsburg, "Case Against Plot," 187.

some conviction: "She had not been prepared for such passionate expressions, and they awakened some natural sparks of feminine pride and joy in her breast. To consider, wrong as he was, that he could care so much for her, and that she had the power to move him so!" (*OMF*, bk. IV, ch. 6, p. 691) Sexist Dickens, who has been both blamed and excused almost equally often, whose treatment of men and women has been discussed so often and with such wonderful insights, nevertheless hits rock-bottom here. His suggestion of her vanity, his suggestion that she cannot help but feel flattered as a victim, is cynical at best. The indirect discourse that reflects the word 'power' in this context may be seen as evidence that this is indeed outward cynicism. Lizzie is completely at the mercy of Eugene at this moment and there is no reader then or now who would not know this.

The doll discourse has prepared the reader to sense the implicit sexual threat and Jenny Wren contributes several remarks that point out the danger Lizzie is in. The text lets her recognise instantly both Eugene's and Headstone's sexual motives and instils in her the moral voice that is supposed to call them to reason and warn Lizzie at the same time: "Jenny tries to warn Lizzie about the appetites men have for women and their need to objectify, control, or commodify them,"[265] and the climax of the topic between Eugene and Lizzie by the river is presented as a logical consequence of the predator's successful hunt. Yet, the text makes light of her distress and sides with Eugene. Although Lizzie is in considerable pain, as much as Lucie Manette during Sydney Carton's confession, in fact, Eugene is allowed to maintain his light-hearted indifference and unscrupulousness. Although the situation clearly presents a relation that relies "on coercion rather than consent, self-interest rather than mutuality,"[266] Eugene's method may prevail. Although the damsel in distress conventionally requires saving, the lawyer unmercifully exploits her dilemma and forces her to admit that she would reciprocate: "There was something in the attitude of her whole figure as he supported it, and she hung her head, which besought him to be merciful and not force her to disclose her heart. He was not merciful with her, and he made her do it" (*OMF*, bk. IV, ch. 6, p. 695). If the discourse on purchasable dolls is as close as the Victorian novel will come to discussing prostitution, this is as close as Dickens will come to openly referring to rape *through a protagonist*. As Brian Cheadle has pointed out, the "cruelly callous fatalism

265 Precious McKenzie Stearns, "'Sex and the City': Charles Dickens's Working Women in *Martin Chuzzlewit* and *Our Mutual Friend*," *English* 61.233 (2012): 137–150, 146.
266 Michael D. Lewis, "The Challenge of Female Homoeroticism in *Our Mutual Friend*," *Dickens Studies Annual* 48 (2017): 207–229, 217.

with which Eugene forces Lizzie to declare her liking for him discomfortingly prefigures a further forcing . . ."[267] If one feels inclined to consider Sydney Carton's confession to Lucie Manette as a metaphorical rape suggested by her utter distress, one has to note that this scene in *Our Mutual Friend* has nothing of metaphor about it. Dickens is as clear as he can be that Eugene's taking physical possession of Lizzie Hexam is only a matter of time. It adds to the reader's discomfort that the lawyer never retreats from his violent endeavour: before he can think better of it or suggest that once again, he is in jest, he is clubbed almost to death and his otherwise impossible redemption is left to higher forces. Thus, Eugene "changes his ways not because of her virtuous pleading but because of Bradley's more masculine chastisement."[268] Eugene's rapist adventure is prevented not because he reforms himself, but because he is brought to justice by the power of man. It certainly leaves no less a sour aftertaste that this force of correction is the last consequential deed of Bradley Headstone, who is for all intents and purposes surely a villain too.

It cannot come as a surprise to anyone who has had an eye on Dickens's construction of the lawyer that Eugene is presented as almost oblivious to how shameful his behaviour is. Moved to tears himself, he dismisses his own emotions with the pleasure of victory: "'I have gained a wonderful power over her, too, let her be as much in earnest as she will!'" (*OMF*, bk. IV, ch. 2, p. 696) Dickens lets Eugene Wrayburn say those things his other lawyers merely imply. Their interest lies in gaining power over a woman and in this late novel the lawyer gains it, enjoys it and boasts of it. Lizzie is an object of desire that Eugene uses to enhance his own self-worth, thereby putting her through pain and coercion, threatening to ruin her in the eyes of society. Once again, the dynamic Dickens imagines between the lawyer and the woman is one of implicit blackmail, for Eugene's pursuit of Lizzie clearly puts her in the same dilemma as Lady Dedlock. She cannot notify others to his advances without implicating herself and thereby ruining her reputation. Eugene admits as much himself when he insists that Bradley not be persecuted for attempted murder, for the story would cast the same shadow on Lizzie's reputation. At the same time, the young woman, who is entirely unprotected, is not in the position to fend him off, as he clearly demands the reciprocation of his feelings without suggesting that he will acknowledge them publicly. The dilemma Lizzie Hexam finds herself in, similar to the female character far above her station, Lady Dedlock, pinpoints the coercive dynamics of sexual harassment and Dickens seems at no pains to conceal his protagonist's intentions.

267 Cheadle, "Improvising Character," 227.
268 Shuman, "Invigilating *Our Mutual Friend*," 160.

In many ways, in this late novel he tells the story of Steerforth and Little Em'ly that he would not tell ten years earlier. Apart from the fact that David Copperfield places a great deal of the blame on Little Em'ly herself very early on in the novel by suggesting that her desire to be a lady is the path towards ill repute, the sexual advances of the idle upper-class gentleman towards the more or less innocent country girl that may or may not end up in the river are two versions of the same story. It is only now that Dickens goes into detail, choosing the sordid interest in a tale of attempted sexual 'seduction' over the delicacy of earlier novels.

Eugene ruthlessly exploits the fact that Lizzie Hexam is without protection in order to please his vanity. Considering the fact that he is saved by her, transformed through his near-death experience and seems reformed in the end, it is easy to buy into the story of love as redemption. This is particularly tempting in the case of a protagonist one cannot imagine as being truly placed on the bad side. It is, however, worth remembering that in his last novel, Dickens would do exactly that: place a more than morally duplicitous character centre-stage and Eugene's inner struggle before he is saved by the novelist is extremely suggestive of his villainous nature. His inner monologue, which is the more significant for the fact that it is the last of his musings before his artificial death, reveals unashamedly that his only motive is vanity. His is "the terrible nature of a sexual will-to-power backed by privilege"[269] and his concerns are solely with himself. In fact, he prides himself on not having 'seduced' her, fabricating this self-constraint as an outward sign of true feeling:

> 'I should like to see the fellow (Mortimer excepted) who would undertake to tell me that this was not a real sentiment on my part, won out of me by her beauty and her worth, in spite of myself, and that I would not be true to her. I should particularly like to the see the fellow to-night who would tell me so, or who would tell me anything that could be construed to her disadvantage . . .' (*OMF*, bk. IV, ch. 2, p. 697)

'That could be construed to her disadvantage' is his self-righteous praise of the fact that he has managed to let her go and has not 'seduced' her, which indicates how low the threshold of expectation here is of himself as suggested by the inner monologue, Dickens's own expectations and, backed by cliché, also the contemporary reader's. Eugene has stopped short of exercising the power he has over Lizzie through gender, class and society; he has for the moment refrained from ruining her for his own pleasure and consoles himself with the fact that this does not mean that he has lost his power over her. The clarity with which Dickens lets this lawyer engage in his sadistic fantasies is astounding. The speech is slightly

269 Cheadle, "Work," 325.

misleading, however, because it suggests that Eugene prides himself on the earnestness of his feelings, while, in fact, the opposite is true. After all, he clearly states that Mortimer would *not* buy into the idea that his sexual restraint here is proof of genuine feelings: "Mortimer excepted," he says. This parenthesis has a prophetic significance and suggests that truly the only thing that can reform Eugene Wrayburn is his consequent suffering and metaphorical death.

Mortimer Lightwood is the other half of this character and he is the half that is endowed with a conscience. The text suggests throughout that the other lawyer is an embodiment of conscience that the character of Eugene simply lacks. Only the two lawyers as a pair make a full character, which is why they are so inseparable. Since Eugene is a protagonist, he has to show a sense of moral obligation sooner or later, but this is almost fully displaced onto Mortimer. As Phoebe Poon has argued, "[t]he voice of his friend and partner in the legal profession [. . .] functions as a kind of external conscience for Eugene."[270] Mortimer Lightwood's existence in the novel is a necessary condition for Eugene's redemption, for the two can only prove worthy in combination. They are two halves of one character. While Eugene shows all the bad traits that are supposed to condition his death at the hands of Bradley Headstone, Mortimer has no psychological traits beyond conscience and therefore provides the morality to balance the other lawyer out. Except for his love of Eugene, which only receives an elaborate image after the latter is supposed to have died already, Mortimer has no interior and constitutes no proper character. He is solely an embodiment of Eugene Wrayburn's Superego.

The construction of the two lawyers is interesting in terms of its duplicity, for Mortimer is an unusual Double. Like many other Victorian novelists, Dickens tends to use the Double to displace the Id unto them, not the Superego. One might think that the Superego is strong enough in the Victorian stories Dickens tells to the middle class, so as readers, we may be more used to the appearance of bad angels. The fact that Vholes acts out Esther Summerson's desires is less surprising than the fact that Mortimer steers against Eugene's. It seems that for the lawyer as protagonist, Dickens needs two in order to balance out the sadistic tendencies he associates with the character. Mortimer Lightwood therefore is an absolute blank, has no desire, no motives and no relationships of his own. He is the good angel on Eugene's shoulder, sometimes echoing Betsey Trotwood's 'blind, blind, blind' for us. He is a personified ritual of morality, testing Eugene for his designs every step of the way and finally acting for him. From the beginning, Mortimer Lightwood is nothing more than a *porte-parole*, who

---

270 Poon, "Trust and Conscience," 18.

delivers the necessary information about the antecedents of the Harmon-plot. His role in the investigation meekly resembles Bucket's, but Mortimer has much less charisma than Dickens's detective figure. Outside his minor role in the novel's main story, Mortimer has only two functions: he increases the comic effect of Eugene and he is the lawyer's voice of conscience. Mortimer is only half a character, but in his function for Eugene, he constitutes his full conscience. At all crucial moments of development, Mortimer asks the necessary questions and confronts Eugene with the fact that he is heading in the morally wrong direction.

Like Agnes, Mortimer is the protagonist's good angel, but in keeping with the idea of male solidarity, Mortimer never stops Eugene – in fact, he merely points out the obvious, which is more often than not a device to lead the reader further into Eugene's initially thinly veiled designs on Lizzie: his charge, "you are withholding something from me," (*OMF*, bk. II, ch. 6, p. 285) functions as an introduction for the entry of Charley Hexam and Bradley Headstone and it alerts the reader to the fact that the plot of Eugene and Lizzie continues in the novel's subtext. The reader is often not privy to crucial moments of their story, such as Eugene's informing her of her father's death, and Mortimer's occasional attempts to draw the truth out of his friend are almost solely constructed for the reader's benefit. Wrayburn is too secretive and unreadable a character not to be accompanied by a spokesperson, who occasionally enters to serve the dialogue that reveals details the reader would otherwise not be able to access. Rosemarie Bodenheimer has emphasised that in *Our Mutual Friend*, all the young men are "doubled and redoubled in ways that display the splits in their inner worlds"[271] and Mortimer fulfils this technical function too. His ritualistic questioning of Eugene's motives is on the surface designed for the reader's understanding of the character and the consequent seduction plot he is headed towards: "I would that you answered me three questions! What is to come of it? What are you doing? Where are you going?" (*OMF*, bk. II, ch. 6, p. 295). Mortimer's interference in the plot barely goes beyond such externalisation of Eugene's motives – otherwise, he is only the embodiment of Eugene's conscience. Thus, caught between his moral obligation as a gentleman and his sadistic desire for the woman, Eugene reiterates Mortimer's presence in his own mind: "'Eugene, Eugene, Eugene, this is a bad business.' Ah! So go the Mortimer Lightwood bells, and they sound melancholy tonight" (*OMF*, bk. IV, ch. 2, p. 697).

As Superego, Mortimer balances out Eugene's depraved tendencies, thus assuring him the right of place as protagonist. Eugene's incapacitation, both

271 Bodenheimer, *Knowing Dickens*, 120.

physically and narratively, moves Mortimer to the forefront of the text not only as his conscience, but towards the conclusion of the narrative also as his voice and hand. While Mortimer has previously only echoed Eugene's dandyesque witticisms with his laughter, he now supplements the protagonist by speaking and acting in his stead. It is reasonable to assume that Eugene's marriage to Lizzie is the ultimate sign of his improvement, because he seems to transcend their class boundary in an act of love: "By offering his hand in marriage to Lizzie Hexam, despite the social chasm between them, Wrayburn assumes a purpose . . ."[272] His marriage to the girl is supposed to set right his injury of her and sanction the sexual union he has sought. Consequently, it is Mortimer, who has to act out the unification for him. The reader steeped in convention easily overlooks the fact that Eugene never offers his hand to Lizzie – Mortimer does. As the protagonist lies incapacitated, the Superego steps up and acts out the necessary rituals that allow the text to redeem Eugene. The reformation of the protagonist is therefore purely exercised by the novelist through handing over the reins to the externally embodied conscience; the character himself can rarely be regarded as reformed only because he has been physically prevented from taking possession of Lizzie unlawfully. His external conscience Mortimer now ensures that all acquisition of female 'property' falls into a properly conjugal category.

It is ironic that even Mortimer Lightwood, the lawyer's conscience, cannot perform anything that would spare Lizzie Hexam a life of pain. After all, Eugene may for once be the man, who has been bent and broken into submission, but in this case, his submission is purely metafictional. Eugene Wrayburn is bent and broken into submission as a proper, morally unambiguous protagonist by the help of his Double – the incompatible evil side to him seems to be extinguished. He is never even close to being a David, but then this is a late Dickens. The important thing is that Eugene is beaten so that his Superego can take over and set things right in order to ensure a proper happy ending. The lawyer's sadistic desire for the woman must be directed into the proper channels by the external conscience that he is given. This separation of the different forces within the self redeems the protagonist, but even Mortimer cannot liberate Lizzie from the hold the novel gives Eugene over her. In fact, even his conscience is an accessory in his crime against her, for Mortimer's execution of the marriage binds Lizzie into a state of submission that has very little to do with the poetic justice that announces a wrong righted through her elevation to wife. In fact, Lizzie Hexam's fate is an ironic echo of Stryver's advice for Carton: his suggestion that the hero

---

272 Gregg A. Hecimovich, "The Cup and the Lip and the Riddle of *Our Mutual Friend*," *ELH* 62.4 (1995): 955–977, 966.

of *A Tale of Two Cities* needs a *nurse* now comes full circle. Evidently, Eugene Wrayburn also needs a nurse, not a wife, and a nurse he gets. The tortured woman is not really rewarded with the status of wife. As much as *Our Mutual Friend* may be indebted to various fairy tales,[273] Lizzie Hexam's story can hardly be described as that of Cinderella. She receives no reward as upper-class wife, she receives a professional promotion to nurse the invalided Eugene within the proper bonds of marriage, thereby extinguishing the sexually sordid association of the union. She does for Eugene what Stryver imagines a woman should do for Sydney Carton and so Eugene is the only one of all of the sadistic lawyers, who finally achieves his goal through marriage. He has Lizzie at his side to dominate as he wishes, the socially acceptable variant of Jaggers's perverted domestic bliss with Molly.

273 See Victoria Williams, "Dickens' Use of the Fairy Tale in *Our Mutual Friend*," *Pennsylvania Literary Journal* 2.2 (2010): 47–75.

6 Afterword

There is more than one lawyer in Dickens, but is there also a lawyer in Dickens? The book's title is deliberately ambivalent, but I hesitate to conclude what it suggests. There is a lawyer in Dickens in the sense that he certainly took an interest in the profession and an extraordinary interest in the system. It may not come as a surprise, however, that Dickens eventually did not become a lawyer. Given the profession's uncertain social status and Dickens's life-long endeavour to be a respected member of the middle classes, it seems fair to assume that the profession simply was not good enough for him. I have tried to show that there is more to the lawyer character than their overt and easily recognisable depravity that is inextricably linked to a corrupt system. Certain lawyers, like Tulkinghorn or Jaggers, are treated with a pinch of admiration for their power and for their capabilities. Even Uriah Heep, who is so clearly a villain, nevertheless shows extraordinary competence within his chosen field that David cannot help but notice. This is a far cry from the reluctant admiration Pip feels for Jaggers, but it would be too simple to argue that all lawyers in Dickens are bad representatives of a bad system. It seems that, for Dickens, the most problematic aspect of the profession was its social ambiguity. I have tried to show that the question of what makes a gentleman looms large over his creation of all his lawyer characters and Eugene's open refusal to identify with his profession comes across as an implicit denunciation of a role in society that is regarded irreconcilable with the position of the gentleman.

The lawyer in Dickens is a literary character that is more complex than he might seem at first sight. The early stereotypes such as Dodson and Fogg or Sampson Brass suggest little more than that the law breeds leeches, irresponsible villains without a conscience, professional men in the worst sense of that word. Their profession allows them to focus solely on the acquisition of money, which is a practice so abject to Dickens's values that it is not surprising that these lawyers are unequivocally unlikeable. Uriah Heep's appearance in Dickens's oeuvre, however, significantly increases the depth with which Dickens perceived of lawyers as cultural agents. Uriah's role in David's life seems to make him nothing but detestable, yet the text cannot help but admire his skills. Micawber's conclusive disgust of HEEP overshadows that David also feels drawn to the creep's capabilities and considerably fears his competence. Uriah is an enigma for David, for he embodies what the narrator aspires to, yet feels too ashamed to admit. I do not try to argue that we should view David's position as inherently Dickens's own, but it might strike one nevertheless as important that one of his most 'personal' villains is also a lawyer. David's struggle to become a

https://doi.org/10.1515/9783110754506-006

respected member of the middle class has often been read as a mirror of Dickens's own wish to advance to the position he would eventually maintain in Victorian society and in this context, it certainly seems important that David turns away from the law in the widest sense and becomes a writer. He is flanked by his two dark angels, Steerforth and Uriah, who both suggest unequivocally, albeit from very different positions, that there is something wrong with the law – it is ungentlemanly. Thus, all of the complex lawyer characters that appear in the Dickens world after *David Copperfield*, have the unmistakeable air of ungentlemanly conduct about them. Their unbashful struggle for money and power simply seems contrary to Victorian values – values, which Dickens tends to uphold throughout his works with sometimes very little subtlety.

It truly seems significant that in a novel, that is so subjective, so meditative and so indicative of such values as *David Copperfield* is, we find the first elaborate lawyer character. This lawyer is representative of the negative forces of the law, yet the legal system garners no position in the novel. This lawyer is representative of the negative forces of ambition next to David's self-professed earnestness. This lawyer does so many things that we know David would like to do that we cannot absolve Copperfield of embarrassing tendencies. Is Uriah the lawyer that presents everything that is wrong with the profession, thereby changing Dickens's mind about working in the law? It is equally possible that the law is the chicken and Uriah the egg, of course. We do not know why Dickens never entered the Bar, we only know that he seriously considered it for a substantial amount of time. We know that he greatly admired successful lawyers and that the novelist had every reason to value the lawyer's 'narrative' or linguistic capabilities. After all, law and literature stand in close proximity and Dickens was never ignorant of this fact. While he might have shared his contemporaries' interest in the power of the law to create narrative suspense and its general suitability for building plots, he also seems aware of the characteristics both disciplines share. It is impossible to overlook that the most successful lawyers in Dickens are fabricators – why would we not assume that the novelist finds this an aspect of the legal profession that he could easily identify with?

The commonality of law and literature is well-established, but it would certainly not be stretching this point too far to see that Dickens and his critics had their hands in this. *Bleak House* and J. Hillis Miller's influential article on interpretation, for instance, only document too well that the two disciplines share such basic characteristics as to see them almost as constitutive of one another. Thus, much more recently, Jonathan Grossman has shown that the novelist can find more aspects in the courtroom indicative of his own profession than elsewhere. So it might be possible to argue that the covert admiration that Dickens's texts express for the lawyer's capabilities is narcissistically turned inward to the novelistic profession itself. Maybe Dickens does not admire the lawyer, but only sees in the profession a mirror of his own. At the same time, the question of power penetrates the text through the entrance of all the lawyers. They pose threats to privacy, to safety, to order – quite absurdly, given that they represent the law that is supposed to ensure all of these three aspects. Yet, a focus on the lawyer in Dickens cannot overlook their constant transgression, their invasion of private spaces, private *minds*, even; their intrusive power to be where they are least expected; their coercion of characters who find themselves helpless in view of such surveillance.

The lawyer's questionable ethics are completely undisguised in most of the texts, but the true extent of the pleasure they find in oppressing others only materialises at such a closer look as I have tried to venture here. Part of the premise of this book, therefore, is that Dickens was not fully in control of the position these seemingly minor characters took in his narratives. Any writer would agree that characters tend to develop a life of their own that may burst the bubble of their intended existence. Dickens himself had an equally democratic view towards his characters, whom he mostly spoke of with great fondness. It cannot come as a surprise that a writer who saw his character creations so vividly in front of his mind's eyes – as anecdotes even from his closest family members affirm – wrote people who slipped from his controlling hand. This is especially obvious in the lawyer character, who is so clearly designed in the initial narratives as a minor character, who has to serve a function. Whether this be Uriah's desire for Agnes or Tulkinghorn's pursuit of Lady Dedlock; Stryver's wish to marry Lucie Manette or Jaggers's revelation, all lawyers are employed to act in very technical terms to advance the plot Dickens has in mind. Within their clearly identifiable function, however, they tend to do things that are not essential to the narrative and they gain a psychological complexity that would be entirely unnecessary. Tulkinghorn especially, possibly, demonstrates what a lawyer can do when left to his own devices. His mental torture of his female superior offers a view of his true desires that is surely astounding – and quite irrelevant in terms of plot. A closer look at these lawyers thus suggests that while Dickens was not looking, they developed a life of their own.

At many points in my analysis it would have been possible to follow the biographical thread as any Dickens scholar who might stoop to read this book can clearly see. There are many parallels to Dickens's own life and problems he struggled with personally at given points of his literary career, but I dare not be presumptuous and conclude that there is a personal Dickens in what I have looked at over the course of this book. This may be most important with regard to his position towards women. I have argued that the lawyer's threatening nature is most apparent in their treatment of women and their transgression of the private sphere. I have claimed that they all exhibit a certain sadistic pleasure in dealing with their female 'clients' – whether they have captured them already or still try to do so. I do not mean to suggest that I see in these instances of coercion any parallels to Dickens's personal life. One might wonder whether there is a covert expression of a wish to control others, but whether or not this is reflective of Charles Dickens may be anyone's guess and certainly not mine. Yet, the consistency with which the lawyer's literal or metaphorical capture of women repeats itself through the oeuvre cannot be a coincidence. From Uriah's wish to possess Agnes to Jaggers's ownership of Molly, such twisted 'relationships' between the lawyer and a respective woman occur over and over again in the middle to late Dickens. The agents of oppression certainly vary in likeability: while we detest Uriah in solidarity with David, we can certainly see what Dickens meant to be sympathetic about Eugene. We cannot overlook that all subsequent lawyer characters have something of Uriah in them and in that sense, they all take a very difficult stance towards women. Heep's wish to acquire Agnes for professional reasons and out of his wish to revenge himself on David re-occurs in his successors, who mostly view women as a delightful piece of property and the more they struggle to protect themselves, the more the lawyers seem adamant to possess them – Eugene Wrayburn is certainly the most obvious example and the epitome of a long thread of this particular kind of narrative.

I have argued in this book that the true victims of the control and coercion the lawyer in Dickens is endowed with are the women. This argument clearly does nothing to absolve the cultural type of the lawyer of their prejudice – at least not in novels that can only ever portray male lawyers long before the profession would even be available to women. However, I never set out to write the cultural history of the lawyer, nor the history of the perpetual prejudice against them. It is far too obvious that Dickens partakes in such prejudice and does little to counter it. It is not that obvious, perhaps, that he imagines the type with a psychological complexity that truly makes them sadists. One might perhaps argue that the women in Dickens who have to fight off the lawyers' advances are more in control of their own situation than I have made them out to be. After all, Lady Dedlock escapes Tulkinghorn and Lizzie Hexam marries Eugene. Sydney Carton even chooses the guillotine to leave Lucie Manette in peace. None of these solutions seem to constitute great victories to me, however, and some of the women, such as Molly or Estella, are granted no such 'liberty.' In fact, the abuse female characters in Dickens experience at the hands of these lawyers is impossible for them to counter, for in each and every case, they would have to speak out to others to seek their help, thereby inadvertently incriminating themselves. All of the women I have focused on in this book more or less find themselves in a situation very similar to Edith Dombey's, who is the only one accepting a fate as a fallen woman to escape Carker – a villain who certainly bears many traits of the lawyer, although it is never mentioned that he may be one.

Uriah's advances to Agnes in her own home; Mr Tulkinghorn's blackmail of Lady Dedlock in her own home; Vholes's taking control of Ada through Richard in his own home; Jaggers's incarceration of Molly in his own home; Sydney's twisted proposal to Lucie in her own home; Lizzie's escape from home – all of these are plot instances in which the lawyer has made the woman's existence in her domestic space unbearable. They have to flee domesticity in a world in which no public space is available to women unless they literally turn to the streets and finish their respectable existence. It is remarkable how consistently Dickens manages to draw attention to the fact that these women can neither speak out for themselves, nor find rescue elsewhere. It is even more remarkable, how openly their lawyers abuse them in front of others, safe in the knowledge that their victims are bound to silence. In court, they might plead the fifth – in Dickens, they have to suffer in silence if they want to avoid incriminating themselves. The lawyer's plotlines and their coercion of women demonstrates quite vividly the restricted position of women in society – in the end, they have to keep silent, if they mean to save themselves. It is just too unfortunate that this silence means suffering. Agnes Wickfield may be the most astonishing of all these women, considering that she suffers not only from Uriah's transgression, but also from David's unrequited love. It is no coincidence that she has hardly ever seemed an actual character to Dickens critics, considering that her endurance does not seem lifelike. Yet, her fate does not necessarily seem such an unusual story if we look even beyond Dickens, so possibly, Agnes is most lifelike after all.

The lawyer in Dickens is certainly a most interesting creature, for while he is of uncertain social status, he nevertheless manages to transcend social boundaries. His treatment of women makes this most obvious, for whether or not Lady Dedlock or Miss Havisham are women of superior rank, they are still liable to oppression. In this sense, the lawyer character in Dickens is of course also a representative of a deeply biased legal system that provided no justice for women. It is even more interesting, therefore, that Dickens uses the lawyer to invade the private sphere – the last domain of the Victorian woman. The lawyer thus manages to use the class system entirely to his advantage and his ghost-like existence in the text demonstrates how a male professional can bend the rules for their purposes. In this aspect of his power then might also lie the text's most intense covert admiration for the lawyer – these characters are manipulators and fabricators; they control narratives and images. They bend the truth to their will and they make people believe what they want them to believe. While this may sound truly unethical in the legal profession, a novelist may certainly and understandably envy such powers.

Works Cited

Alter, Robert, "The Demons of History in Dickens' *Tale*," *Novel: A Forum on Fiction* 2.2 (1969): 135–142.

Axton, William, "Unity and Coherence in *The Pickwick Papers*," *Studies in English Literature* 5.4 (1965): 663–676.

Baker, J. H., *An Introduction to English Legal History*. Second Edition. London: Butterworths, 1979.

Baker, Robert, "Imagination and Literacy in Dickens' *Our Mutual Friend*," *Criticism* 18.1 (1976): 57–72.

Baldridge, Cates, "Alternatives to Bourgeois Individualism in *A Tale of Two Cities*," *SEL* 30.4 (1990): 633–654.

Birks, Michael, *Gentlemen of the Law*. Stevens & Sons Limited, 1960.

Blain, Virginia, "Double Vision and the Double Standard in *Bleak House*: A Feminist Perspective" in *Bleak* House. *Contemporary Critical Essays*, ed. Jeremy Tambling. Basingstoke: Macmillan, 1998: 65–86.

Boasberg, James E., "Chancery as Megalosaurus: Lawyers, Courts, and Society in *Bleak House*," *University of Hartford Studies in Literature* 21 (1989): 38–60.

Bodenheimer, Rosemarie, *Knowing Dickens*. Ithaca, N.Y.: Cornell University Press, 2007.

Bodenheimer, Rosemarie, "Dickens and the Identical Man: *Our Mutual Friend* Doubled," *Dickens Studies Annual* 31 (2002): 159–174.

Boheemen-Saaf, Christine Van, "'The Universe Makes an Indifferent Parent': *Bleak House* and the Victorian Family Romance" in *Bleak House. Contemporary Critical Essays*, ed. Jeremy Tambling. Basingstoke: Macmillan, 1999: 54–64.

Bowen, John, *Other Dickens. Pickwick to Chuzzlewit*. Oxford: OUP, 2000.

Buzard, James, "Enumeration and Exhaustion: Taking Inventory in *The Old Curiosity Shop*," *Dickens Studies Annual* 39 (2008): 17–41.

Cheadle, Brian, "Improvising Character in *Our Mutual Friend*," *Essays in Criticism* 59.3 (2009): 211–233.

Cheadle, Brian, "The Late Novels: *Great Expectations* and *Our Mutual Friend*" in *The Cambridge Companion to Charles Dickens*, ed. John O. Jordan. Cambridge: CUP, 2001: 78–91.

Cheadle, Brian, "Work in *Our Mutual Friend*," *Essays in Criticism* 51.3 (2001): 308–329.

Cixous, Hélène, "The Character of 'Character'," *New Literary History* 5.2 (1974): 383–402.

Cocks, Raymond, *Foundations of the Modern Bar*. London: Sweet & Maxwell, 1983.

Coleman, Rosemary, "Nell and Sophronia – Catherine, Mary, and Georgina: Solving the Female Puzzle and the Gender Conundrum in *The Old Curiosity Shop*," *Dickens Studies Annual* 36 (2005): 33–55.

Collins, Philip (ed.), *Dickens: The Critical Heritage*. London: Routledge and Kegan Paul, 1971.

Collins, Philip, "A Tale of Two Novels: *A Tale of Two Cities* and *Great Expectations* in Dickens' Career," *Dickens Studies Annual* 2 (1972): 336–351.

Cook, Susan, "Season of Light and Darkness: *A Tale of Two Cities* and the Daguerrean Imagination," *Dickens Studies Annual* 42 (2011): 237–260.

Crawford, Iain, "Pip and the Monster: The Joys of Bondage," *SEL* 28.4 (1988): 625–648.

Crawford, Iain, "Sex and Seriousness in *David Copperfield*," *The Journal of Narrative Technique* 16.1 (1986): 41–57.

https://doi.org/10.1515/9783110754506-007

Crompton, Louis, "Satire and Symbolism in *Bleak House*," *Nineteenth-Century Fiction* 12.4 (1958): 284–303.
Crosby, Christina, "Financial" in *A Companion to Victorian Literature and Culture*, ed. Herbert F. Tucker. Oxford: Wiley-Blackwell, 1999: 225–243.
Daly, Suzanne, "Belligerent Instruments: The Documentary Violence of *Bleak House*," *Studies in the Novel* 47.1 (2015): 20–42.
DiBattista, Maria, *Novel Characters. A Genealogy*. Oxford: Wiley-Blackwell, 2010.
Dickens, Charles, *A Tale of Two Cities*. Penguin English Library. London: Penguin Books Ltd., 2012.
Dickens, Charles, *David Copperfield*. Penguin English Library. London: Penguin Books Ltd., 2012.
Dickens, Charles, *Our Mutual Friend*. Oxford World's Classics. Oxford: OUP, 2008.
Dickens, Charles, *Great Expectations*, ed. Edgar Rosenberg. Norton Critical Editions. New York and London: W. W. Norton & Company, 1999.
Dickens, Charles, *Bleak House*. Wordsworth Classics. Ware: Wordsworth Editions Limited, 1993.
Dolin, Kieran, *Fiction and the Law. Legal Discourse in Victorian and Modernist Literature*. Cambridge: CUP, 1999.
Donovan, Robert A., "Structure and Idea in *Bleak House*," *ELH* 29.2 (1962): 175–201.
Easley, Keith, "Caught in Time: Performance and Spectatorship in *Our Mutual Friend*," *Dickens Studies Annual* 50.2 (2019): 295–362.
Eigner, Edwin M., "Charles Darnay and Revolutionary Identity," *Dickens Studies Annual* 12 (1983): 147–159.
Fein, Mara H., "The Politics of Family in *The Pickwick Papers*," *ELH* 61.2 (1994): 363–379.
Ferguson, Frances, "On Terrorism and Morals: Dickens's *A Tale of Two Cities*," *Partial Answers* 3.2 (2005): 49–74.
Forker, Charles, R., "The Language of Hands in *Great Expectations*," *Texas Studies in Literature and Language* 3.2 (1961): 280–293.
Forster, E. M., *Aspects of the Novel*, ed. Oliver Stallybrass. London: Penguin Books, 2005.
Fradin, Joseph I., "Will and Society in *Bleak House*," *PMLA* 81.1 (1966): 95–109.
French, A. L., "Beating and Cringing: *Great Expectations*" in *Great* Expectations. *Contemporary Critical Essays*, ed. Roger D. Sell. Basingstoke: Macmillan, 1994: 41–59.
Frost, Lucy, "Taming to Improve. Dickens and the Women in *Great Expectations*" in *Great* Expectations. *Contemporary Critical Essays*, ed. Roger D. Sell. Basingstoke: Macmillan, 1994: 60–78.
Galanter, Marc, *Lowering the Bar. Lawyer Jokes & Legal Culture*. Madison: The University of Wisconsin Press, 2005.
Gallagher, Catherine, *The Body Economic: Life, Death, and Sensation in Political Economy and the Victorian Novel*. Princeton, N.J.: Princeton University Press; 2006.
Garis, Robert, *The Dickens Theatre. A Reassessment of the Novels*. Oxford: Clarendon Press, 1965.
Georgas, Marilyn, "Dickens, Defoe, the Devil and the Dedlocks: The 'Faust Motif' in *Bleak House*," *Dickens Studies Annual* 10 (1982): 23–44.
Gibson, Anna, "*Our Mutual Friend* and Network Form," *Novel* 48.1 (2015): 63–84.
Gilmour, Robin, *The Idea of the Gentleman in the Victorian Novel*. London: George Allen & Unwin, 1981.

Ginsburg, Michal Peled, "Dickens and the Scene of Recognition," *Partial Answers* 3.2 (2005): 75–97.
Ginsburg, Michal Peled, "The Case Against Plot in *Bleak House* and *Our Mutual Friend*," *ELH* 59.1 (1992): 175–195.
Glatt, Carra, "Genre and the Counterfactual in *The Old Curiosity Shop*," *Dickens Quarterly* 31.2 (2014): 113–126.
Grass, Sean, "Pickwick, the Past, and the Prison," *Dickens Studies Annual* 29 (2000): 17–39.
Gribble, Jennifer, "Depth and Surface in *Our Mutual Friend*," *Essays in Criticism* 25 (1975): 197–214.
Grossman, Jonathan, "*Two Cities* Networked: The Historical Novel and Form in French Revolutionary Politics," *Novel* 50.2 (2017): 176–196.
Grossman, Jonathan, *The Art of Alibi. English Law Courts and the Novel*. Baltimore and London: The Johns Hopkins University Press, 2002.
Hamdi, Saber, "Of 'Household Gods' and Devils: Fetishism in *The Old Curiosity Shop*," *Anglia* 137.3 (2019): 411–433.
Hara, Eiichi, "Stories Absent and Present in *Great Expectations*," *ELH* 53.3 (1986): 593–614.
Harvey, William R., "Charles Dickens and the Byronic Hero," *Nineteenth-Century Fiction* 24.3 (1969): 305–316.
Hecimovich, Gregg A., "The Cup and the Lip and the Riddle of *Our Mutual Friend*," *ELH* 62.4 (1995): 955–977.
Herst, Beth F., *The Dickens Hero. Selfhood and Alienation in the Dickens World*. London: Weidenfeld and Nicolson, 1990.
Holdsworth, William S., *Charles Dickens as a Legal Historian*. New Haven: Yale University Press, 1929.
Hutter, Albert D., "Nation and Generation in *A Tale of Two Cities*," *PMLA* 93.3 (1978): 448–462.
Jaffe, Audrey, *Vanishing Points. Dickens, Narrative, and the Subject of Omniscience*. Berkeley: University of California Press, 1991.
James, Stephen, "Repetition, Rumination, Superstition: The Rituals of *Our Mutual Friend*," *English* 61.234 (2012): 214–233.
Jordan, John O., *Supposing Bleak House*. Charlottesville and London: University of Virginia Press, 2011.
Jordan, John O., "The Social Sub-text of *David Copperfield*," *Dickens Studies Annual* 14 (1985): 61–92.
Jordan, John O., "The Medium of *Great Expectations*," *Dickens Studies Annual* 11 (1983): 73–88.
Kettle, Arnold, "Dickens and the Popular Tradition" in *Marxists on Literature. An Anthology*, ed. David Craig. London: Penguin, 1975: 214–244.
Kincaid, James R., "The Education of Mr. Pickwick," *Nineteenth-Century Fiction* 24.2 (1969): 127–141.
Kirk, Harry, *Portrait of a Profession. A History of the Solicitor's Profession, 1100 to the Present Day*. London: Oyez Publishing, 1976.
Kucich, John, "Dickens' Fantastic Rhetoric: The Semantics of Reality and Unreality in *Our Mutual Friend*," *Dickens Studies Annual* 14 (1985): 167–189.
Kucich, John, *Excess and Restraint in the Novels of Charles Dickens*. Athens, Ga.: University of Georgia Press, 1981.
Kucich, John, "The Purity of Violence: *A Tale of Two Cities*," *Dickens Studies Annual* 8 (1980): 119–137.

Ledger, Sally, "Dickens, Natural History, and *Our Mutual Friend*," *Partial Answers* 9.2 (2011): 363–378.
Lewis, Michael D., "The Challenge of Female Homoeroticism in *Our Mutual Friend*," *Dickens Studies Annual* 48 (2017): 207–229.
Litvack, Leon, "*Our Mutual Friend*" in *A* Companion *to Charles Dickens*, ed. David Paroissien. Oxford: Wiley-Blackwell, 2011: 422–432.
Macdonald, Tara, "'red-headed animal': Race, Sexuality and Dickens's Uriah Heep," *Critical Survey* 17.2 (2005): 48–62.
Marcus, David, "The Carlylean Vision of *A Tale of Two Cities*," *Studies in the Novel* 8.1 (1976): 56–68.
Marcus, Steven, "Language into Structure: Pickwick Revisited," *Daedalus* 101.1 (1972): 183–202.
McKenzie Stearns, Precious, "'Sex and the City': Charles Dickens's Working Women in *Martin Chuzzlewit* and *Our Mutual Friend*," *English* 61.233 (2012): 137–150.
McKnight, Natalie, "Dickens and Gender" in *A* Companion *to Charles Dickens*, ed. David Paroissien. Oxford: Wiley-Blackwell, 2011: 186–198.
McKnight, Natalie, *Idiots, Madmen and Other Prisoners in Dickens*. New York: St. Martin's Press, 1993.
McMaster, Juliet, *Dickens the Designer*. Basingstoke: Macmillan, 1987.
McMaster, Juliet, "Visual Design in *Pickwick Papers*," *Studies in English Literature* 23.4 (1983): 595–614.
Michie, Helen, "'Who Is This in Pain?': Scarring, Disfigurement, and Female Identity in *Bleak House* and *Our Mutual Friend*," *Novel: A Forum on Fiction* 22.2 (1989): 199–212.
Miller, D. A., *The Novel and the Police*. Berkeley: University of California Press, 1988.
Miller, J. Hillis, "Moments of Decision in *Bleak House" in The Cambridge Companion to Charles Dickens*, ed. John O. Jordan. Cambridge: CUP, 2001: 49–63.
Miller, J. Hillis, "Interpretation in *Bleak House*" in *Bleak* House. *Contemporary Critical Essays*, ed. Jeremy Tambling. New Casebooks. Basingstoke: Macmillan, 1998: 29–53.
Newsom, Robert, *Dickens on the Romantic Side of Familiar Things: Bleak House and the Novel Tradition*. New York: Columbia University Press, 1977.
Palmer, William J., "The Movement of History in *Our Mutual Friend*," *PMLA* 89.3 (1974): 487–495.
Peltason, Timothy, "Esther's Will" in *Bleak* House. *Contemporary Critical Essays*, ed. Jeremy Tambling. Basingstoke: Macmillan, 1999: 205–227.
Petch, Simon, "The Business of the Barrister in *A Tale of Two Cities*," *Criticism* 44.1 (2002): 27–42.
Polloczek, Dieter Paul, *Literature and Legal Discourse. Equity and Ethics from Sterne to Conrad*. Cambridge: CUP, 1999.
Poon, Phoebe, "Trust and Conscience in *Bleak House* and *Our Mutual Friend*," *Dickens Quarterly* 28.1 (2011): 3–21.
Qualls, Barry V., "Savages in a 'Bran-New' World: Carlyle and *Our Mutual Friend*," *Studies in the Novel* 10.2 (1978): 199–217.
Quirk, Eugene F., "Tulkinghorn's Buried Life: A Study of Character in *Bleak House*," *The Journal of English and Germanic Philology* 72.4 (1973): 526–535.
Rainsford, Dominic, "*Our Mutual Friend* and Victorian Moral Philosophy," *Dickens Quarterly* 27.4 (2010): 273–291.

Rawlins, Jack, "Great Expiations: Dickens and the Betrayal of the Child" in *Great* Expectations. *Contemporary Critical Essays*, ed. Roger D. Sell. Basingstoke: Macmillan, 1994: 79–97.

Rignall, J. M., "Dickens and the Catastrophic Continuum of History in *A Tale of Two Cities*," *ELH* 51.3 (1984): 575–587.

Robbins, Bruce, "Telescopic Philanthropy: Professionalism and Responsibility in *Bleak House*" in *Bleak House*, ed. Jeremy Tambling. New Casebooks. Basingstoke: Macmillan, 1998: 139–162.

Rosenberg, Brian, *Little Dorrit's Shadows. Character and Contradiction in Dickens*. Columbia, Mo. and London: University of Missouri Press, 1996.

Rosenfield, Claire, "The Shadow Within: The Conscious and Unconscious Use of the Double" in *Stories of the Double*, ed. Albert J. Guerard. Philadelphia and New York: J. B. Lippincott Company, 1967: 311–331.

Sadoff, Dianne F., *Monster of Affection. Dickens, Eliot & Brontë on Fatherhood*. Baltimore and London: The Johns Hopkins University Press, 1982.

Scheckner, Peter, "Gender and Class in Dickens: Making Connections," *Midwest Quarterly* 41.3 (2000): 236–250.

Schiffman, Robyn L., "Wax-Work, Clock-Work, and Puppet-Shews: *Bleak House* and the Uncanny," *Dickens Studies Annual* 30 (2001): 159–171.

Schlicke, Paul (ed.), *The Oxford Reader's Companion to Dickens*. Oxford: OUP, 1999.

Schlicke, Paul, "Embracing the New Spirit of the Age: Dickens and the Evolution of *The Old Curiosity Shop*," *Dickens Studies Annual* 32 (2002): 1–35.

Schramm, Jan-Melissa, "Dickens and the Law" in *A* Companion *to Charles Dickens*, ed. David Paroissien. Oxford: Wiley-Blackwell, 2011: 277–293.

Schramm, Jan-Melissa, "Is Literature More Ethical Than Law? Fitzjames Stephen and Literary Responses to the Advent of Full Legal Representation for Felons" in *Law and Literature. Current Legal Issues 1999, Vol. 2*, eds. Michael Freeman and Andrew D. E. Lewis. Oxford: OUP, 1999: 417–435.

Sherer, Ray J., "Laughter in *Our Mutual Friend*," *Texas Studies in Literature and Language* 13.3 (1971): 509–521.

Showalter, Elaine, *The Female Malady. Women, Madness and English Culture, 1830–1980*. London: Virago Press, 1987.

Shuman, Cathy, "Invigilating *Our Mutual Friend* – Gender and the Legitimation of Professional Authority," *Novel* 28.2 (1995): 154–172.

Slater, Michael, *Charles Dickens*. New Haven and London: Yale University Press, 2009.

Smith, Peter, "The Aestheticist Argument of *Our Mutual Friend*," *The Cambridge Quarterly* 18.4 (1989): 363–382.

Steig, Michael and F. A. C. Wilson, "Hortense versus Bucket. The Ambiguity of Order in *Bleak House*," *Modern Language Quarterly* 33 (1972): 289–299.

Stewart, Garrett, "The New Mortality of *Bleak House*," *ELH* 45.3 (1978): 443–487.

Stoehr, Taylor, *Dickens: The Dreamer's Stance*. Ithaca, N.Y.: Cornell University Press, 1965.

Stout, Daniel, "Nothing Personal: The Decapitation of Character in *A Tale of Two Cities*," *Novel* 41.1 (2007): 29–52.

Storey, Graham, *Charles Dickens. Bleak House*. Landmarks of World Literature. Cambridge: CUP, 1987.

Surridge, Lisa, "'John Rokesmith's Secret': Sensation, Detection, and the Policing of the Feminine in *Our Mutual Friend*," *Dickens Studies Annual* 26 (1998): 265–284.

Tambling, Jeremy, "Prison-Bound: Dickens and Foucault," *Essays in Criticism* 36.1 (1986): 11–31.

Thiele, David, "The 'transcendent and immortal . . . HEEP!': Class Consciousness, Narrative Authority, and the Gothic in *David Copperfield*," *Texas Studies in Literature and Language* 42.3 (2000): 201–222.

Watt, Gary, *Equity Stirring. The Story of Justice Beyond Law*. Hart: Oxford and Portland, 2009.

Welch, Brenda, "Tulkinghorn and Professional Responsibility in *Bleak House*," *Dickens Quarterly* 35.1 (2018): 47–62.

Welsh, Alexander, *Dickens Redressed. The Art of Bleak House and Hard Times*. New Haven and London: Yale University Press, 2000.

Welsh, Alexander, *From Copyright to Copperfield. The Identity of Dickens*. Cambridge, Mass.: Harvard University Press, 1987.

Welsh, Alexander, "Waverley, Pickwick, and Don Quixote," *Nineteenth-Century Fiction* 22.1 (1967): 19–30.

Williams, Victoria, "Dickens' Use of the Fairy Tale in *Our Mutual Friend*," *Pennsylvania Literary Journal* 2.2 (2010): 47–75.

Winner, Anthony, "Character and Knowledge in Dickens: The Enigma of Jaggers," *Dickens Studies Annual* 3 (1974): 100–121.

Winter, Sarah, "Curiosity as Didacticism in *The Old Curiosity Shop*," *Novel* 34.1 (2000): 28–55.

Woloch, Alex, *The One vs. the Many. Minor Characters and the Space of the Protagonist in the Novel*. Princeton and Oxford: Princeton University Press, 2003.

Wright, Terence, "Caresses that Comfort, Blows that Bind – Sex, Sentiment and the Sense of Touch in *David Copperfield*," *English* 48.190 (1999): 1–16.

Index

https://doi.org/10.1515/9783110754506-008